Praise for *On the Line*

'Compelling . . . a portrait of the frontline which will fill you with admiration for those who, like Vinten, daily risk life and limb to keep us safe.'
Sunday Express

'Extraordinary'
Mail on Sunday

'A humane but unflinching look at the sharp end of contemporary policing. Vinten has a compassionate eye, and gives a human face to those charged with our safety.'
Luke Jennings, author of the *Killing Eve* novels

'I loved this book. Gritty and gripping, moving and shocking, this brilliant police memoir shows that life on the force really is different for girls.'
Erin Kelly, author of *He Said/She Said*

'Alice Vinten is the real deal – all the thrills of a crime novel, only true. Required reading for anyone interested in what the police really do.'
Mel McGrath, author of *Give Me the Child*

Alice Vinten

On the Line

Life – and death – in the Metropolitan Police

www.tworoadsbooks.com

First published as *Girl on the Line* in 2018 by Two Roads
An imprint of John Murray Press
An Hachette UK company

This paperback edition first published in 2019

1

A CIP catalogue record for this title is available from the British Library

Paperback ISBN 978 1 473 65884 4
eBook ISBN 978 1 473 65883 7

Typeset in Celeste by Hewer Text UK Ltd, Edinburgh
Printed and bound in Great Britain by Clays Ltd, Elcograf S.p.A

Hodder & Stoughton policy is to use papers that are natural, renewable
and recyclable products and made from wood grown in sustainable
forests. The logging and manufacturing processes are expected to
conform to the environmental regulations of the country of origin.

Hodder & Stoughton Ltd
Carmelite House
50 Victoria Embankment
London EC4Y 0DZ

I dedicate this book to all the coppers out there who are still doing the job that I wasn't strong enough to continue.

Contents

1

Leanne

Wide-eyed and excited, we file into the lecture theatre. I try not to fidget in my stiff new uniform. The coarse blue jumper, just like the ones I wore at school, is making me itch. It's October and the room is stifling with dry, heated air. I gaze around the theatre and resist the urge to pinch myself at the thought that I'm sitting slap bang in the middle of Hendon Police College, the Metropolitan Police's iconic training centre. A single bead of sweat runs down the small of my back. I'm exhausted from the 'introductory drinks' of the night before, but there's nowhere else I want to be. I've waited two years to get here. Two years working for the local council, assessing the needs of homeless applicants. Interviewing drunks, vagrants and domestic violence victims. Little do I know I'm facing more of the same.

We sit down in the stiff plastic chairs and look at each other. I glance across the faces of my new colleagues and fellow probationers. Mostly men, mostly white men. Not even a third of us are women. A buzzing murmur fills the room as people talk in animated whispers. We've made it. It's the first day of the rest of our lives. The first day of the career we all know we'll be in for the next thirty years. Yesterday we moved into our rooms in Hendon's notorious tower blocks – the first things you see as you approach Colindale tube station on the Northern Line – eager to begin our eighteen weeks of training. Even the sight of the previous occupant's hair in my sink hadn't dampened my spirits. This morning we were allocated our uniforms. For the first time in my life (except possibly for a few university fancy dress parties) I was dressed as a police officer. The trousers fasten above my belly button and give me the longest-looking bottom in history. But we all look the same. And I already feel the sense of unity that will become familiar. *One for all.*

A hush falls as the teachers walk in. From that day on we will refer to them as 'staff'. We look at them with barely concealed awe. These people have been there and done it all and come back to teach *us* how to be there and do it all. I click my biro on and clutch my pad, my eyes barely leaving the front as I lean forward. After the formalities of fire exits and laundry rooms, of parade times and uniform expectations, the male probationers are asked to leave the room. They file out in silence, and the male sergeants and inspector leave with them. With the majority of cadets now gone, the hall seems suddenly sparse. As we glance at each other nervously I realise that I'm in the minority. Then they give us 'the talk'.

I roll my eyes as the female staff lecture us about relationships with fellow cadets (not a good idea), relationships with staff *(really* not a good idea) and contraception.

They tell tales of women gone before us, women who have come away from training with a nasty case of the clap. Or a baby. Honestly, do they think I'm stupid? I've got through twenty-four years of life so far without getting pregnant, I think I can manage eighteen weeks more. Besides, I have a boyfriend and I'm on the pill.

It's pointed out to us that there are 'no days off' in training. No days to pop to the doctor's and get a new prescription. So we'd better have enough birth control with us. A tiny voice in the back of my head. *How many pills have I got left?* I ignore it. I've waited two years to get here, I'm not going to mess it up now. If I run out, then we'll just use a condom. No condom, no sex. Simple. My mind skips from the warning to the next item on our agenda: being assigned our boroughs.

When I filled out my application form I had little knowledge of London's boroughs, a fact that hasn't changed much. So when it's announced that I'll be joining Brixley with eight other trainee constables I'm perfectly happy. It's North London, at least, and relatively easy to get to from my parents' house in Cheshunt. Not that I intend to live there for long. We wander out of the lecture theatre and I head back up to my small room on the thirteenth floor. In my room is a small single bed, a desk, some drawers and a wardrobe. Next to the wardrobe is a metal sink and a mirror. I leave my room and wander down the halls, stopping to speak to the other girls on the corridor, introducing myself to anyone I've not already met. It's agreed that we're all going to the Peel Bar, the only bar on site, and then I feel like I'm at university again as we all start flitting in and out of each other's rooms borrowing hair straighteners and make-up.

I can feel the sexual tension as soon as we walk into the bar. It's dimly lit and full to the brim. The majority of recruits are in their early twenties and I feel a little like I'm on display in a meat market as tables of blokes turn to look at us. I feel like they may hold up score cards at any point and I don't want to know what my total is. I swallow down my nerves and head for the bar. The décor is tired – green sofas and dark varnished wood, with green panelled walls and an old-fashioned jukebox in one corner – and the clientele are a mixture of brand–new recruits like me and other intakes. A new intake joins Hendon every five weeks as the oldest intake graduates, and there are approximately two hundred recruits in each. We are the purple intake. There are always four intakes training at any one time and the other colours are green, red and blue. Already we feel the superiority of the trainees that have been here longer than us, and I can't wait until I can lord it over recruits who are younger in service than me. *Bottom of the pile.* Only way is up.

* * *

I can still taste the bacon from my bacon roll as I quick-step towards my classroom. Smoothing down the coarse blue stomach of my Met jumper, I sigh as my fingers catch on the new bulge of podge that is growing over the waistband of my trousers. I've been at Hendon for seven weeks and I've got another eleven to go. *Got to stop having cooked breakfasts every day.* Hot food is available in the canteen three times a day and it seems that I just can't bring myself to head to the salad trolley. Apparently Met canteens aren't known for their healthy options. I make a mental note to try and cut back as I push into my classroom. Staff aren't here yet, phew, and I take my seat.

There's not been a morning yet that I haven't wanted to start the day. I'm loving every minute; the shouting at officer safety training, the role-plays and even the study. It seems like ages since I've written notes and, being a bit of a stationery freak, I'm in my element when creating multi-coloured, highly highlighted revision sheets. I love being tested. An approval seeker, I remind myself of Lisa Simpson in the episode where Springfield Elementary is closed down and she's desperate to be graded by anyone, for anything. *Grade me!* We've settled into a routine that involves a week of early shifts, followed by a week of lates. Earlies are 6 a.m. until 2 p.m. and lates are 2 p.m. until 10 p.m. The purpose is to get us used to the shifts we'll be working in the real world. Unlike real-world policing, however, our weekends are free. Most people, including me, travel home at the weekends to see friends and family. I see my boyfriend. I met him at university and we've been dating for five years. He's black and lives on a notorious estate in Tottenham. Facts I'd never considered much of a talking point until I started discussing it with other recruits. He's now referred to as my 'gangster boyfriend'. But I tell myself they're only joking.

The class stands as Sergeant Gracie walks through the door. A relic from the tradition of standing when a higher rank enters the room, it strikes me as overly military. He tells us to sit and as I lower myself into my chair I remember what this class is going to be covering: Dead bodies and death messages. Nerves start to wriggle in my belly as I consider what I'm about to see. I've never seen a dead body. Sure, I've seen plenty of bloody recreations in violent movies, I've seen blurred and grainy images on the news, but I've never seen a real body. Sgt Gracie has his arms wrapped round a thick black ring binder. He places it on the desk in front of him. Twenty-eight pairs of eyes follow the folder to the desk. We all know what's in there.

He starts the lesson. His Northern Irish accent sounds both harsh and rounded in equal measures. There's no mistaking when he's pissed off, though. First up is the usual welfare spiel. We get it every time we're about to discuss something that could upset or offend anyone. *You can leave the room at any time.* There's no way I'll be walking out of that door. I'm apprehensive about what I'm going to see, yes, but I'm absolutely sure I can handle it. I've never been queasy. Blood doesn't bother me. I've never turned away at the gruesome bits in horror movies; if anything, I lean in for a better view. He tells us that we'll be viewing the photos in groups of four. They start at one end of the tables and work their way round. We chat quietly while waiting for our turn – idle chat to pass the time while our eyes flick constantly towards the folder. I try not to look at the other recruits as they view the photos. I don't want to see their reactions. I want the way I react to be totally uninfluenced by them. By the time the folder has reached my group, about two-thirds of the class have already seen it. No one has left the room.

Sgt Gracie places the folder on the table between the four of us. He opens the plastic cover to reveal the first photograph. It's a man. He's old and fat, lying on his back, wearing a brown cardigan over a blue shirt, beige trousers and brown shoes. A large black knife-handle protrudes from the centre of his chest. A trickle of blood runs from the corner of his mouth to the floor. It's dark brown. His eyes are wide and staring, his mouth hangs open and his skin is completely white. At the top of the page, on the right, some details are printed:

```
RODRIGUES, Arthur — 63 —
alcoholic, murdered by lodger.
```

It's only as I read his name that a lump starts to form in my throat. This is – was – a real person. We nod between ourselves and someone turns the page. We turn again and again – limbs and torsos, dark smudges on walls, vacant eyes, open mouths and frozen faces. With each photo my jaw sets tighter and tighter, but I'm fine. I'm holding it together. *I can do this.*

We're nearly at the end and Sgt Gracie turns the page again. This time the photo shows a woman lying in a hallway, at the bottom of a flight of stairs. Around her neck is

7

a rope, which winds around her throat, the skin there bulging and blackened. Her face is turned away and her curly auburn hair is raked upwards beneath her head so that her neck is visible. The end of the rope twists out from under her shoulder and ends in a wild fray on the carpet. The carpet looks thick and clean. In the corner of the hallway is a table with a pot plant. Beneath the table are two pairs of shoes. Adult trainers sit neatly next to tiny wellies. *She was a mother.* I feel the first prickles of tears in my eyes. *Stop.* She lies mostly on her back, her legs twisted to one side. Above her, hanging from the banister, is the other half of the rope, wrapped thickly around one of the spindles. Beside her, around a metre from her head, is a steak knife.

COLLINS, Leanne — 31 — domestic murder.

But the image doesn't fit the description. Did she hang herself? Did someone else do it? Why is the knife there?

I look up at Sgt Gracie. 'She was strangled by her estranged and abusive husband. He panicked and tried to make it look like a suicide; hung her from the banisters. Her four-year-old son found her and ran to a neighbour's house. When police arrived, they cut her down. The presence of the knife was a puzzle for detectives.' He pauses, four faces turned up towards him, hanging on his every word. 'It was only when Leanne's son was spoken to by specially trained officers the next day that they discovered why the knife was there. He said that he had brought Mummy the knife so that she could cut off the rope when she woke up.'

My hands are across my mouth. Suddenly all I can see is that four-year-old, standing in a hallway with a knife in his hand. The tears spill from my eyes and my cheeks burn in embarrassment as I dash from the room. I cover my face entirely with my hands as I sob in the corridor outside the classroom. The tragedy of it tears through my chest as I try and get a hold of myself. *What the hell is wrong with me?* I imagine what the other recruits are thinking. *Does she honestly think she can be a good copper? She can't even look at dead bodies without* crying. *Pathetic.* But this isn't me. I wanted to shout it at them. *This is not me.* I've heard tragic stories before. The world is full of them. The whole reason I joined the police is to try and stop those tragedies from happening, or to at least catch the perpetrators responsible. Maybe I've got it all wrong. Maybe I can't do this.

* * *

Tears well in my eyes as I look down at the stick. Nine weeks into training and I'm pregnant. Pregnant and sitting in the urine-scented toilets at Metropolitan Police training college, Hendon. I think back to my smugness in the welcome lecture and shudder. How could I have been so reckless? I knew something was different – I hadn't been myself for the last few weeks. But how could I be pregnant? I only ran out of pills a few weeks back and we've been careful since then. Those immortal words from all the teen magazines I have ever read flood through my head. *It only takes one time.* But I'm not a teen, am I? I'm a grown woman, a woman supposed to be responsible enough to become a police officer.

I walk back into my room. Dropping the stick on my desk I sink onto my bed next to my boyfriend. 'It's positive.' I can't bring myself to say the word 'pregnant'.

'I won't stay with you if you keep it.' He sits on the edge of the bed. 'You won't be a good mother. You're not ready.' His fingers twist together.

'But we could do it together,' I hear myself say, my voice high and wheedling, and it makes me cringe. 'We love each other. We could make it work.'

'No, we couldn't, and you can kiss goodbye to all this.' He gestures to my training room, my white notes, my polished boots. 'You'll have to stop your training. You've waited two years for this. You'll resent it.'

The next day and I'm sitting in a small room with two comfy armchairs in it. I can tell it's the bad news room. The welfare room. Calm colours, soft furnishings. There are rooms like it all across the Met. I had reached the staff room early this morning, careful to slip out before the other recruits. As soon as I'd opened my mouth to tell them the tears had started to flow.

I sit clutching a soggy tissue, tears dripping onto my stiff blue jumper, as I wait for Sgt Gracie. He is well respected by the recruits and you can tell that the rest of the staff feel the same. I like him. I respect him and trust him. I look to him for guidance and I want to impress him. I have been that way since school. *Always searching for a gold star or a smiley face.*

He walks into the room and sits down in front of me. I tell him that I've made up my mind. He nods and gets straight down to business. 'We'll say you've had a family emergency.'

'OK.'

'You can have two days, but you'll have to come to Hendon at some point and cover what you've missed.'

'Thank you.'

'One more thing.' He leans forward, his elbows resting on his pressed black trousers, silver sergeant stripes glinting on his shoulders. 'I don't think you should tell your parents.'

'Why?' I hear myself ask, my voice claggy and wet.

'I just think it will be easier if you don't.'

And just like that, I make a decision that I will regret for another twelve years of my life. A decision that will fester, getting bigger and bigger the longer it sits in my belly. I don't know why I listened to him. Every other piece of advice he ever gave me was sound. He didn't voice his opinions on what I should do, he didn't judge me; he just listened and assured me that he could give me the time to do what I needed to. But that one sentence, that one small piece of advice, that's what I regret more than anything. Because I had a great relationship with my parents, still do. I knew I could tell them anything and that they would still be there for me. Still love me. And the longer I hadn't said it, the more hurt they would be that I hadn't. But every time I opened my mouth to try, nothing came out.

*   *   *

'From the date of your last period, I would say you are six weeks' pregnant.' The doctor has a thick Nigerian accent. It reminds me of my boyfriend and his family, which is really not what I need right now. He sits behind a large desk. Surrounding him, and on the walls of his office, are photographs of his family. His many children smile at me from their wooden frames. I look at the crucifix behind his head and swallow.

'I've made up my mind.' My voice is firm.

'Why would you do this?' He shakes his head and tuts. A bolt of rage. This isn't what doctors are supposed to do. It's my right to choose. I feel my cheeks glow hot and wish I could conceal the blush. But anger comes from shame. And I am ashamed. Ashamed and furious.

'It's not the right time for me.' I say the words as quickly as I can, hoping that I can hold my voice steady. He looks down. The conversation appears to be over and I've never been so grateful. He scribbles on a piece of paper, reaches into his drawers for a leaflet and gives both to me.

'Everything you need is on there.'

'Thank you.' *Fuck you.*

Later on, with the leaflet in my hand and my boyfriend by my side, I call and make the appointment. I will have to wait a week. There's nothing sooner.

'I'll pay for it all,' he says, keen to help. *Keen to get rid of it.*

Each day during that long week I tell myself I'm doing the right thing. I throw myself into my training during the day and the team bonding during the evenings. Each day I remind myself where I'm going with my life, that I want to be a police officer. That I want nothing to slow me down. That I want to help people. I often think of Leanne. Of how maybe, just maybe, I'll one day be able to prevent that happening to someone else.

*   *   *

After my family emergency I returned to my training. Most of the recruits accepted my refusal to answer questions about where I'd been, but there were rumours. I got lower test results than before, my enthusiasm for study dampened. But I could forgive myself for that. I got myself through it. I pushed it to the back of my mind and focused on my career. After all, that was what it had all been for. The recruits in my class bonded well. We'd celebrate small milestones and big. We'd go to the local pub often and I drank a lot – often. I loved my classmates, and I loved my new career.

But later, after the pub had chucked us out and the laughing had stopped, when I was alone in the dark, the tears would come.

'I'm sorry,' I'd say.

I knew exactly who I was talking to as I repeated it over

and over again. Even though they didn't exist any more. My jaw and eyes ached from crying.

And every night I made a promise that I'd be the best police officer I could be.

That I'd help as many people as I could.

That I'd make up for it.

2

Wayne

The SOCO (scenes of crime officer) walks into her office at 9 a.m. on the dot. I'd probably be more pleased to see her if I hadn't been waiting since 6.30 a.m. I'm a brand-new probationary constable and have been told to parade for early turn, so that's jolly well what I've done. Except today I'm supposed to be shadowing the SOCO, and they don't start until 9. *Basics.* Still, one of the main talents of a probationary police constable seems to be 'taking it on the chin', so I'm off to a good start. Plus, it's my birthday, and I'm actually really keen to witness the forensic experts in action. Mum's planned me a birthday tea for when I get home, which is usually around 4 p.m. on an early shift, and I'm looking forward to it. Six weeks after leaving Hendon and I'm loving every minute of my street duties course. Ten weeks of being paired with experienced officers, taking reports, searching suspects and plenty of shoplifters. Getting to grips with the radio and starting to learn your borough. Only two weeks before the puppy-walking ends and I'm placed on a response team for real. I feel a little jolt of excitement in my tummy just thinking about it. Real

999 calls, real policing. *But no street duties instructors to walk you through it.*

I jump up as she enters and introduce myself. *Always be keen.* She's warm and friendly, introduces herself as Michelle and asks me if I've been waiting long. Not at all, I answer with a smile. She tells me that we've got a list of crime scenes to go to and quickly packs up her kit. We're out in the yard just as fast and getting into her van. It's unmarked, white, with a very small Metropolitan Police emblem on the side. I look to the emergency response cars parked around me and grin as a bubble of anticipation pops in my stomach. *Soon.* As I settle into the front passenger seat I double-check that my radio is on the correct channel: BX1. I twist the volume dial and cock my head to listen as the current response team go about their calls. I love listening to what's going on, tuning into a channel previously unavailable to me and altogether unavailable to the public. I feel pride prickle in my chest as I consider the fact that I'm now part of this very exclusive club.

I run my finger over the various knobs and buttons, trying to remember the feel of them all without having to look. The tip of my index finger lingers on the soft rubber pad of the emergency button. It's bright orange and, without doubt, the most important button on your radio. Referred to as the 'emer' button, when pressed it triggers an alarm that sounds on every radio within your borough. Cutting across the airways so that your radio has priority over everyone else, even Control, it gives you ten seconds of airtime to ask for help. Everybody jumps when the emer button sounds. It usually means one thing: your colleagues are in trouble and they need help. If you press the emer button you'll have every available police officer on their way to your location in seconds, discarding their lunch, dumping cups of tea and running to the yard. It's a reassuring button to have.

We pull out of the yard and Michelle starts making small talk. She's dressed in plain clothes with a Met vest, the kevlar body armour issued to all front-line Metropolitan police staff, over the top of her thin jumper. The sickly scent of her vanilla perfume wafts up my nose as we pull out of the yard and I reach into my pocket for some lip-gloss. I can feel my Met vest digging into me as Michelle weaves through the busy London traffic. It's a feeling I'm yet to get used to. It's tighter than normal as, unlike the usual thin cotton of my white shirt, today I'm wearing a red hoody underneath. I'm also in plain clothes, except for my kit-belt and Met vest, of course. It does feel good to be in jeans and trainers.

We soon arrive at the location of a burglary and head in to find the officers on scene. It's a small flat, basement level, with a front window that's completely obscured from the street. Someone could have worked away at that window for as long as they wanted without being disturbed, and they've obviously done just that. The uniformed officers direct us to some obvious evidence opportunities; the broken window and some clean shiny surfaces that may have been touched by the suspects. Michelle explains that clean and shiny is good for fingerprints. Then the officers get called to a 'fight in progress' and leave us to it. I look longingly at their backs as they rush to their car, envying their sense of urgency. *They're needed.*

I soon forget them, however, as I'm fascinated by Michelle's job. We're encouraged by some small drops of blood on the broken window, the best evidence we're likely to find at a scene like this. She swabs it and seals it. She works quickly and efficiently, talking enthusiastically about everything she's doing. Before long we're packing up and I find myself hoping that we're heading to a grisly scene next. We head out to the car and are so busy chatting that we miss the fluorescent yellow metal at first. *Oh shit.* We've been clamped. The van looks forlorn sitting by the kerb with a penalty notice strapped to its windshield. Michelle turns red as she explains that she must have forgotten to display the log book in the window, and starts to make the necessary phone calls. I feel the rain start to spit, so we get into the car and wait for the clampers to come and remove their shackle.

Two hours later, and I'm stifling a yawn as Michelle launches into the story of 'boyfriend number three.' It's only 11 a.m. but it's four-and-a-half hours into my shift and I've been up since 4.30. I despair as I work out that half of my shift is gone already and I've hardly seen any forensic action. In an effort to keep myself amused, I'm listening to my police radio while grunting the occasional 'uh-huh' in response to Michelle's monologue. Listening to all the calls that I'm not on my way to, I lean my head back and close my eyes, thinking about the delicious meal ahead of me, the presents and the now definitely 'necessary' drinks to celebrate my twenty-five years on this planet. The thought of a drink cheers me up and I straighten up as my attention gets drawn by something moving farther down the street.

It's a car. A jeep, to be precise, and it's moving fast. Straight towards us. It screeches up the road and blasts past, causing our van to shake in its wake. I see a flash of white face and a shaved head as the driver's window is framed in mine for a less than a millisecond. Michelle's shocked into a refreshing silence and I twist in my seat to try and catch the registration. I only catch the first half.

'He's going to wind up in a crash if he's not careful,' I mutter to Michelle as I crane around for a street sign. Being new to the borough has many disadvantages. I wipe my brow in the stuffy car as the voice of my reporting sergeant echoes through my mind. *Always make sure you know where you are.* I'm instantly annoyed with myself for not noting our address. Finally, I see it on the side of a house near the end of the street. *St Peter's Crescent.* I'm just lifting my personal radio to my lips to circulate the speeding car when an emergency call broadcast stops me.

'Call on an "I grade" now to St Peter's Crescent, road traffic accident, injured parties on scene, police assistance requested.'

'I grade'. *Immediate.* My heart skips a beat. I sit up and look at Michelle as I hear the location of the call. *That's us. That's where we are. Take the call!* Again I reach for my radio but a voice at the back of my mind is saying, *Wait.*

You don't know what you're doing. There's no experienced officer to give me advice. It's my decision and I'm on my own. I can feel Michelle watching me as I sit staring into space, expecting another unit to pipe up and answer the call. But it's been a busy early turn and the airwaves remain silent. What if someone's seriously hurt? The thought clears all the doubt from my mind and I press the button on the side of my PR (personal radio). I wait for the bleep and the echo that tells me I'm on the air.

'NI from 215NI.'

'Go ahead, 215 . . .'

The sound of my high-pitched and slightly shaky voice over the airwaves distracts me. I try not to think about the fact that every police officer in the borough, plus the entire control room, can hear everything I'm saying.

'I'm . . . um, I'm street duties and I'm on St Peter's Crescent now. I can go and take a look?' Hoping simultaneously to be told that I can't go on my own, while also quietly respected for my bravery, I hold my breath as another silent beat passes.

'Street duties . . . received. Do we have another unit that can attend to assist 215?'

Again the control room's request remains unanswered.

'Got to go.' I glance at Michelle, who is still staring blankly at me, and push open my door. The fresh April air feels cool on my clammy face as I look up the crescent. I can't see anything from where I'm standing, but I just about hear it as I turn my head to look around. Someone's shouting. I start to jog in the direction of the noise. As I run into the curve, more and more of the road ahead opens up to me and suddenly I can see the crash. It's 20 metres away and I see fluorescent jackets, scattered traffic cones and the rear of the jeep, in the air, wheels spinning. I quicken my pace as the shouting gets louder. It's coming from a man who's lying on the floor. He's splayed on his side next to the jeep, and at either end of him burly-looking builders are kneeling. *Is he injured? Is a head injury making him lash out?* I run straight into the middle of the scene and have maybe half a second to grasp what has happened before everybody starts shouting at once. *At me.* They must have clocked the Met vest and cuffs then.

'He drove straight into the hole.'

'He's a fucking nutcase!'

'Lucky no one was hit.'

The words jumble together as I try and figure out what to do next. What to do first. The jeep's rear wheels are suspended in the air, still spinning. Its bonnet is pointing down into the road and obscured by the hole it's driven into. The driver's door hangs open, a few feet away from where he has wound up on the floor. There are red and white barriers scattered around and a number of shocked-looking residents have come out of their houses. I assume that the driver, the skinhead I saw before, has lost control and driven into a hole. I walk over as the builders look up at me. The look of disappointment is etched across their faces.

'Are you *it*?' the builder on the left asks, eyebrows raised. *Hold it together. You can do this.*

'I'm a police officer, yes,' I answer him and nod to the driver. 'Do you need an ambulance?'

This time it's the other builder who speaks. His hat is skewed sideways and he's panting like a dog. 'An ambulance?' he wheezes, as if it's the most ridiculous suggestion he's ever heard. 'Listen, love, the only thing you need is back-up!'

And it's only as he says it that I begin to fully comprehend the situation. The driver's not hurt, he's being prevented from running off. The builders are restraining him, not tending to his wounds. As my mind slows slightly from its whirring panic I can finally hear what the driver's saying. And it's not nice.

'You fucking Paki prick.' He spits the words out like venom, saliva bubbling at the corner of his mouth. 'Fucking let go of me, you fucking pricks.'

I bend over and take a proper look at him. He's about my age. His T-shirt is like a saggy tent around his torso and his tracksuit bottoms drape over thin legs. He's out of breath, but seriously agitated. I take my cuffs from their holster on my belt and motion to the builders to bring the suspect's wrists together. They achieve this easily and I breathe a secret sigh of relief as I manage to get the cuffs on without looking like a novice. And then it happens. The police are here. *They can deal with it now.* Both burly builders let go of the man and stand up, stepping away from him and brushing themselves down. *Now it's just me and him.* The suspect has gone quiet and I stand there for a moment, holding him by the cuffs, him still on his side on the floor. He twists his head towards me and I can see grazes on the right side of his face, where it has been rubbed into the road.

'Can I stand up, miss? Please?' Later on in my service, the word 'miss' would have flashed as a warning that this suspect had been in prison. That's what the inmates call the female prison guards. But I wasn't late in my service. I was three weeks in.

He's calmed down. He's skinny. Why not?

'OK.' I pull on the cuffs and the suspect stands up. And before he's even reached his full height I realise my mistake. He may be slight, but he's tall. Really tall. Around 6 foot 7 to be precise. I look up at him as he towers over me. *Oh shit.*

My radio screeches to life and I can hear the control room calling my number.

'215 receiving NI? Are you on scene?

I take one hand off of the cuffs to answer and the suspect sees his opportunity. He lunges towards the builders, lashing his head forwards as they jump out of the way.

'I'm gonna fucking have you. You messed with the wrong fucker today, blud.'

I've got both hands on the cuffs again as he starts to pull away from me. I can't get to my radio. It takes all of my strength to hold onto the cuffs, and as the suspect keeps pulling I try and dig the treads of my trainers into the tarmac. The builders are back on the pavement and it's just me and the suspect in the middle of the road. The onlookers blur into streaks of colour as the suspect starts to pull me round in a circle.

'I'm not going back inside,' he shouts as he tries to yank his hands away from me.

With bright and brutal clarity I can now see the prison tattoos on the back of his neck. I can see the needle marks on his bare arms as they twist round his back into the cuffs. I can see a large scar twisting its way across his scalp. It looks like a knife wound. I realise that it's the rookie in me that stopped me seeing these details before. Globs of spit fly from his mouth as he shouts obscenities at anyone and everyone. He's pulling in every direction to get away. Again, the faint sound of the radio reaches my ringing ears.

'215 from NI? . . . 215, are you receiving?'

I can't get to it. Sweat is making my fingers slip on the cuffs. The soles of my trainers drag over the road surface as I lean away from the suspect and I wish I was wearing my boots. I'm trying with all my strength to stop him moving, but he's not giving in. *He knows you're weak. He can see right through you.* I push my self-doubt to the back of my mind and focus on his wrists in the cuffs. We twist in circles as he continues to pull and my hair streaks across my face as it starts to come loose from the bun I tied this morning. It sticks to my forehead and hazes my vision and I'm desperate to wipe it away. But I will not let go of these cuffs.

'All units, all units now please to attend St Peter's Crescent, officer in need of urgent assistance.'

I swipe my head to the left and see one of the builders. Phone pressed to his ear. Eyes glued to us. *Thank God.* There's no radio silence this time. I hear the call signs of the response units as they each answer in turn, responding to a colleague in need. I'm one of them now, and they look after their own. I close my eyes as relief runs through me. *They'll be here soon.* But the suspect has heard them too. I step backwards sharply as he stops pulling, and instead tries to twist round and face me.

'I'm not going back inside,' he growls at me through gritted teeth. He lashes round with his torso, trying again to break my grasp. *Thank God I put the cuffs up his back.* He can't face me because I get pulled around behind him every time he tries.

'If you weren't a fucking woman you'd be on the floor by now.'

My blood runs cold. *Please don't attack me.* The veins in his temples bulge against his fatless skin. His wrists have started to bleed and the metal scrapes at his raw skin each time he pulls away. Then I hear the sirens in the distance and for the first time in our struggle I find my voice, my strength. Back-up is on the way.

'Stop resisting,' I shout, full and loud.

I feel the fight go out of him as the sirens quickly get closer. He is still pulling away from me by the time three police cars screech onto the crescent, but it is half-hearted at most. Two male PCs are with us seconds later. They take the man from me, like adults confiscating scissors from a child, and fold him over the front of a parked van, barking loud orders and pushing his head into the metal. I try not to look shaky as a sergeant approaches me. I straighten and bend my fingers as, for the first time, they start to ache. As the response team take over I feel like a toddler. A toddler who's just been rescued by the big boys.

'NI from 84.'

'Go ahead, 84.'

'I'm here with 215. She's fine.' I'm not sure if it's his tone or his thick Scottish accent that makes me think he's pissed off.

I explain what happened and am puppy-walked through taking an accident report, told what to arrest the suspect for. I mouth the caution with as much confidence as I can muster. The driver has suddenly developed a sore neck and we are forced to take him to hospital for a check-up before we can safely take him to custody. I stand with him for over four hours in A&E, where he is given a neck X-ray to rule out any fractures. He is handcuffed to his trolley the whole time. Bored of threatening and insulting me, he tells me that his name is Wayne and that he only has half a lung on one side, due to being stabbed. If it wasn't for that, he winks, he would've got away. He also says that I'm pretty fit for a copper, wonders if I'd like to go out for a drink. I politely decline. Eventually I am joined by a street duties instructor and, once Wayne has been given the all clear, we transport him back to the custody suite in the marked police van.

I write out my statement, interview Wayne and complete the relevant case files. I take a look at his PNC (police national computer) record and find out that he is one of the borough's most prolific burglars, and is known for police assault and violence. He is released on bail and I walk him out of custody and through to the front office. He waves casually to me as he leaves, as if we were old friends who'd just caught up over a cup of coffee. I shake my head as I consider the drastic shift in his behaviour.

Once I've filed my paperwork I leave the station. It's 10.30 p.m. and I've got plenty of time before my last train. It's a Friday night and the tube is packed with revellers. I'm not envious, I just want my bed. I lean my head onto the vibrating Perspex that separates the doors from the seats and close my eyes. I listen as the rattle of the rails merges and transforms into the interference of my radio. I hear the muted tones of the control room and the echo of replies over the air, despite the fact that my radio is back in my locker at the police station. My mind assesses and reassesses the events of the day. *I could have done better.* I think about what the response officers must have thought of me. *Another useless Doris joins the force.* I think about telling the other new recruits, of explaining it all to my reporting sergeant. And I think about Wayne. I think about how two people of roughly the same age could be so different. Of how I would have turned out if I'd had his life, and vice versa.

I think about what he's taught me. *Assess the scene before you run in. Always err on the side of caution if you're on your own. If someone's already on the ground, just keep them there.* I stride from the tube to my train and from the station to my house and open the front door gently, careful not to wake my sleeping parents. No one has waited up for me, and nor would I want them to. A small pile of presents lies on the breakfast bar, with a note. I pick it up.

Dinner's in the fridge. Shall we do your birthday tomorrow?
Love, Mum xxx

3

Francine

I can smell the custody suite before I've even opened the door to the entry cage. Stale alcohol, acrid body odour, old boots, and an underlying note of something rotting. That thick odour that seems to ooze from the cells. Sullying everything it touches. I sigh as I grudgingly accept that I'll still be smelling it on my skin and hair long after my shift finishes. I finger-stab the entry code into the key-pad and push open the main door.

Once through, I find myself contained between the entry door behind me, and a large, floor to ceiling metal gate, about a metre in front. I enter the code into a second keypad and, as the door clunks home behind me, I hear the solid metal click of the gate releasing. Never open at the same time, the doors into Custody provide an extra layer of security against those who may wish to leave at short notice. Not for the first time, I wonder who chose to paint the bars of the gate cream. A passive colour for the medieval-looking bars. *Come! Take a stay in our custody 'suite', where the beds smell of piss and our waiters will serve you endless cups of seven-spoon sugared tea!* Raising an eyebrow at the thought, I walk along the short corridor, passing two empty interview rooms on my left. I shoulder-barge yet another door and then I'm twisting the cool, metal handle of the inner sanctum, as the fetid air meets my face and the murmur of noise clarifies into banging, laughing and shouting.

The banging is coming from the cells. A monotonous thud. I imagine a prisoner lying on the floor, repeatedly smacking the soles of his socked feet against the metal of his cell door. The shouting is coming from a charmingly agitated detainee, who seems to be trying to head-butt the custody sergeants' desk. His uniformed captors stand either side, taking an arm each, rolling their eyes. And the laughing is coming from Tony, who is partially hidden inside the small kitchen area, staring at his phone. I ram myself into the tiny space, filled with pre-powdered tea and coffee cups, microwave meals for the prisoners and a small basin.

'Big Al!' Tony chuckles. 'You need to see this.' He passes me the phone and I smile in confusion as I watch a man in very tight swimming trunks jump into a frozen pool. Instead of smashing through the ice, he lands on his coccyx and writhes around in agony, much to the delight of his hysterical friends. It's funny, and a hell of a lot nicer than some of the videos I've had shoved in my face since I joined the Met. I'd probably laugh louder if I didn't have the prospect of eight hours in the custody suite ahead of me. After completing my street duties training I had been assigned to D Team, a response team that I was still getting to know

– I'd been with them for just under two months when I was told it was my turn to spend four weeks doing jailer duties. It meant eight hours a day, every day, in the cells. But I wasn't about to let my disappointment show. *Always be keen.* Each probationer has their turn, and I was eager to learn more about Custody, even if it was hard listening to all the excitement going on over the radio when you were stuck in a dank, windowless hole that stank of rotten feet.

'You jailer tonight?' I ask Tony as I pass back his phone.

'For my sins.' He nods towards the goldfish bowl, and we head over.

I find my spirits rise slightly at the prospect of good company, before taking a sharp nose-dive as I enter the goldfish bowl and see the skippers in charge tonight. I've quickly got used to addressing them as 'sarge' or 'skip', depending on their individual temperaments. There's usually four assigned to the custody suite during a late turn. I take in the four sergeants, matching their faces with their names in my head, noting their shoulder numbers, and then I try not to sigh like an insolent teenager at the sight of PS Debden. There's nothing quite as bad as being jailer on a Friday late turn, unless you're jailer on a Friday late turn with an absolute prick of a sergeant. That's definitely worse. I smile politely at him and make a mental note to try and stay out of his way.

The 'Jailer's Office' is small and central, stationed right in the middle of custody and walled, on three out of four sides, by glass. Hence its nickname. It's in here that each shift must 'hand over' to the next, imparting critical information about current detainees, and any incidents that may have happened throughout the morning. We're the late shift – 2 p.m. to 10 p.m.; traditionally the busiest shift of the day.

'Right then, listen in, guys,' one of the skippers from the previous custody team begins. The chatter dies as Tony pulls the office door closed, dulling the roar of the detained. There are twelve people in the small room, most leaning casually on various desks, drawers and filing units around the edges. Two sergeants and three jailers from early turn, the four new late-turn skippers, a dedicated detention officer, me and Tony. The skipper leading the handover stands directly in front of a large white board that lists the cell numbers and which prisoner is where. It also has room for any details such as medical issues, officer safety concerns, and what the suspects have been arrested for. As usual, the board is full of angular letters, blurred edits and multiple red warning marks. Nearly every prisoner that we deal with has some kind of medical condition; drink or drug related. And many are violent.

'So, we've currently got seven in, including one female in F3, and two youths in MD1 and MD2.' He pauses to consider his clipboard and one of the early-turn jailers yawns widely. I envy her for finishing her shift.

'I'll only mention the prisoners of note,' he continues, clearing his throat. 'We've got three on fifteens. Mr Trangmere in M3, an alcoholic-diabetic, which must be tricky.'

A short laugh around the room.

'Brought in for drunk and dis, he's been placid enough since he got here. He's on fifteens for his health conditions. Then there's Mr Brown in M7' – he flashes M for Mental and S for Suicide, no need to explain that one – 'And then there's Adam Lacey in MD1. I'm sure you've all heard of him, one of our prolific burglars. Gives it the big 'un while he's out with his mates but cries like a baby in the cells. He's only thirteen so he's on fifteens, just in case.'

I raise the clipboard that I'd grabbed on my way in and make a note against Trangmere, Brown and Lacey. 'Fifteens' meant that, as jailer, I'd be responsible for checking on their welfare every fifteen minutes. And not just peering through the wicket at them, but actually rousing them, noting movements and interacting. There had been too many junkies and drunks die in police custody to take the risk of letting them lie, undisturbed, in their cells for too long. Reserved for the drunks, addicts and suicidal detainees, the responsibility of the checks would ensure I was constantly on the go throughout the shift. I preferred it that way. There's nothing worse than a slow shift in the cells.

Everyone starts to fidget as the skipper nears the end of the list.

'Hang on, guys, one more here that I should mention.' He wipes his brow as he stares briefly at the board, presumably to remind himself where he is. 'Ah, yes. M10. Mr Dixon.'

Tony groans loudly.

'Sounds like you've already had the pleasure, Tony?'

Tony snorts. 'Guy's a fucking waste of space.'

'Quite,' the skipper continues. 'Dixon is incredibly violent and known for assault on police. The best bit is he only assaults female officers.'

I feel a wave of dread ripple across my stomach.

'I don't want any female officers dealing with him without assistance, and absolutely no one opens that cell door without back-up, understood?'

A murmur of assent across the room.

'OK, ladies and gents, we're outta here.' And with that the skipper hands the custody baton to his late-turn counterparts, and the early-turn jailers head for the door. The chunky cell keys are placed in my upturned palm and I close my hand around the sturdy fish knife that acts as a key ring. The bright yellow plastic screams its importance. There's a razor blade tucked into a hook at one end, making it impossible to cut your fingers on, but handy if you need to cut a ligature from the neck of a suicidal detainee. There's supposed to be one on each set of cell keys. The keys themselves are just what you'd imagine them to be: long, antiquated-looking, dark metal and chunky teeth. The early-turn jailers bolt from the room, already imagining the clean air of outside world, as I drop the keys into the deep pockets of my Met trousers.

'Tea?' I ask my team. There's no one who refuses, and I walk around the group with a stack of Styrofoam cups, marking each person's preference on the soft white sides as I go. I like the feel of the biro sliding across the yielding surface. I don't mind making the teas. It's practically expected of probationers, plus it's quick, easy, and it keeps you in the skippers' good books if you keep them well lubricated throughout the shift. There's also something about, at twenty-four, being the youngest copper in custody that makes me feel it ought to be me. I ignore the fact that I'm also the only woman.

It's getting late by the time Francine is brought in. It's just past 9 p.m. when the big metal door that leads out to the back yard swings open, and she shuffles through, tiny between the two giant constables that flank her. I don't recognise them, and a glance at their shoulder numbers tells me that they're Camden officers. It's not unusual for Brixley to open up our cells to other boroughs if we have the space. Tony appears beside me and nods towards her.

'Whaddya reckon?'

I suck in my bottom lip as I look at the three of them. The officers are calm and relaxed; she poses no threat to them. Her clothes are clean, fashionable, and they fit her properly. She has a beautiful silk scarf draped across her shoulders, and small ballerina shoes that make her look almost doll-like. She's young, not more than nineteen years old, and very thin. But she's not an addict. Her skin is clear and gleams pinkish in the strip lights of Custody.

'A tom?' Tony nudges me to illicit my guess. He uses the common police-speak for prostitute.

'No way.' She's not a tom. She's terrified. She's never been in a custody suite before – of that I feel certain.

I glance at the clear plastic bag that swings from the fist of one of the officers that brought her in. It twists as he walks her towards the custody desk and I glimpse a set of car keys amongst the various items of make-up.

'Drink-drive,' I say, before wandering towards the cells, the next set of checks on my mind. As I drift into the claustrophobic corridor that leads towards the male cells, I glance back at the girl as she leans forward on the sergeant's desk to spell her name. *Francine.* Her accent is more London plum than cockney, and she speaks politely. Her voice breaks as she tries to speak through her sobs. I watch her shoulders hitching and can't help thinking that she doesn't belong in the cells. I shake my head slightly, reminding myself that there's probably a good reason that she's here. Although I've been in the police for nearly six months now – almost at the end of my probation – I still have to constantly fight against my belief that most people are good. There are only so many times people can lie to your face before it starts getting through. But will I ever stop feeling sorry for people locked in cells?

I'm nearly finished my checks of the male occupants when Tony appears at the end of the corridor with a cup of tea in his hand. He thrusts it towards me.

'What's this for?' I say. Tony's not known for his generosity in the tea-making department.

'You were right, she's in for drink-drive. Nice one, Probbie!' He laughs as he lopes off, and I begin to follow him out of the cells. I consider telling him that I saw the car keys, but then decide that I'll keep it to myself. There's nothing wrong with one of the more experienced members of my team thinking that I'm learning.

As I pass the skippers' desks, PS Debden leans over and beckons me with a cocked finger.

'That tea for me, Doris?'

I take a deep breath and force a smile. 'No, Sarge, but I can make you one if you like?'

'About time! I'm parched. Two sugars and easy on the milk this time.' He winks in a way that makes me want to shudder. 'Also, the bird I've just checked in, she's on half-hour checks, bloody hysterical. Serves her right for driving pissed, silly tart.'

I wince at his use of the word. At his use of all the words that come out of his mouth. I imagine that PS Debden would get on rather well with the woman-hating Mr Dixon. I turn around and walk towards the kitchen as the image of me spitting in his tea flashes across my mind. Once I've plonked it on his desk my thoughts stray again to Francine. She was so upset. *So fragile.* She's been put in F4, the F marking the female end of the custody suite. I make a mental note to try and check on her more frequently than every half-hour and head in her direction, with the intention of offering her a cup of tea. I now know why she's here, and I frown as I consider the worrying numbers of drivers that still drive whilst drunk. I don't agree with what she's done and I do think she deserves to be here. To be processed and punished for the risk she has taken with public safety, and her own. But that doesn't mean that I can't feel sorry for her. And it doesn't mean that I can't offer her a friendly face.

As I approach her cell, shouting erupts behind me and

she is wiped from my mind as a large, angry detainee is dragged in by four officers. A shout goes up for a jailer and I am there, leading them straight to an available cell. Usually suspects are 'checked in' at the desk before being allocated a cell, but in some cases they are too violent to do this. PS Clarke follows us down to the corridor to supervise the suspect as he's put into the cell. Once his roaring has died down, and I've completed my next set of checks, I again think of the small girl in F4.

This time I make it all the way to her door without being called away. I slide down the solid plastic cover to reveal the clear Perspex of the wicket. It's this small window that lets us peer into a cell without opening the door. I am smiling, ready to reassure, when the sight of her face shocks my smile frozen.

She is red and gasping. Her hair is matted with sweat and her eyes are wide and bulging as she slips forward off the bunk, landing heavily on her knees. They crack against the concrete floor as I realise what she's done. My hand gropes in my pocket for the keys. But they're not there. *Shit.* A memory of handing them to a detective earlier flits into my mind.

I shout as loud as I can. Just one word. 'KEYS!'

The shout rings in my ears as Tony appears from the goldfish bowl. He must have heard the urgency in my voice because he's running so fast that he almost skids into the wall beside me. He flings the keys as he stumbles. I grapple them into the lock and shove against the cold, heavy handle of the cell door. The slow, ponderous swing of it as I push inwards seems to last an eternity and then I am with her, skidding to my knees, my face level with hers.

Her eyes bulge at me, pleading. The beautiful scarf is pulled taut around her neck. So tight that it's rolled in on itself and feels thick and gnarly as I try and push my fingers beneath it. I can hear Tony yelling for the sergeants behind me, and the echo of his deep voice throbs in my ears as it reverberates around the cell. The sound of boots stomping, Tony shouting, someone hits the cell alarm and it wails, pitching into the rising wave of noise.

Everything muffles as my fingers dig into the soft skin of her neck. All I can hear is the rasp of her breaths, *her last breaths*, as she leans into me. It takes all my strength to hold her up until Tony is there, wrenching her up from beneath her armpits. He leans back on the bed and props her in front of him, her limbs flopping like a sickening ventriloquist's dummy as he moves her. I kneel in front of them as I try and tug the fabric away from the front of her neck, trying to take the pressure off her windpipe. The cartilage of her trachea rubs against the back of my knuckles as I finally get purchase beneath the silk. She is gurgling now. A rasping, desperate sound. Her eyes are wide and bloodshot and pinned on mine.

Save me.

Her skin is already darkening from red to purple above the scarf at her neck. *I need to be faster.* I grab the chunky plastic of the cell keys and ram the cutting end underneath the stretched fabric. I wince as it pushes roughly against her neck. I can feel her tense beneath me and I know that

39

I am hurting her. I can almost see the bruising that will appear on her neck. But if I don't cut this scarf she will die. It seems to take an age but finally it is up and under her chin and I push the silk towards the blade that sits within the crook of the plastic. What if it doesn't work? *It has to.* I push the doubts aside as I tug the plastic down, forcing the material up against the blade.

It's not instantaneous. There's no sudden slackening, and for a terrifying moment I think it's not working, that we really are going to lose her. And then the silk starts to hitch and fray, unfurling from the blade as I work it quickly up and down, sawing through the tortuous fabric, until there is just a thread, and it breaks away from her raw neck. She slumps forwards into my arms and it's the sweetest of sounds as she gulps, the air sucking and wheezing into her desperate lungs. I wipe the sweaty hair from her brow and sit there, panting, on the cold concrete floor of her cell.

'Ambulance is on its way. Stay with her until it arrives.' I nod up to PS Debden and get an unguarded glimpse of his pale, drawn face. I barely have the chance to consider whether it's contrition I'm witnessing before he straightens his shoulders once more and marches back towards the sergeants' desk. *Good job, constable. Way to save a life. As if.*

I gently help Francine to her feet and she sits on the edge of the bed. My hands tremble and I clasp them behind my back as the adrenalin courses through my veins. I look at her swollen throat. There are bright red welts where I was forced to shove the fish knife under the scarf. Claw marks where I tried to wrench the fabric free. All encircled by a thick, darkening bruise that marks where the scarf was positioned. Standing beside her seems too formal so I perch on the other side of the long wooden bench. I can usually find the words to reassure, but my mind is searching for something and coming up empty. Francine sniffs and swipes at her nose with a balled-up fist.

'I'm sorry.' Her voice is a rasp.

I start to tell her it's fine, that I'm just glad she's OK, when I realise she's still talking.

'I didn't mean to – I mean, I wasn't trying to –,' she falters, pushing a shaky palm into her forehead and screwing up her eyes before blowing out her breath in a long, shuddering sigh. 'I don't know why I did that.'

I want her to know that I understand. That we all have moments of despair, moments where we feel alone and our minds are clamouring, screaming, for someone to notice, for someone to come. Moments where we consider the inconceivable. I also want to shout at her. *You stupid girl!* Does she know how close she really came? I imagine telling her family. I imagine the endless questions, the inquest; the braying press. BREAKING: *Another death in police custody.* The public's shock at her young age, her pretty face staring out at them from the tabloids; *that could be our daughter.* Not a criminal, with so much promise, a life of opportunities ahead of her. Cut short by negligence. I imagine her purple face and bulging eyes joining my mind's inventory of the dead. Yet another face that will appear late at night when I close my eyes.

But she's not dead. We saved her. *I* saved her.

I slide across the plastic-wrapped foam mattress and put an arm around her trembling shoulders.

'It's OK,' I murmur. She nods as silent tears fall from her swollen lids. Her breath is steadying, but there is still a dragging rasp with each inhalation. I think of the swollen tissues in her throat and silently pray that she stays stable until the ambulance arrives. She'll have torn the muscles in her throat, shredded tissues swelling to constrict her airways. I'm not sure how long we sit there, me minutely aware of every change in her wretched breathing, but when I look up the paramedics are walking into the cell. The sense of relief throughout the custody suite is almost palpable. The professionals are here. She will go to hospital, she will live. *We are off the hook.*

I give her hand a squeeze and leave the paramedics to do their job. Heading straight for the kitchen, I wedge myself in by the taps, pouring and gulping a tepid cup of water. I wipe the sweat from my brow and clasp my hands together, breathing deeply. I am just about to head back to Francine when PS Debden spots me.

'Male three needs taking out for a phone call.' If he has been affected by what has just happened, he shows no sign of it.

'Sarge.' I nod at him and head to the cells, taking a long look back towards Francine's cell before I go. *Chin up, officer, carry on.*

I stride into the corridor leading to the male cells and start reaching for my keys. But the image of Francine's choking face is swimming before my eyes. I realise that I am still shaking slightly and pause, halfway down the cells, to steady myself. As I lean against the wall a wave of hopelessness catches me by the throat. I glance into an empty cell. The smell of it, bleach mixed with piss mixed with stale booze. The cold tiles, the seatless toilet. The shoes and belts outside cell doors; laces and leather ligatures. The despair of being closed into such a hard, unforgiving hole. I think of the children in the 'detention rooms'. Exactly the same cells given a different name. They may be burglars, but they're still children. And what kind of life have they had to wind up in here?

I shake my head to clear it. My boots scuff against the floor as I start to select the cell key. Then a scraping sound makes me turn to the cell behind me and I realise that I have stopped outside M10.

Dixon.

His voice wheedles through the metal. 'What's up, little girlie? Tired of playing with the big boys, are we?'

It sounds like he's right behind the door. I imagine him pressed up against it, a mere metre from where I stand. A bolt of fear grips my stomach and put my hands to my mouth. I know he can't see me. The wicket to his cell is closed and there are no windows. He must have heard me. I try to remember if I've made any sound. Have I been breathing loudly? How does he know I'm upset?

He doesn't know, he's just winding you up. Get a grip.

I straighten my back and push back my shoulders. My cheeks feel hot and I realise with a burning anger that he has made me feel ashamed of myself. Ashamed of being scared of him. Another slither from the cell and he speaks again.

'I know you're there, girlie. I can smell your perfume.'

I open my mouth but nothing comes out. I stand, gaping like a fish, my anger building inside me.

'I know you're there.' He speaks in a sing-song voice that almost makes me shudder. 'Don't pretend you're not, I can hear you – or do you think I'm stupid?'

And I don't know what makes me say it. I've never been bothered by cons before. The things they say have never hurt me, and I've certainly never satisfied them with a reply. I don't know why, on this particular shift, at this particular moment, I snap.

'Yes, I *do* think you're fucking stupid.' It comes out as a whisper. But Dixon hears it.

'You fucking bitch!' His cell explodes with noise and I jump back as his door begins to vibrate with the force of him kicking it. The force of him trying to get to me. I am surprised to feel a dark kind of satisfaction at his distress. He roars with rage as I turn my back on his cell and walk towards M7. I open the wicket calmly and see that Mr Trangmere is sitting on his bunk. Satisfied that he's placid, I unlock the door and swing it open.

'You waiting for a phone call?' I smile my sweetest smile.

Trangmere shuffles towards the door and turns right down the corridor. He knows the way. I follow him towards the phones and as we pass Dixon's vibrating door Trangmere shakes his head. 'Someone's not happy,' he mutters to me.

'Seems that way.' A small smile on my lips.

As we reach the front desk I glimpse the back of Francine as she is led out by the paramedics. I later find out that she has been bailed. It's easier than sending an officer to watch her while she's in hospital, especially when we need all the coppers we have out on the streets. She'll be charged with drink-drive on her return to custody in a few weeks' time.

*   *   *

I'm changing in the locker room at the end of my shift when I think again about that small girl in the cells. Mere seconds making the difference between life and death. Was it pure luck that I chose to look into her cell at that precise moment?

I don't believe in God. But, sometimes, when I think on the moments like back there in Francine's cell, where life was stretched so thin and all it would have taken to pierce through the tracing paper of her existence was one sharp nail, one distraction, I know that there must be something more to life than just biology.

It's 10.30 p.m., and I sigh as I look out of the second-floor window onto the black London skyline. I won't make it back to Mum and Dad's until way after midnight and my body sags, visualising my comfortable bed. But then a thought occurs to me. *You saved someone's life today*. My shoulders square and I raise my chin. Suddenly it doesn't matter how far my bed is or how weary my legs feel. Because I've finally done it. I've done what I joined up to do. I've made it so a daughter gets to return to her family.

4

Wormwood Scrubs

I slam my locker door and hold it shut while I force the old lock round into place. The screech of metal on metal doesn't even cause me to wince any more. It's 23 July 2005 and I've been in the Met for nine months. I'm still a probationer, technically not yet a full-blown police constable. But I'm certainly doing the job of one. It's been two weeks and two days since terrorists blew up London's transport systems, killing fifty-two people. I walk to the mirrors and zip up my Met vest. Just two days ago, a second attack was launched. It failed when the bombs didn't detonate. The Met's in crisis mode and the security level is 'critical', the highest it gets. I stare at my face in the mirror. Jaw set, eyes rimmed with dark circles. I twist my cravat so that it sits neatly in the centre of my collar. I've hardly left work since the 7th. But I don't mind. In fact, nobody minds.

I glance at my watch. 8.30 p.m. Up until last night, I was working a late turn today; 2.30 p.m. to 10.30 p.m., responding to 999 calls on my borough. But shifts change quickly at the moment. Now I've been told that I'm on a night shift heading to Wormwood Scrubs. A suspect package has been found in the woods. They must be taking it seriously if they're sending a carrier-load of coppers up there for the night. I grab my kitbag and head for the stairs. Down two at a time to the yard, where my carrier's waiting. I smile at the governor, police-speak for inspector, and give a silent thank you that it's him. Night shifts in a carrier with a 'jobsworth' inspector are not fun. I'm happy with the skipper, too. My spirits lift. In all, there are eight of us: one inspector, one sergeant and six constables. The rest of the PCs and I bundle into the carrier and choose our seats; there's plenty of room. The metal beasts are designed for public order events. Designed to be rammed-full of large officers in riot gear, shields, helmets and all. Metal grilles sit raised over the windscreen and rear doors. Not necessary for tonight's deployment. I scrape some crumbs from somebody's lunch off my seat and sit down. Lunch and dinner are 'refs' to me now. Another piece of police-talk that has become ingrained in my head. I assume it stands for refreshments but I've never asked. If someone gets a 'body' it means they've arrested someone, not found a corpse. Criminals are referred to as 'slags'. Funnily enough that wasn't included in the police speak they taught us at Hendon. It's a term I now use to fit in but it doesn't sit easy with me.

My booted foot crackles on empty crisp packets and I shake my head in disgust. The seat covers have been worn shiny and stained by years of use. The seatbelts hang forlornly from their housings, resigned to being rarely worn. The air inside is stuffy and tinged with sweat. I'm the only girl on the bus and the air has turned blue before we even hit the tarmac.

The skipper's driving and the governor takes the front seat. I stifle a yawn as we head towards West London. It's going to be a long night. Shifting inside my stab-vest, I can already feel a layer of sweat sticking my shirt to my back. I stare out at the traffic, wondering where each car is going. I bet none of them are going to guard a bomb. Not for the first time, I think how awesome my job is. Not just awesome, but damn cool. There's nothing like blatting round London in a police car. The governor's voice pulls me back to the musty interior of the carrier.

'Right. Does everyone know where we're going?' A murmur in reply.

The inspector rolls his eyes. 'What an enthusiastic bunch.' He's got a dry humour that I enjoy. He also refuses to call anyone by their first name, instead barking surnames and shoulder numbers. I like his old-school approach. Unlike many of his contemporaries, he's got the balance of discipline and respect just right.

'OK. For those who don't know, an unexploded bomb has been found in a bin at Little Wormwood Scrubs, which is a small patch of scrubland on the opposite side of the park from the prison. Apparently a park keeper found a rucksack, yanked it out and gave it a bit of a shake, before shitting himself when a bunch of wires and some explosives fell out.'

'Bloody hell,' I mutter.

'Bloody hell indeed, 215.' He continues. 'The device has

49

been made safe by the EXPOs and now, needless to say, it's a pretty important crime scene. Obviously there could be a link to the attempted bombings two days ago, so the Anti-Terrorism branch are all over it.'

A brief silence on the bus before the usual banter resumes. The EXPOs that the governor is referring to are specialised explosives officers. My pulse quickens as I think about the night ahead. Usually, sitting on a crime scene is the most mind-numbing job in the world. Not tonight. I'm happy just to be involved. If this dumped ruck-sack could lead us to the bombers, well, it's a scene worth sitting on. I feel oddly proud at the thought that I'll be one of the few chosen to stand guard. I look out of the window and realise that we've reached the river.

'Crossing over to the dark side, boys,' shouts the skipper from the front.

A mock groan goes up from 'the boys', and I don't even bother to point out that I'm not one of them.

'Andy, you got the time?' It's Joseph. A nice bloke who's been in the job for years. Before that he was in the army. Institutionalised through and through and proud of it. Plus, he tells some great stories. I look at him from my seat and he smirks in reply. Andy's the new guy, been on our team for about two weeks. The rest of the carrier holds its breath to see what Andy will do. It's an old trick. I notice that even the governor has an ear cocked, head tilted towards us from the front seat.

I watch the back of Andy's head from my position in the middle of the carrier. He looks down, shoulders shuffling a bit, and I can imagine him pushing his jumper up away from his wrist. *Don't do it, Andy.* But I know he will. This is probably his first trip in a carrier. He's just glad to be asked a direct question.

'It's nine on the dot, Joseph.' Andy looks up and throws Joseph a wide, trusting smile. His innocent face looks confused as the bus explodes into laughter. I can't help but join in. He looks to me for enlightenment.

'Look up, Andy.' I point out of the window next to him. And we all gaze up into the giant face of Big Ben, beaming down at us with its vertiginous face. It's a classic trick played on the new guys. I learnt it, and now Andy has too.

'Coffees are on you,' Joseph laughs as he pats Andy on the back.

We're still teasing Andy as we cruise over the bridge towards our destination. He seems to be taking it on the chin. I gaze out of the window and yawn again, my eyes bouncing around the London skyline. There's no architecture in the world that pleases me so. Such a muddle of new and old, each building different from the last. A brief stop at Buckingham Gate to get our refreshments and on we go. Naturally the skipper and governor get to rummage through the box first, then it's lobbed in the back for us to fight over.

'Ladies first, lads,' I shout as I swipe the box from Andy. I may be nice to the newbies, but when it comes to food I show no mercy. I scoop out a tired-looking BLT, the best I can hope for tonight. Together with the standard bottle of water, crisps and a chocolate bar, it's a depressing prospect.

And I doubt we'll be able to stop off anywhere to get something hot. There's nothing like the lack of good food to put me in a bad mood. I force my mind to focus on what we're doing and why. It keeps me positive.

Eventually we arrive at the Scrubs. It's 9.30 p.m. and we're assigned to start at 10 p.m. So we've got half an hour to kill before we start. I spend most of it hovering next to the EXPOs, quizzing them on what they've found, pretending to act cool when really I'm screaming *you guys are so awesome* inside my head. My mind squeals at their fatigues and equipment. They're all ex-army, of course, and Joseph gets much further with them than I do. I listen to everything, sucking up every detail. They've made the bomb safe and now it needs forensics to see if we can find anything. Soon they've packed up and are loading their van. Nothing will be progressing overnight – it'll just be us and the bomb.

'Have fun bomb-sitting,' laughs one of the EXPOs as he gets into the van. 'Honestly, it's completely safe. Just don't poke it, OK?' He winks at me and slides the door shut. I can hear the laughter fade as the van starts up and drives off. For a moment, I envy them, heading off towards their warm beds. It suddenly feels chilly as the last rays of summer sun disappear behind the tall blocks of flats that surround us. I rub my arms as I walk back to the carrier.

'Right. Now that 215 has finished flirting,' the governor gives me a pointed look as he continues, 'we're needed to station two points in the Scrubs. The first is that Portakabin,' he points with a straight arm, open palm, as if he's directing traffic. We all twist around and gaze at a dingy-looking temporary cabin at the entrance to the park. 'The second, next to the package itself.'

The skipper carries on from the governor's lead. 'I've worked it so that we can each do one hour on, two hours off. Hopefully that'll give some of you a chance to have a kip in between shifts. I know we're all working tomorrow.'

This goes down well with the rest of us. We've been told to expect a twelve-hour shift, so the hope that we'll get some downtime is a relief. Of course, when the skipper says 'we', he actually means 'you', just us PCs. He and the governor will probably spend the entire shift in the carrier; no getting out in the cold for them. This is so ingrained that it isn't even questioned.

'215,' the skipper barks. 'You're up first in the Portakabin.'

'Sarge,' I nod, before turning and striding towards it.

Its windows glow in the dusk. They're all open and so is the door. I hop up the steps and walk into the cabin. It's a perfect square. There are rectangular tables running along each side and the door opens up in the middle. The tables are already littered with debris, despite its being here for only eight hours or so. Magazines, newspapers, polystyrene cups and fast food wrappers almost completely cover the table-tops. A packet of half-eaten doughnuts sits in front of a large officer with jam at the corner of his mouth. He stands up slowly, wipes his lips with the back of his hand and reaches his arms to the roof, his stretch revealing a large gut that protrudes beneath his Met vest.

'At bloody last,' he grunts as he walks past me and down the steps, sugar falling from his chest as he moves. 'I've signed my statement, crime scene log is on the table.' The cabin shakes as he steps off the last step and the door slams shut behind him.

I look at the mess. *Where on the bloody table?* I sigh as I start to rummage through the magazines, looking for the white booklet that holds the all-important crime scene details. As soon as I start to move things about, I realise my mistake. *It's a summer evening. It's dark outside, the lights are on in here, and the windows are open.* A giant daddy-long-legs flies into my face as I sense the terrifying erratic flapping all around me. The cabin is full of them. Burglars I can handle, but daddy-long-legs are a step too far. I let out an embarrassingly loud scream and flap my arms like a woman on fire. I grab a copy of the *Sun* and start whacking randomly in every direction. It's no good. There are too many of them. I feel one land on my hair and shivers rush through my body. I start to pant as my irrational fear drives me to the door. It's stuck. *Fucking open, you shitting thing!* I pull at the useless handle and the whole cabin shakes as I rock forwards and backwards, desperately trying to get the door open. I just need to get out. Finally, after what seems like an eternity of insect-infested hell, the door pops open and I launch myself out of the cabin. My legs are like jelly and I miss the top step, rolling forward over myself and landing in a heap at the shiny-shoed feet of my inspector.

I look up at him through my glasses, now steamed up and wonky. I try a smile. He looks down at me with his arms crossed.

'215, what in God's name are you doing?' he barks, unamused.

I can see the rest of the carrier huddled behind him. Joseph is actually bent double with laughter. I stand up and dust myself down, sighing.

I'll never live this down.

*   *   *

Four hours later, I'm nudged awake by the skipper. I lift my head from the stained seat and rub my eyes, feel dried saliva on my cheek and quickly scrub it away with the coarse sleeve of my Met jumper. Thank God it's dark in here.

'You're up.' He nods towards the Scrubs outside.

I force myself upright and yawn, before shivering. It's a horrible feeling to be wrenched out of a deep sleep. Worse when you realise that you're still on a carrier and it's 2 a.m. I shrug on my lightweight jacket and step down off the carrier steps. The thought crosses my mind that I may have something written on my face – a real risk when sleeping on a carrier – but I'm too disorientated to really care. I shuffle through the woods in the general direction of the bomb. It's pitch black. The trees are blocking out any light from the moon and I strain my eyes as I try and see through the blackness. Up ahead I catch a glimpse of a tiny light. As

I get closer I can see that it's Joseph's phone. His face is lit up from below like a ghoul in a scary movie.

'Did you look at it?' I ask him.

'Yeah, 'course,' he replies. He gets up and pats me on the back. 'Watch out for the daddy-long-legs.' His chuckling fades into the night air as he walks away.

I roll my eyes and sit down on the plastic folding chair. It's still warm. Using my phone as a light, I search around me for the crime scene log. I balance it on my lap as I sign it, and screw up my face as I realise my signature looks like it's been scrawled by a two-year-old. I've now officially taken over the scene from Joseph. The log will be used in court as proof that the scene hasn't been contaminated. And in a case like this one, it's pretty important. You log visitors in and out; forensics, detectives and the like. I doubt there'll be any tonight, and shove the log back on the tarpaulin beneath my seat. As soon as my phone light dies, the darkness creeps back in. I look around, blinking and waiting for my eyes to adjust. A crack in the twigs behind me makes me whip my head around. It's nothing. I chastise myself for being afraid of the dark. But it's damn creepy sitting in the middle of the woods alone.

As my eyes get used to the lack of light I start to pick out the shapes around me. I can see the crime scene tent a few feet away, its front flaps moving ever so slightly in the gentle breeze. The zip is undone. I wish I'd brought a torch, or at least borrowed one from one of the guys. My phone will have to do. I tiptoe over to the tent and poke my head in through the open zip. I point my phone inside and look at the bomb. I've never seen a real one before, not counting photos from training. It's a clear plastic tub, the type used in catering maybe, and it's full of a yellowish material that looks like mashed potato. I'm not sure what I had expected, but it wasn't this. I feel a little deflated that there's no 'countdown clock'. Then my cheeks grow hot as I think about how childish I'm being. I raise my phone closer and peer harder, noticing for the first time that there are little objects taped all around the sides of the tub. My stomach churns as I realise what I'm looking at. They are metal bolts and screws. Lots of them. And they're secured all around the tub, with what looks like tape.

Temporarily blinded by the light of my phone, I stumble back to my seat and sink down into it. I know what those bolts and screws are for. They're for hurting people. No, not hurting. Killing. They're taped onto that bomb to create shrapnel. To rip through limbs and torsos. To cause maximum pain. The most horrific injuries. Suddenly nothing seems exciting any more. Not sitting here next to a bomb. Not wearing the uniform or doing my duty. Suddenly all I can feel is despair at the thought of those poor people. *Did they feel it? Did they hear the bang or just see the explosion?* I close my eyes and hope that all they did was hear a bang. That shock numbed their pain. That a warm light surrounded them and took them softly away. But my head shakes at the thought.

My head drops as the images run through my mind. In my short time as a probationary officer I've already seen enough death to provide me with plenty of material. I sit like that for a long time, head bowed, arms wrapped around my body, boots firm on the ground. I think of travelling on the tube later this morning, of the looks that will pass between travellers. The nervous glances. *Will we ever feel safe? How can we defend ourselves against people who are so sure of their beliefs that they are prepared to die for them?* There's a part of me that wants to leave London and never come back.

I must have sat like that for an hour because the next thing I know, Andy is standing beside me and my time's up. I get up and smooth out my trousers.

'You OK?' Andy asks, his eyes on mine.

'Yeah, I'm fine.' I force out a smile. 'Do you know what you're doing with the log?'

'Yup, did one last week.' His eyes are shining with excitement. Even a long boring night shift hasn't dampened his spirits. I smile again, and this time it's genuine.

'Don't forget . . .' I whisper, holding my phone under my chin and walking backwards, 'try not to poke the bomb.'

Andy laughs as I walk away. And as I tread silently through the Scrubs I realise that it's Andy's enthusiasm that has rallied me. Not just enthusiasm, but dedication. Determination to get the job done. It's the same determination that got Londoners back on the tubes as soon as they were running again. It's the same spirit that bound all of London together on 7 July. The spirit that made officers on their day off drop everything and rush to their stations to report for duty. Without being asked. As I step out of the clearing I think of London's top forensics experts and know that they will be here at first light. There's no scene more important than this one, right now.

As the carrier comes into view I head towards it, yawning. Climbing up onto the metal grated step of the carrier, I look at the horizon, an early morning sunset just beginning to colour the sky.

5
Ben

I stare at myself in the bathroom mirror. The lights are muted and the rough brick walls are painted purple. Paired with the gaudy gold mirrors and horrific 'fake candle' sconces, it's more like a tom's boudoir than a pub toilet. It's only 5 p.m. but, along with the rest of my team, I've been drinking since we came off shift two hours ago. I'm about fifteen months into my career and feel like one of the team. Gone are the probationer nerves, replaced by a healthy enthusiasm for my job. I know it won't last – one look at the coppers who have been around a few years tells me that – but I'm relishing loving my job while I still do. I cast a critical eye over my reflection and deduce that my critical eye is too tipsy to care what I look like. A quick fingertip wipe under each eye to stay my spreading mascara and I'm heading back to the tables.

The bar is long but narrow, a typical North London venue with bare brick, exposed wooden beams and mismatched salvaged furniture. The windows are high and leaded and I love the reality that they've probably been that way for nearly a century. The walk back from the toilets gives me ample time to observe my team from the outside. We are the only ones here, for now, and perhaps this knowledge is what emboldens us to be so loud at such an early hour. For the present, at least, we own this bar. We own this borough. We've commandeered three tables, which have been pushed together in a lopsided fashion, and even these provide insufficient seating space. Each chair is occupied, and yet more of us crowd around the table. It's the end of a nine-day week for us, prompting a turnout that's larger than usual, and I smile to myself as I stride towards the table. *This is going to be a good night.*

'Would you jump in my grave so quick?' I say, as I see that Ralph has nicked my chair.

'Probably, but I'd jump your bones quicker.' He delivers it deadpan, and is rewarded with a raucous eruption of laughter from around the table.

I brush his comment off easily with a theatrical eye-roll, the three double vodkas I've already consumed helping to douse the flame of embarrassment that I would usually feel. I'd learned early on that, as a woman in the force, you had two choices against the constant barrage of sexual innuendos and sexist remarks. Take them, or get ostracised. The rest of them have already moved on, distracted by someone getting drinks orders at the bar. Emboldened by the alcohol singing in my veins, I lean forward, stretching to get my drink from in front of Ralph, and giving him a long eyeful of my cleavage. And when he finally drags his eyes from between my breasts, I meet them with a hard stare.

'Try it,' I murmur, 'and I'll rip your cock off.'

With that, I drain my glass and head to the bar.

*   *   *

It's two hours later and we've swapped shabby chic for plain old shabby. Although situated on a bustling London street packed with wine bars and trendy restaurants, the pub we're in seems to have missed the last decade or so and be stuck in a rather sticky rendition of the 1990s. And not in a cool way.

I'm at the bar with Ben, Graeme and Ralph. It's Graeme's round and I've ordered a Vodka Cranberry. It comes in an odd shade of purple, and after tasting it I suspect that the cranberry juice may, in actual fact, be Ribena. But as the vodka starts to numb the back of my throat I decide I don't care. I turn back to Ralph, who's in the middle of a rendition of his latest arrest. Because what else would coppers possibly talk about after a nine-day stint of exhausting police work?

Ralph's face glows from the beer and he's captivating us all. Short and built like a bulldog, he's surprisingly fast on his feet. He's one of the team veterans, and a well-respected officer. And it's well deserved. I like him, despite the occasional inappropriate comment, and as I listen to his anecdote, I realise that my eyes are wide and my mouth is hanging slightly open. I start to adjust my expression before I realise that everyone else is doing the same. I notice that a couple of new probationers are straggling the outside of our group, straining to hear.

'So he's come out the door at me, and he must be like 6 foot 7 or something ridiculous, right? Fucking massive.' His beer slops as he gesticulates the sheer size of the suspect. 'And I'm thinking, fuck, right? I mean, I need to get these cuffs on, like, yesterday.' We all nod, urging him to continue.

'So I know, I mean *I just know*, that this guy is going to kick off when I try and nick him. So what do I do?' Our group bundles inwards, no one is drinking, seven suspended pints in mid-air.

'So I ask him the time.' Graeme and Ben let out a laugh and nod enthusiastically. I have no idea what Ralph is talking about, but I smile and nod along, not wanting to be the one who doesn't get it.

Ralph continues. 'I ask him the time. And when he lifts up his wrist to look at his watch, I snap on a cuff.'

An exhalation of understanding from those in the group that were lost. Including me.

'Now. I've done this a million times, right? Always works. Once you have one cuff on you have them under control. You take them to the floor – sorted.'

'Nice one, Ralph.' Ben slaps him on the back.

'Yeah, but that's not how it went down this time.' A pause. 'See, I was standing at the top of about five concrete steps that led up to his front door. I realised too late that there was nowhere to go. And this guy, he saw what I'd done, and he went fucking berserk.'

'He shoves into me hard, and I'm thinking two things. One, I'm going backwards down these steps, and two, this is going to fucking hurt. Like, do I hold on to the cuffs or do I let go and try and stop my skull getting smashed in?'

'What did you do?' This from one of the probbies at the back.

Ralph grins and takes a long swig of his lager. He's making us wait and he loves it.

'I let go of the cuffs, of course. Do you think I'm nuts?' He shakes his head as the rest of us laugh loudly. 'Off that fucker goes with my cuffs dangling from his wrist.'

The laughter dies and, sensing that the tale is over, the stragglers wander off.

'Oh my God, Ralph,' I say, my hands covering my mouth. 'What did the skipper say?' At this, Graeme, Ralph and Ben groan and roll their eyes. Graeme puts an affectionate arm around me and pulls me in for a hug. 'You're such a goody two shoes, Alice.'

'What?' I look from one face to the other, wondering what I've missed.

'The skipper said fuck all,' Ralph chuckles, 'cos I didn't fucking tell him.'

And before I can wonder where Ralph is going to get another pair of handcuffs without telling a sergeant, we're ordering shots and the handcuffs fly from my mind like they flew from Ralph's grasp.

*　　*　　*

The soles of my ballet pumps stick to the floor as I stand at the bar, and I have to keep schlepping them free, for fear of being permanently rooted to this spot. I suspect that my right elbow is also superglued to the stainless steel bar surface, but after countless double vodkas I need to lean. I try and ignore the slightly clouded stain on my glass and decide it's not worth bothering the gruff-looking bartender with. He's glaring at us from his position by the taps, leaning back against the bar with his tattooed arms crossed across a giant beer belly. He's already taken a dislike to our group, although obviously not enough of a dislike to actually refuse our money. I wonder if he's sussed us already. It's not that hard to guess what we do. One glaring denominator gives us away to anyone whose glance lingers a little longer: most of my team are tall white males with close-cropped short hair, wearing Superdry jeans and North Face jackets. I smile at the irony that, since the main North Face warehouse was burgled a year or so ago, the same jackets have now become a common choice for our local slags.

This is not a bar that any of us would have chosen to drink in alone. It may be a line from a tacky movie to say that a copper never switches off, but to a certain extent it's true. We're always on duty. If something happens and we don't take action at best we could lose our job. At worst, we could be sent down for gross misconduct. So when we walk into a bar we start sussing out the clientele before we even order our first drink. We decide which table would give us the tactical advantage should anything go wrong, and ultimately, if we get that feeling then we don't stay. That's what we'd usually do. But strength in numbers, hours of drinking and multiple rounds mean that we don't really care any more. We've wandered into another small, quiet pub and basically taken over the bar. *We're untouchable.*

I'm thinking about suggesting we move on when a pretty blonde girl squeezes up to the bar, sandwiching herself between Ben and Graeme. She doesn't seem to mind the close proximity, and smiles up as Ben starts to talk to her ample chest. Immediately Ralph appears beside them and I roll my eyes as I watch him check out her arse from behind. His exaggerated eyebrow-raising tells me he approves, and he starts nudging Graeme and winking at Ben from behind the girl's back. I feel briefly agitated, but before I can really grasp the reason for this, something starts to tug at my subconscious. A little warning light, bleak and dulled by the vodka, is insistently trying to get my attention.

My eyes flit to the back of the bar and, as the door to the men's room swings open, I instantly realise what it is that my brain is trying to tell me. *She has a boyfriend. And he looks like a bloody Rottweiler.* I remember now that they've been at the back of the bar, sitting opposite each other across a small table for two. From her frown, and his gesticulating, I'd gathered that they were having some kind of row. He was roped with muscle, the sinews of his neck straining as he aggressively arrowed his fingers towards her, jabbing each word he said towards her like darts. Her shoulders were hunched and her head was down. I'd noted their domestic at the time, as I do every time I see a couple rowing. Because it so often turns nasty, and we were all far too drunk to deal with it if it did. He stands now, all Alpha male with his legs apart, hands on hips, pelvis thrust forward, looking at his empty table. I see the storm cloud pass his face as he raises his gaze to the bar. I once again clock his shaven head, striped with whitened scars, and tattooed knuckles. *He's a fighter.* I lurch towards Ben and grab him by the shoulder. Blondie's boyfriend strides towards our group and just as I manage to get Ben's attention, he reaches into their circle of four and grabs Blondie by the arm.

She immediately tries to placate him, but he drags her towards him roughly, and her drink splays from her hand and falls to the ground. The smash of breaking glass brings everyone to a stop, and I feel the cold liquid splash against my feet as ice cubes skitter across the floor.

His voice is as rough as his appearance as he growls at Blondie, before pushing her away towards their vacated table. There are four of us at the bar and one of him. The rest of the team are only metres away and everyone is watching. Graeme and Ralph are already shaking their heads, palms up and facing the Fighter. *You've got the wrong idea.* But Ben's hands are fisted by his side and I only need a glimpse of his face to see that the shutters have already slammed down. And they're painted red.

'What the fuck are you doing talking to my girlfriend?' The Fighter raises his voice. He wants everyone to hear. Seeing that he's found himself a willing opponent, he ignores Graeme and Ralph and steps up to Ben. Every muscle in his neck is veined and taut, his chin jutted and sharp. Ben responds in kind, pushing his chest out and lowering his brow, until they are just inches apart, grunting angry breaths in each other's faces. And as I look at them I imagine peacocks in their place. *Men.*

'I think you should apologise to the lady for spilling her drink.' Ben's voice is low and menacing. There's something about his Northern accent that makes it even more so. He stands a good foot taller than the fighter, but he's easily outweighed in terms of sheer bulk.

'You know nothing about it, mate.' His rough cockney is a jarring contrast to Ben's northern baritone. 'So why don't you just fuck off back to your mates?'

Ben doesn't move an inch. The team are closer now, edging towards the stand-off so that Ben and the Fighter are almost completely surrounded. Blondie is back at the table for two, sniffling into her handbag.

Ralph calls towards Ben, 'Come on, mate, he's really not worth it.'

'Listen to your mate and fuck off.' The Fighter smirks as he says it. I cannot believe the guts of him, and I'm not the only one who's realised that he must have a screw loose. And maybe it's not just that. I watch as his eyes jump around Ben's face and notice that his jaw is working away. *Is he grinding his teeth?* Ralph and Graeme move to stand either side of Ben.

'Looks like you're outnumbered,' Ben cocks an eyebrow. 'So why don't *you* fuck off?' The tension curls through the air as cigarette smoke would have before the ban.

To my amazement, the Fighter just shrugs. 'Whatever,' he mutters, and turns away from Ben.

The breath that I haven't even realised I am holding whooshes out of my mouth in a grateful sigh. The bar swings to life again and my team soften their stances and start finishing their drinks. Conversations spring to life once more and Graeme and Ralph are laughing at something Ben has said. But Ben doesn't laugh, the tension still steaming from his back. I glance back to the Fighter as he strolls slowly to his table, swinging his arms in exaggerated casualness. Something stops me from looking away and I watch as he leans down and plants a kiss on his girlfriend's cheek. Then he picks up an empty pint glass. He raises it so that it's level with his eyes and studies it, turning it this way and that. His girlfriend takes him by the wrist and tries to bring him back to her, but in his head he's still face to face with Ben.

He grips the pint glass at the base, large hand almost encompassing it completely, and punches his hand down towards the table-top. The top of the pint glass explodes as it hits the wood and then the Fighter is walking back towards Ben, the jagged remains of his pint glass glinting in his hand.

The realisation of what's about to happen hits our group and travels like a wave through us to Graeme, Ben and Ralph at the bar. I catch a glimpse of the bartender with the landline phone clutched to his ear, his free hand cupped around the mouthpiece. Ben spins around as the Fighter starts to shout.

'I'm going to open you up like a tin of beans.' He roars it across the bar towards Ben. And he stands, jagged glass extended towards Ben, feet spread, spit flying from his mouth as he accentuates the word beans. I have a brief moment to consider just how ridiculous he sounds before everyone jumps to life around me. Graeme and Ralph grapple with Ben as he lunges towards the Fighter. I've seen Ben's temper before and it's no different now. Seemingly oblivious to the jagged glass and the risk of losing his job, not to mention serious injury, Ben struggles to get to him. Two more of our team join Graeme and Ralph and, as a group, they manage to hold Ben back.

'I've called the police!' shouts the barman and, almost on cue, I hear the sirens. We're only a few minutes away from the station. From *our* station. I grab the boys' jackets from their beer stools as they shove Ben roughly from the pub. I burst into the fresh night air just as Ralph is loudly reminding Ben that we do not want to be here when the police arrive. As I look towards the station I can make out blue lights reflecting on the shop windows. They're nearly round the corner – they'll be able to see us in a matter of seconds. For a moment I pause, unsure of what we're doing. *Are we staying to report the man's behaviour?* And I do what I always do in moments of confusion; I look to the senior members of my team. Ralph is shouting 'Let's go, let's go' and I shove the jackets towards him as he starts backing away. The probbies shoot confused looks at me and I shrug before following Ralph and the others.

And then we're down a side-alley and running. It hits me that I've never run away from police officers before and the sheer irony of it makes me laugh. The hysterical giggles bubble out of me as I run with my team. And the blood pumps in our veins and the cool air wipes the bar funk from our faces and we're sprinting and soaring and whooping. Left down a cut-through road, right through a dark estate. We run until the sirens have died into the distance, until we're laughing so much that our breath comes in gulps and gasps and we have to stop and hold our knees. Panting and crying with laughter, the tension slips from us like oil slicking over water. The tension of eight days of shifts; eight days of risk. Of being a copper. And in that moment, standing with my team under a humming street light in Brixley, I feel *untouchable. Invincible.*

We saunter towards another bar, arms thrown around each other. Walking as one.

6

Hilda

The radio crackles into life.

'Suspected sudden death, neighbours reporting foul smell coming from property next door . . .'

I sigh loudly. I've recently become a police driver, stepping up a rung from unskilled probationer to slightly skilled probationer. It's September, and my two years are up in October. I'll finally be a full constable and I'm counting down the days. Not that it seems to be such a big deal any more – to anyone else apart from me, that is. With the speed that officers come on and off team at the moment I've managed to feel quite experienced already. I'm frequently paired with probationers younger in service than me and I'm next in line for a response driving course. The thought of driving an emergency response vehicle for real, of actually using the lights and sirens, or blues and twos as they're more commonly known, fills me with anticipation. But, right now, it seems that I'm forever doomed to drive 'the death car': a panda, and the most likely unit to be assigned to attend a sudden death call.

Although my vehicle is equipped with lights and sirens, I'm not yet qualified to use them in pursuit, or to progress to a call. Basically, I'm driving the 'slow' car responsible for reporting all of the non-emergency crimes. Still, it's better than being stuck in the cells looking after the guests, or standing on a crime scene in the rain.

I still start my shift each day with a smile and a thank you. The thank you is for being part of the best police service in the world. The smile – well, surely a smiling copper is less likely to get punched in the mouth? For all of my griping, I love my job. Every day brings something different and each call dangles the possibility of excitement just ahead of me. Will this be *the* call? The call I will remember for the rest of my life? The call that makes a difference? I highly doubt it.

Reaching for my radio, I press the button and wait for the bleep that tells me I'm on the airway, 'Show November India 81.'

I accept the call in my 'radio drawl'. Everybody has one. Everybody with sense, anyway. For a woman, like myself, it's important not to sound like a 'Doris' on the radio. Oh yes, even in this day and age, female officers collectively still get referred to as 'Doris'. The more monotone your voice and the more bored you sound, the better. I still remember the piss-taking I suffered after my first few days on the beat; my high-pitched, quaky voice shivering out over the airways. It didn't take me long to learn.

I turn to my operator, the officer who sits in the passenger seat. They call them operators because they are

supposed to assist the driver, provide directions if necessary and generally be helpful, hardworking and focused.
My operator is Liz. I've only worked with her a couple of
times before and from what I've seen and heard, she's
keen. Which is a good start.

'You been to a sudden death before?'

Liz shakes her head.

'Ever seen a dead body before?

Another silent shake.

'OK, well, don't worry, I'll guide you through it.'

Liz nods, wide-eyed, her brown hair bobbing slightly as
she does so. A quick raise of the hand to smooth a fly-away
strand, a gesture of practicality rather than vanity. Apparently
Liz likes to box and it doesn't surprise me. Her moves are
sharp, calculated. As I drive towards the address, she sits
rigid, with her hands clasped in her lap. I can feel the nervous
tension coming off her like heat from a radiator. My first
sudden death call was a man living in a hostel for alcoholics.
He had basically coughed up his own lungs. We found him
kneeling at the small sink in his room, with foamy black
blood coagulating down his chin. The bulbous purple splat-
ters in the sink were his alveoli, according to the doctor who
attended the scene. He was pale and solid. I remember looking at his hands, frozen in a literal death-grip onto the rim of
the sink, thinking how about awful his last moments must
have been, the pain he must have felt. His feet were bare and
blue, where the blood had pooled at the bottom of his body.

Although it was entirely certain that he was dead, way
past saving, I still found myself thinking, why are we all

doing nothing? Why is everyone just standing around? Of course, as I would quickly learn, this was the way of the job. Insecurities and fears, feelings and pain were to be shoved deep down to the pit of the stomach, only to be thought about late at night, when you were drunk and alone. Or maybe that's just me.

We arrive at the address and Liz knocks on the door of the informant, the neighbour who made the call. As she waits for a reply I knock on the door of the suspected death. After a few loud knocks I bend down and open the letter-box. The air hits my face and I take a cautious sniff. The familiar smell of rotten flesh is seeping from the flat, and I turn to Liz and nod.

'She's dead all right,' I say quietly, as the informant's door pops open.

'Oh, finally,' is the greeting from Mrs Gayton, our dead body's kindly next-door neighbour. 'I called you lot hours ago.' It hasn't been hours, it's been about thirty minutes.

'Sorry for the delay,' says Liz. 'Can you tell me when you last saw your neighbour?'

Mrs Gayton rolls her eyes to the top of her head and sighs loudly, her jowly chin quivering as she does so. 'I already told the bloke on the phone, I ain't seen her for nearly a month.' She takes her hands from the hips of her velour tracksuit and wafts them in front of her puffy face. 'And then there's *the smell.*'

'What's your neighbour's name, please?' I ask, as a waft of stale cigarettes reaches my nostrils. Mrs Gayton's flat doesn't smell too nice either.

75

'Hilda, I think.'

'Does Hilda often go out?'

'Never. Only see her when she peeks out of her window, or comes to get the milk. She can't walk far, poor love.' Mrs Gayton pouts and tilts her head, and I find myself staring at the deep drag wrinkles around her thin lips. The concerned look doesn't really sit right on her mascara-smeared face.

I glance at the full milk bottles lined up by the door. 'Does she have any family nearby?' I ask, nodding to Liz that she should be writing all this down. Liz starts fumbling for her pocket book.

'Nope, no one ever visits, poor thing.'

'Except you?'

A short silence.

'Me?' Mrs Gayton gasps, puffing out her chest slightly. 'Well, I don't even know her.'

'I'm sure,' I say with a practised fake smile, not particularly caring whether she thinks I'm genuine or not.

'I don't suppose you have a spare key?' I'm pretty sure I know what the answer's going to be, and Mrs Gayton confirms it with a shake of her head.

'We may need to speak to you again, but we've got all your details. We'll take it from here. Thanks for calling.' I turn to Liz as Mrs Gayton shuts the door behind me.

'Right then,' I rub my hands together. 'Shall we try and get in?'

The door is wooden, thankfully, and secured by a single Yale lock. I give a tug on the letter-box and am pleased to feel the door jiggle. It won't take much to open it. Sure, we could smash it open, but then we'd be stuck on scene for hours waiting for a service to come and board it up. I'd much rather get in without damaging the lock, so that we can shut it behind us ourselves when we leave. Slipping the lock is frighteningly easy to do. In fact, it's exactly why I tell people to double-lock their doors at night.

Once I've slipped the lock, I open the door slowly, trying not to breathe through my nose. The air that greets us is so thick you can almost see it. Ahead of me is a short hallway that leads to a set of stairs. And so it begins. The search for the corpse. I've done it more times than I care to remember but it still unsettles me, every time. You never know where it's going to be. You don't know how it's going to look. You just wander reluctantly from room to room until you find it.

As I pass the radiator in the hallway I can feel it's on full-blast. The air is so still and viscous that I'm pretty sure there are no windows open. The perfect conditions for decomposition.

'You OK?' I whisper to Liz, who's coming up the stairs behind me.

'Yeah.' Her voice is muffled through the arm of her police jumper, which she is pressing to her nose and mouth.

I've reached the top of the stairs. There are four doors off the hallway ahead of me. Two on the left, one dead ahead and one on the right. I start with the closest room. I'm aware of my boots as they skim across the thick carpet. They feel heavy, but I push them forwards. The intensity of the smell has wiped from my mind any possibility that she might still be alive. There's no rush. There's no urgency, no chance to save life or limb. Just death. I stand in the first doorway and stare into an empty bedroom. Neat and tidy, bed made. I notice that Liz is holding back, hovering at the top of the stairs.

'This isn't going to be a nice one, Liz,' I say, moving forwards to the next door. 'Stay there. I'll find her.'

Of course, once she's found, Liz will have to look. She'll have to do all the unpleasant things that coppers have to do. But there's no harm in delaying it slightly. Because once you've seen your first dead body, there's no going back. I stand at the end of the hallway, where I can see into the next two rooms. An empty kitchen and bathroom. One door left. It's almost closed – just the smallest of gaps separate it from the frame. I can feel the heat hit my palm as I reach my hand across to push it open. The room opens up before me and the first thing I see are the flies. They cover the curtains like moving mould. I can hear their buzz and a few shoot past me as I step into the room, causing me to wave my arms about. I shudder as I think about what they've been feeding on. *I don't want them to touch me.*

Time slows as my vision turns towards the chair in the corner of the room. And there she is. Hilda. Or rather, where Hilda used to live. In one quick glance my eyes take in so many things and the images shoot through my mind, buzzing and itching like the flies that surround me. *Maggots, rot, fluid, seeping, swollen, blackened.* Images I can never erase.

My mind gathers itself and I'm back to the job in hand. At each sudden death we have to justify why we don't do CPR. *How did we know they were dead? Why didn't we try and save them?* It shouldn't be necessary in this case, but it will still need to be documented. *Note the state of the body, the rot. The smell.* They are difficult details to write down as it's done with the knowledge that, somewhere down the line, those details may be read out in a coroner's court in front of the deceased's family.

'Got her,' I call to Liz, who I imagine is still standing at the top of the stairs.

I hear her slow steps approaching the room. As she reaches the door she steps quickly in, and I get the opinion that she has had to force herself to take that last step. Like a shy performer being shoved onto the stage. Liz's eyes rest on the body and she goes very still. Straight back, chin tucked in, the only movement she makes is the clenching and unclenching of her fists. *The boxer.*

'You OK?' I ask, placing a hand on her arm.

'Yep.' The reply is short.

'Right then.' I reach into my pocket and pull out some rubber gloves. The flies buzz around me as I walk to the windows and open them as wide as they go. Relieved as the bluebottles begin to stream out of the window, I turn back to the corpse. There are certain things you need to do at sudden deaths. You need to look for any signs that the death could be suspicious. You need to try and find contact details for friends and family, so that a death message can be given. You need to inform a supervisor, check the property for medication and valuables, record the scene in a detailed statement and 'roll the body'. It's called 'rolling the body' because, most of the time, that's exactly what you do. You turn it over to check for any signs of trauma, or injuries that may have caused death. It would be quite embarrassing if you called the undertakers and they rolled the body themselves, only to find a massive knife sticking out of its back. It has happened.

So we stand in front of the body, gloves on, sweating and breathing through our mouths. *How the hell are we going to do this?* The body is so decomposed that it has no eyes. As I look at it, I make an assumption that she has died sitting upright in her chair, and then slid forwards, so that her knees are now resting on the carpet. Her hands have remained on the armrests, and her arms are pulled up behind her so that she is stretched into an unnatural position. Her legs have spread open and her nightdress has ridden up to just below her breasts. I wince as I look at her, as I invade her by seeing her in this most vulnerable of positions. *Hilda's gone. She doesn't care.* The lower half of her body is mostly dark blue, where gravity has pulled all of her blood down towards the floor.

There are transparent sheets of what looks like clingfilm, flaying away from her legs and stuck to the feet of the chair.

'What is that?' Liz whispers, leaning down to have a closer look. 'Was she wearing tights, do you think?'

I eye the delicate layers and sigh. 'I think it's her skin.' Liz gulps as she straightens up.

Between Hilda's legs is a large sac of skin, bulging outwards. I can't make sense of it. My gaze slips from it like oil over water each time I try and take it in, and so I just stop looking. Later, I learn from the undertakers that all of the liquid, blood and organs have slipped downwards through her body, effectively turning her inside out. Gathering in the sac between her legs.

'We need to check for injuries,' I mumble. Liz doesn't move.

I don't blame her. I don't want to take another step towards Hilda's corpse, let alone touch it. But there's always a chance she's been murdered. Doesn't she deserve to be checked? Steeling myself, I step towards her and bend over to look at her shoulders. They are pressed against the front edge of the seat. Taking a deep breath, I put my hand on the shoulder that is closest to me, and pull. I'm trying to move her forward slightly, so that I can see her back. She moves surprisingly easily, rigor mortis having long since passed. My gloved fingers sink into her flesh and it feels like cold play-dough. A fresh wave of pungent rot catches in my throat and I whip my hand away, stumbling backwards. My head spins slightly as I taste bile in my throat.

'Fuck that,' I pant. I can't do it. Resisting the urge to vomit like a rookie, I rip off my glove and throw it on the floor. Not for the first time, I think about how cruelly death can steal our dignity. I usher Liz outside with me, where I spend the rest of our time helping her with her statement for the coroner. Our skipper arrives and I tell her that we haven't been able to check the corpse due to severe decomposition. To be honest, even if I had been able to check her back, it would have been difficult to differentiate any injury from the decomposition.

We search the flat for any clues that could lead us to her next of kin, but find little to go on. One solitary card sits on the mantelpiece, a floral scene on the front. It's impossible to tell how long it's been there. The flat is mostly neat and tidy, clean apart from the film of dust that has settled in the weeks since Hilda died.

'Hilda. I miss you. Jack.'

Standing there, reading those words, it hits me that I am witnessing the end of a life. Not just the decay of a body, but the departure of a real person. Someone who has loved and lost. Someone who ended up terribly alone. There are no family photos, no evidence of grandchildren. I wonder if Hilda ever had any children. Then I see a small black and white photo, tucked behind a box of tissues. A slim woman poses for the camera in a fitted dress. She's shading her eyes from the sun, hair pulled back, except for a few strands that fly loose around her cheeks. She is smiling. A smile that reaches all the way to her eyes. As I look at it I know it's Hilda. And I smile, happy that she was happy, even if only for a while.

Once the undertakers have taken her away, we secure the flat and head back to the station. Liz finishes her statement for the coroner and I complete a 'body found' report on the computer. And the whole time I'm thinking how awful it is that Hilda's death went unnoticed. That her body was left to get in that state. Living in London, one of the busiest cities in the world, surrounded by people, crammed into flats, one piled on top of each other, and yet so completely alone. So forgotten that only one of her neighbours noticed she was gone, and even then, she only really rang us because of the smell.

So, no, it isn't the call. It isn't the call that changes my career, or the call where I make a difference. There has been no shouting, running or fighting. Instead, I have seen death at its most silent, most lonely, its most degrading. I have seen the power it has to call people to witness its destruction. So, although it isn't the call, I'll never forget it. And sometimes, in the dark of night, it's Hilda I see when I close my eyes.

7

Rosa

I'm trying to stay positive as I shoulder-barge my way into the custody suite. My early-turn shift has been going well up until now. The sun is shining and Londoners are out in force, enjoying the Saturday sun. There's been a lot of bare skin on show, which the male officers have been readily enjoying as they cruise around the borough. There's been slightly less eye candy for the female members of the team, however, as every Tom, Dick and Harry who owns a shirt has decided to take theirs off, without giving much thought, it seems, to whether or not they really should. I've been up and down the borough, mainly reporting non-emergency crimes, chatting to the public and getting my hands in the pockets of some of the less desirable residents of Brixley.

We are planning on grabbing some refs as the request from Custody comes out over the radio.

'All cars, all cars, from Bravo X-ray – is there an available female officer to assist in custody with a strip search?'

I groan loudly and wait as the radio silence stretches out between me and the control room, imagining tumbleweeds rolling across arid vistas.

'Surely there's some free probationers that need experience of a strip search?' I lament to Joseph, my operator for the day. Despite being longer in service than me, at seven years in, Joseph has never wanted to drive for the Met. *They'll do your legs every opportunity they get.* There are a small few who refuse to drive for fear of being done over by the Met if something goes wrong. You knock someone over while on an emergency run? You're on your own. I still hope that I won't grow to be so cynical. My two years' probation was officially over last month. My certificate is at home at my mum's. I've finally found a flat and am living with two other coppers, who work in a different borough to me. We're like ships in the night, which is actually quite nice, since my time at home is the only escape I get from the job. When I'm not at work or doing overtime, I'm usually out drinking with my workmates. I live and breathe the job and I love it.

When I was new in service, the one thing I was told was *be keen.* Stick your neck out, volunteer for the shit jobs, grab any chance you have at doing something new. Not only would it mean that you learnt quickly, but also, and maybe more importantly, that your team would recognise you were willing to pitch in. That you wanted to be there. That you'd waited two years to get into Hendon and would do those eighteen weeks in the tower blocks from hell all over again if it meant you got to stay. You can say what you like about a newbie, but if they're keen, if they volunteer time and time again throughout those first two years, for the weary jobs, reporting jobs, the sudden deaths and the strip-searches, then a grudging respect will develop. Maybe even turn into a mutual respect. Trouble was, we seemed to be getting more and more probationers who weren't willing, or were too nervous, to put themselves forwards. First, forcing a probationer to make the tea for the rest of their team had been deemed 'bullying'. And now, probbies were racing through their two years as mentees and disappearing off to CID before they'd even learnt the basics of street policing.

We continue to listen to the silence until the thought of my colleagues waiting in Custody pushes away my reluctance.

'BX – show 215.'

'Received, 215. And thanks.'

And now I'm strolling towards the skippers' desks trying to keep the scowl from my face. Ahead of me stands Julia, a two-weeks-in fledgling, and Liz, who went through Hendon with me. Between them, a scrawny-looking female lolls forwards against the custody desk. She's growling at the custody sergeant in a gravelly hack.

'Every fucking time. Every *fucking* time I come in here you strip me.' Her dry knuckles are white with dead skin and pressure as she fists them against the counter. 'I've told you, I've got nothing on me.'

Liz raises a weary hand in gesture and rolls her eyes.

'Sorry about this, mate, but something tells me I'll need another pair of hands. It's Julia's first strip-search.'

I nod a reply that says *don't worry about it*, as the detainee continues to bend the skipper's ear. Liz hands me a printed sheet of paper and I see the summarised details of Rosa's police record. A long life of misery cramped onto half a page of A4. She's mostly been arrested for drugs offences: Class A, crack and heroin. Lots of shop-lifting. I shake my head slightly as I notice a few old counts of soliciting. I've never understood the point of arresting prostitutes. In fact, the only time I do it is if they're wanted for an outstanding warrant, or they're carrying drugs. I've never arrested anyone for the offence of soliciting, and I don't intend to ever do so. Don't get me wrong, I'll nick a John every day of the week. Dirty bastards, perpetuating the crime with their custom. But 99 per cent of prostitutes are also drug addicts. They're stuck in a harrowing cycle of soliciting to pay for drugs. When they get arrested for soliciting, they get sent to court. The court gives them a fine. And then they go out and solicit, double-time, to pay off the fine *and* buy their drugs. There's something wrong with the logic of that. Rosa's agitated voice brings me back into the room.

'I'm not fucking doing it! You're not strip-searching me again.' Her last words are spat rather than spoken, and she pushes herself off of the counter and upright, crossing her arms defiantly across her chest. She juts out her chin and stands at full height, but she is tiny even still. Her 5 ft 4 inch frame is wired and tense, each wasted muscle defined on her skin, which is bluish-white in the fluorescent glare of the custody lights. She is wearing the standard garb of a Brixley hooker, scuffed skinny jeans and a tight white vest top. Well, maybe it used to be white. Most of the make-up caking on her face seems to have ended up around the neck of the vest, and a bright pink bra-strap sticks out across one of her shoulders. The lace looks crisp and new, at odds with the rest of her outfit. *Someone's been shoplifting again.* Her arms are bare and bruised, dotted with scabs and scratches, and her feet sit in tiny, hideously grubby ballet pumps.

The skipper's face is impassive. 'Rosa, you know the drill. You're a Class A drug addict with a history of self-harm. I'm not putting you in a cell without strip-searching you first.'

Rosa twists her face into a grimace. 'I'm not having it. How the fuck would you like it?'

She has a point. I doubt the custody sergeant would like it very much at all. I doubt anyone would. The fact that none of us likes doing it means nothing to Rosa, and so it shouldn't. Whichever way you look at it, being forced to strip naked, in front of strangers, in a small dank cell is nobody's idea of pleasant. Nobody reasonable anyway.

The skipper's face softens. 'Rosa, come on. My officers are professionals, they do this all the time. If you play along then it'll be over before you know it and we'll let you out for a fag, make you a nice cuppa?' Rosa snorts deridingly and shakes her head.

'Look, Rosa, if I send you into that cell and you end up cutting yourself with a razor or overdosing on some dodgy gear, then it's my job on the line. I just can't do it.' The skipper is the face of reason. His body language is open, his palms face the sky in a *WhatCanIDo?* pose. I'm impressed.

But Rosa's gone past reasonable and has entered a fury all of her own. She leans towards the custody desk and points a bony finger at the skipper's face. I notice the dirt under her long, ragged fingernail as she begins to wheeze, in a guttural rant.

'Fuck your job, Sarge, and fuck you dykes. Any excuse for a bit of pussy, eh?' Her lip is taut and twisted in a snarl as she directs this towards Liz, Julia and myself. 'You'll have to fucking drag me down there 'cos I ain't fucking going!'

The skipper looks at me and Liz. He's done all he can. 'Female Cell 4 please, ladies.'

I nod to Liz, and without speaking we take hold of Rosa, gently, taking an arm each. I place one hand around her right arm, just above the elbow, and rest the other on her shoulder. Liz does the same on Rosa's left, so that we border her on each side and she stands in between and slightly in front of us. We begin to push her gently in the direction of Female Cell 4. I glance at Julia's pale face as we pass, and she steps in behind us.

After a few shuffled steps, Rosa starts to writhe and kick out against us in earnest. The closer we get to F4, the harder it becomes to move her without strong force. And as I open my mouth to try and calm her, I hear a distinct sound in her throat. I immediately shove her shoulders forward and twist my face away from her. She is bent forward by the movement and the viscous lump of phlegm and saliva that she's just tried to spit in my face sails past me and hits the custody walls with a tiny splat. White-hot rage rips through me. *How dare she try and spit in my face.* I clamp my mouth shut and push my anger down into the pit of my stomach. *Hepatitis, herpes, risk of infection.*

'Let's just get her to the cell,' I mutter to Liz through my clenched jaw, and we walk her, still bent forward, down the corridor.

'Julia, get the door,' Liz orders.

We pause as Julia scurries around us and rushes ahead to F4. She swings the heavy metal door back and we walk Rosa into the cell and push her towards the bed. Liz swings the door almost shut behind us, leaving it open an inch or so. It's never safe to lock yourself in a cell with a detainee, but equally we need to ensure Rosa has privacy during the search.

She's got all of our backs up and I'm getting more than a bit impatient with her. But as she flops onto the hard plastic mattress she puts her head in her hands and starts to cry. I put my hands on my hips and take a breath. I try and remind myself how horrifying her life is. And when I speak, I manage to sound calm.

'Rosa. We have to do this. It's going to be so much easier if you cooperate with us. I know this sucks. We think so too.'

'I don't want to.' Her voice is small and childlike as she sniffs, wiping her balled fists across her nose.

'I know.' I feel genuine sympathy for her, and I try and

let it show in my voice. 'But let's just get it over with. We'll do one piece of clothing at a time, top, then bottoms, so you'll never be completely undressed.'

'Oooo, lucky fucking me.'

She's changed once again from little girl lost into a vicious, withered hag. She's so up and down I wonder if she's taken a hit of something just before getting nicked. And with the reappearance of Hyde, my patience wears dangerously thin. 'Look, Rosa, we've all got stuff to do, OK?' I take a pair of silicone gloves out of the small Personal Protection Kit pouch on my belt. Liz's already got hers on and I look to Julia. I pat my PPK and she immediately starts fishing around in hers. Tugging the purple powdered latex on, I nod towards Rosa again. 'Come on, Rosa, on your feet. Let's get this over with.'

Rosa stuffs her balled fists between her thighs and hunkers down. 'Fuck you, dyke.'

Liz lets out a frustrated groan and Julia's eyes flick from me to Rosa and back again. Maybe it's the stench of the custody suite. Maybe it's the flickering cell light irritating my eyes, or the fact that I'd rather be out on the streets getting my hands in pockets. Maybe it's the fact that no other fucker volunteered, or the memory of Rosa trying to spit in my face that slams my shutters down – I can't say I honestly know. But whatever it is, I change. I change from the copper who would rather talk a situation through, build a rapport, take the long way round, the copper who would choose time over force; to the copper who marches over to Rosa and pulls her upright.

She promptly begins to shriek like she's being murdered. As I grapple with her left arm Liz takes her right, and as we pull her to the centre of the cell I can feel the sharp heat of her armpit through my gloved fingers. It's at this point that Rosa decides to change tack, from rigid jerking to total floppiness. We struggle to hold her up momentarily, before slowly lowering her to the floor. It's an awkward manoeuvre, and Rosa ends up prone, with her arms twisting backwards, caught in our swan-neck grips. Her grubby cheek looks like an undercooked, flaccid pancake, pressed against the floor tiles, and I think how filthy they must be. *I couldn't bear to have my face there.*

'Julia – shoes.' I jerk my head towards Rosa's feet, and Julia startles forward, bending down to reach for Rosa's shoes. Rosa starts to kick out furiously, and I twist myself round so that I can press my knee into the back of her calf. Liz mimics my position, and Rosa is now pressed into the floor tiles from chest to shin. She is groaning and swearing and I can hear her breath coming in ragged gulps. We can't keep her in this position for long. Every copper that pays attention in officer safety training should know that forcing a prisoner into a prone position is extremely high-risk. Especially an agitated prisoner. The weight of restraint starts to restrict the chest movements, and the more distressed the detainee becomes, the harder they find it to breathe.

Julia has successfully removed Rosa's shoes and a wad of crumpled-up tissue falls out of one of them.

'Search it,' Liz says, as Julia obediently rifles through the tissues.

'Nothing here.'

Rosa has stopped swearing and her struggling has reduced to weak twitching.

'Rosa?' I lean forward and talk directly into her ear. My left knee aches as it presses into the cold hard tiles. My thigh is beginning to shake with the effort of balancing on one knee while pushing my other into Rosa's lower leg. 'I want to get you up so you're more comfortable. Will you please stop struggling so I can do that?'

A muffled reply, and I look to Liz. 'We can't keep her on her chest. Let's take her on her side.'

Liz nods and replies, 'Towards me, then.'

A quick nod to show I agree and then I'm lifting Rosa from the shoulder, up and over so that she rolls backwards towards Liz, her back pushed into Liz's knees, her chest facing me. Liz takes control of both of Rosa's arms, and I release my grip on her completely, but remain squatted in front of her. She is laid out on her right side, her arms pulled behind her by Liz, her legs straight down, blackened toes pointing towards Julia. She immediately tries to curl her knees up to her chest, move herself into a more comfortable position, but I push them back down with my foot.

'If you try and kick us again you'll go back on your front.' My voice is stern.

Another nod from Rosa. She seems to be catching her breath and lets her head loll sideways so that the top of it rests on the floor. I feel that some of the fight has left her and hope that I might be able to reach her this time.

'So, if we sit you up we can just get this done? Are you going to let us do this now?'

Her head stays lolled but her eyes swivel up to meet mine. And her expression tells me that the fight hasn't left her at all, that we've just allowed her a respite to catch her breath, and now she's ready for round two. 'Fuck. You. Dyke.'

'Jesus Christ,' Liz sighs.

'Fine,' I sigh. 'Have it your way.' I reach for the waist of her jeans, and as my fingers connect with the cold metal of the button, she violently shoves her pelvis towards me.

'You like that, do you, dyke?' Her voice is raw and it bounces around the walls of the small hard cell. 'You like forcing women's clothes off, yeah? Bet you're getting a right fucking kick out of this, aren't you?'

She writhes on the floor in front of me as I struggle to undo the button, the denim tight and thick around her waistband. I can feel sweat beading on my brow as I finally get the button loose and zip down her fly. She's not wearing any knickers and her pubic hair is instantly exposed as the zip fully opens.

'This is assault!' Rosa wails and continues to writhe. I can hear Liz panting, exhausted with the effort of trying to restrain her. I grab the waistband of Rosa's jeans and start to push them down. It's almost impossible to wrench them downwards while she's on her side, pressed against the floor. I have one knee bent beneath me in a squat, and the other straightened out to the side and forwards, still restraining her legs. My legs are burning and my arms feel weak and I can't get the anchorage I need to push her jeans down further. I can feel my face heating up and I hope it's the physical effort that's making my cheeks redden and not the shame of what I'm doing.

'Julia!' It comes out gruffer than I want to sound. 'Pull her jeans down.'

Julia just stares at me like a blinded rabbit. And I know what she's thinking, because I'm thinking it too. Rosa's no bigger than a girl. She's a prostitute and a drug addict, her body carved and wasted by her sickness. She's never had a chance to be anything else because her life has been shit from day dot and no one has ever cared enough about her for her to care about herself. We're holding her down on a hard filthy floor, in a horrible place that smells of violent men. We're holding her down and we're stripping her. And each violent scene of rape that I've ever watched on TV flickers and rolls across my mind like an old-fashioned movie reel. I shake the images out of my mind and look at Julia.

'Julia, we need to do this. Pull off her jeans.'

Julia reaches for the knees of Rosa's jeans and starts tugging them down. Her face is white and she looks like she might cry. Rosa has gone silent and I almost wish she was still shouting at me. She stares straight ahead of her. I catch Liz's eye and she meets my gaze with a look that means she'd rather be anywhere else but here. Julia is working Rosa's jeans off of her legs, one ankle at a time, and then Rosa is bare from the waist down. I move my right foot from her legs and her knees shoot up to her chest. Julia stands up and starts feeling around the fabric of Rosa's jeans.

'Make sure you check the waistband, the crotch, and all of the pockets really well.' Julia nods and continues her search. I watch her for a moment before turning back to Liz.

'What are we going to do about the squat?' I ask. It's procedure to ask detainees to squat during their search so that a visual inspection can be made to rule out items concealed in their genital area. Something makes me think that Rosa won't be agreeing to this request.

Liz's mouth twists as she considers. It's not just Rosa who's at risk if we fail to find something she's concealed. It's our jobs on the line, too. 'Well, she's kind of squatting on her side now, isn't she?' She has a good point. I stand up and move next to Julia, who's just finished up with the jeans.

'They're clear.' She hands them to me, and her eyes rest everywhere in the cell that isn't Rosa.

'OK.' I kneel at Rosa's feet and start to put her jeans back on. She is still curled in a foetal position. Her legs are limp and she lets me manoeuvre her ankles into the thin denim. Once each foot is in, I begin to push the jeans up her legs, but before I reach the top I look directly at her exposed crotch. It's not because I want to. It's because I have to. I satisfy myself that there is nothing concealed between her legs and then look away. Liz has released Rosa's arms now that all the fight has left her, and Rosa reaches down and pulls her jeans up the rest of the way.

I stand and address Julia, 'Usually, if the suspect was cooperating, we'd ask them to squat so that we can check there's nothing hidden between their legs.'

'Right,' Julia nods.

'It's really important that you make an actual visual inspection. You can't afford to miss anything.'

'Of course.' Julia looks at Rosa, who is now fully sitting on the floor. Liz has stood up behind her and is stretching out her legs. But we're not finished yet.

'OK, Rosa.' I try and sound cheery and hope Rosa will just play along. 'Let's quickly get your top half done and get you that cuppa, shall we?'

Rosa just shrugs and I feel myself sag with relief.

'Top off, then,' I say, keeping my voice light. Rosa stands up and sways a little. Liz reaches out a hand and supports her with an upturned palm just under her elbow. 'Whoa, don't fall over on us now. We're nearly done.' Her voice is soft and kind. None of us are in the mood to hold a grudge.

Rosa reaches down and pulls her top up and over her head. I take it from her and pass it to Julia, watching as she searches it. It doesn't take long to establish that there's nothing hidden in the small scrap of stretchy fabric. I face Rosa again and she's already un-hooking her bra. She hands it to me and raises her arms, negating the need for me to ask her to. Again, procedure dictates that we visually inspect the areas under the breasts and armpits. The bra is still warm from the heat of her body as I turn it over in my hands. Immediately I feel a spike in my pulse as I notice some frayed edges around the base of the cups, where the padding meets the underwire. *This bra looks far too new to be fraying.*

I beckon to Julia, holding the bra out so that she can see the tiny ragged threads. I point to the underwire and carefully push into the frayed material with my finger. 'Look here,' I say, already pretty certain of what I'm going to find. And at that moment my finger connects with something sharp. I pull at the fabric until the cool glint of the razor blade is visible. 'This is a common place to hide sharps.'

Julia gasps as I pull out the razor blade. It's the type with a triangular point, designed to slot into a Stanley knife or something similar. I repeat the process on the other cup, then hold out a pair of razor blades. 'This is why you never run your fingers underneath someone's bra during a search.' Julia clasps her hands into fists as she thinks about what I've said.

'These are nasty, Rosa.' I keep my voice level, although another spike of rage shoots through me. I've seen the damage razor blades can do to police officers. 'Are they for you, or us?'

Rosa smirks. 'Depends what kind of mood I'm in.'

I fold my hand over the blades carefully, and let my arm hang by my side. 'You know, this is exactly why we needed to strip-search you, Rosa.'

'You fucking loved it, dyke.'

I roll my eyes and turn to leave the cell. 'I'll get these into a sharps tube and let the skipper know.'

'Thanks,' Liz calls, as I leave them to escort Rosa back to the custody desk. I head to the property store in search of a weapons tube. As I step into the confined space of the property cupboard I look down and open my hand. The blades glint in the harsh strip lighting, dirty but sharp. I shudder as I think of the germs they could spread – a vision of soft flesh gaping open, skin splitting like butter at their lightest of touches. Spraying blood, stitches; milky-white scars. The sympathy I felt for Rosa has all but disappeared as I find a clear plastic tube and drop the blades inside. I consider the strong possibility that she would have used them on herself. Late at night in her cold, hard cell. When the withdrawal shakes had kicked in and the burning started up in her limbs. How she might have tried to dig that burning out with one of these blades. How we would have found her. Cold and bloodless.

I close my eyes and see Rosa curled foetal on the cell floor. Sighing, I feel a sense of relief that the search was justified. *Thank God it wasn't for nothing.* I wander to the custody desk and hand over the weapons tube. If the skipper is surprised he shows no sign of it. Before I leave Custody I let Liz know that I'll do the intelligence report. It's important that Rosa's predilection for carrying razors in her bra is recorded and shared with other officers who may have to deal with her in the future. It's probably the most important thing to come out of her whole sorry arrest.

'Thanks, mate,' she smiles. 'I owe you one.'

'You can bring a cuppa to the writing room,' I call over my shoulder as I swing the custody door open. 'White – no sugar. Then we can call it even.'

8

Lennox

The call is on and there's no time to think. We're about three minutes from the hospital; less than a minute with lights and sirens.

> *'Call on to female armed with knife, now outside*
> *the hospital. She's threatened staff in A&E,*
> *wearing stained jeans and white vest top.'*

I light them up as soon as the call comes through, before the dispatcher has even finished her sentence. I still get a kick from pressing the big red button that activates the lights and sirens. I passed my response driving course just over a month ago and the thrill of driving on blues and twos still hasn't worn off. I'm hoping it never will. We're an all-female crew today, and I breathe a sigh of relief that the suspect is female too. It's a secret sigh. No female officer worth her salt would ever admit to being anything less than her male counterparts. But the fact remains. I can make myself as strong as I can possibly be, but my male equal will still be stronger. Cerys, my operator, clicks off her seatbelt as we approach the hospital, and I reach to do the same. She's got a similar amount of service to me and it's nice to be partnered with someone who knows what they're doing. *Ready to go.*

There's no time to get the suspect's name, no time to ask the dispatchers to talk to the staff. No time for background checks, officer safety risk assessments or strategy. Because before we can think we're rounding the corner to the hospital entrance. It's a fly-by-the-seat-of-your-pants call. It's a get-there-and-deal-with-it call. It's a cross-your-fingers-and-hope-you-don't-get-stabbed kind of call. I pull up in the ambulance bay and there she is. Standing on a grass bank opposite the A&E entrance. It's a sunny day and I can see the light glinting off the knife as it waves above her head.

Me and Cerys are out of the car and running towards her. I wave the keys behind me as I run, hoping vaguely that the car will lock as I squeeze the button. I shove the keys back in my pocket and stop about 3 metres away from the suspect. She's hysterical. And pregnant. Her wasted frame makes it impossible not to notice the perfect, football-sized bump. It doesn't sit well on her; she's a drug addict. I need only one look to confirm this. Her hair is matted to her head and her face is sunken. Her skin has the grey, dull pallor of an addict, and there are scabs around her mouth. She's so thin that I can see every vein in her arms, every straining muscle, as she waves the knife and screams. Her teeth are brown and her dry lips stretch back over her mouth so tightly as she wails, that I think they may split open.

'NI22 also on scene outside the hospital.'

I hear the message without needing to listen for it. Another unit has arrived.

What happens next plays out in the blink of an eye. That's the thing that's hard to understand when you're on the outside, watching YouTube. Police pile in, jump on, grab, pull and restrain. When our actions are watched on the news it's with the sage wisdom of hindsight. Hindsight, and full knowledge of the facts at hand. What the public don't get to see is the explosions of thought inside our heads. The risk assessments, the 'what ifs', the 'fucking hell, she's going to stab mes'. They don't see what we've seen before. They don't see the stories of dead colleagues that flash in our minds. *That won't be me.* In training, we're taught to be strong, shout loud. *Trust no one. Act first, think later.* It's pounded into us from the first moment we lace up those boots. *Pre-emptive strike.*

'Drop it,' we shout in unison. We work well together, and we don't need to look at each other to know that we're both slowly approaching the suspect, imperceptibly closing the gap between us and her. She's crying. The blood is rushing in my ears and the adrenalin is blinding me to everything else but the knife in her hand. But something about her makes me wait. *She's pregnant.* The hand that would usually be on my baton right now is empty at my side. *She's pregnant.* Yes, she's holding a knife, but her arms have dropped and her shoulders have sagged. She continues to cry as she moans, softer now. Snot and tears smudge on her face and she suddenly looks smaller. I sense that the risk has lowered significantly as the glinting knife lowers towards the ground. And, as my screaming brain slows slightly, I can see that it's not a knife at all. It's a corkscrew. Still potent enough to cause a nasty injury, but it's not going to kill me or my colleague.

'Put it down,' I say. We're now only around a metre away from her and she looks right into my eyes. I raise my hands, palms facing her.

'It's OK,' I say, 'put it down and let's talk.'

As the words come out of my mouth I know she'll do what I ask. The relief I feel makes me exhale. *I don't want to tackle a pregnant woman.* But before she can put the corkscrew down, and before I can say another word, a flash of black and white stops me in my tracks. It's running at the woman from behind, quick and quiet. It's Lee. *The other unit.* He's seen his chance and he's taken it. Before I can even move to react he's on her and they crash to the ground. Face first. As he takes her down he shouts 'Drop the knife!' at the top of his voice. She wails as she crashes forward, Lee on her back. He takes her left hand and slams it on the ground; the corkscrew skitters across the paving stones. I kneel down beside them. It's over. The time slows and we're back to reality.

'Lee. She's pregnant.'

'Shit!' He reacts immediately, shifting his weight off her back and twisting her up on her side. She's shouting, full volume, and a crowd has started to gather. Now that she's on the ground and the 'knife' has gone, I can finally hear

what she's saying. The words hidden in her awful screams.
And, although I'm not a mother yet, it still breaks my heart.

'My baby.'

My baby.

'Let us take her,' I say to Lee, reaching for the woman's
scrawny arms. Cerys is beside me as we take an arm each
and sit the woman up. Lee releases her eagerly. Most male
coppers feel the same about restraining women. It doesn't
look good. *But sometimes it's necessary.*

I'm not angry with Lee. I don't even feel that he did the
wrong thing. It's not what I was planning to do, but he's a
good policeman and I trust his judgement. Until I see what
he saw, through his eyes, I can't judge the decisions he
made. And I'm guessing he saw something like this: two of
his colleagues facing down an aggressive woman with a
knife. He made his decision in a split second like the rest of
us. He did his job, disarming an armed suspect, protecting
the public and his colleagues.

The woman whimpers. I place my hand on her shoulder,
feeling the sharpness of her bones and the dampness of
her sweat as I do so. Willing her to calm down, I look into
her frightened eyes.

'It's OK, it's OK. What's your name?'

'Fuck off.'

'We're not going to hurt you,' I say loudly. Partly for the
gathered crowd, and partly for the woman. She's stopped
crying now and her eyes are glassy and still. The fight has
left her and she hunches between me and Cerys. She really
is tiny, barely 5 feet tall and completely ravaged.

'Have you got anything else on you that could hurt us?' I ask, expecting no response. I don't get any. I can't take her back into the hospital without searching her first. 'We're going to have to search you for weapons. Can you stand up for us please?' Again, no response. She stares into the distance, her cheeks shining with the slick of her tears. Cerys and I gently pull her upright. She offers no resistance.

I pat her down. It doesn't take long. Her jeans are grubby and tight, each pocket stuffed with dirty tissues but nothing else. I run the back of my hands down each leg, and up in between her thighs. Her feet are sockless in trainers. I run my bare fingers into each side of her shoes, wishing I'd put my gloves on first as my fingers rub against her sweaty feet. *God, she stinks.* Cerys swipes around her top for signs of hidden objects. Her breasts are small and she's not wearing a bra. There's nowhere to hide anything. Not for the first time in my career, I think how degrading it must feel to be searched in the street. In this case, in front of a crowd. *We need to get her inside.*

'We'll get you checked out inside, shall we?' I nod at her bump. Her face crumples. And in that instant, I know what she's about to say.

'He's dead,' she whispers.

Oh.

I turn to Cerys and I can see she's heard it too. I don't know what to say.

How awful. I'm sorry. That baby had a lucky escape. The thought pops into my mind before I can censor it away.

Most of me is horrified but there's a part that won't shut up. *You know how awful that baby's life would have been, you've seen it.* I don't deserve to comment on her suffering when I have awful thoughts like that. So I say nothing. *And I still feel bad about it.*

We walk slowly towards the entrance to A&E, me and Cerys bracketing her with our uniforms.

'They wouldn't let me see him.'

'Your baby?'

She nods. 'I just wanted to see him again. They don't fucking care.'

'Why wouldn't they let you?'

'They said I was too high and to come back when I had calmed down.' Her voice cracks as she talks. 'Maybe if they'd helped me in the first place he'd still be alive.'

'Have you taken anything today?' I ask, guiding her through the automatic doors.

'Yeah, this morning.'

'What did you take?'

'Some brown.' *Heroin.*

'OK.' We approach the desk in the majors area, where a sister has already seen us and is waving us over.

'Selina,' she says in a soft voice as we draw close to her, 'have you calmed down now, love?'

I've always envied the Irish accent. Nearly everything said in it sounds genuine and heartfelt, while I struggle to make my English anything but cold. The nurse's arms are crossed and she tilts her head at Selina – the way you might look at a child who's just scribbled on your bedroom wall.

But in her eyes there is concern, and care. And standing there, looking into her caring eyes, is where it first hits me. It's where I first fully begin to comprehend the loss that Selina has suffered.

We are still holding her by the arms. I want to let her go, sit her down. Give her a hug. But I'm strapped in behind my vest and laces. I'm working. The mere fact that I'm here, in uniform, means that I've become responsible for Selina, and the people around her. *What if I let her go and she lashes out again?*

'I've arranged for Lennox to be brought to you, but you must stay calm for me while you're waiting. Is that OK?'

She turns away from me as she speaks, making it clear that her words are meant for Selina. I can tell that she's seen what happened outside. *We're the bad guys.* Usually, this attitude gets right up my nose. We get called to deal with violent people because the caller shouldn't have to – it's our job. Agreed. It's what we signed up for. So, we turn up and 'deal' with the violent person in whatever way we can. Then we get criticised for doing it. Usually, that's the way it goes. But right now, I couldn't agree with her more. I feel like the bad guy. I look at the floor. *I wish Lee hadn't taken her down.*

'Room 3, please.' And she nods towards the 'mental health' holding units behind her. Not fit for purpose, they are just small waiting rooms. There's no padding and plenty of movable furniture, some of which I've had thrown at me in the past. We walk Selina towards Room 3 and I think to myself, *here we are again.* I think about how much of our time is wasted in hospital, baby-sitting violent or suicidal mental health patients who we've had to section for their own safety. We have to stay because the security guards at the hospital can't or won't restrain people. We have to stay and ensure they don't hurt themselves or the staff, until they're passed safely into the hands of the professionals. Who usually turf them out half an hour later. It's not their fault. There are not enough of them and mental health facilities in this country are laughable. People who are mentally ill don't deserve to be dealt with by police officers, and police officers don't deserve to deal with them as much as they do.

Today, however, I can't resent being here. Today I feel that we're genuinely needed. After all, what are we here for if it's not to get people through the most traumatic experiences of their lives? Selina sits on a chair in the corner of Room 3 and curls in on herself. Cerys leaves the room to update Brixley Control of the situation. I doubt anybody will be interested in getting Selina arrested now that we all know the full circumstances. I stand at the door of the room feeling stiff and formal.

Then Selina starts to talk.

'It was going to be different,' she mutters quietly. Her voice is thick with mucus and grief. 'I was going to straighten myself out, for him.' She looks down and holds her bump. 'I came to A&E and they just didn't want to know. You could tell from their faces what they were thinking. Another crack-whore pregnant. Fucking great. They put me in a cubicle and just left me there. I was in so much pain.' I don't say anything, not wanting to stop her mid-flow. I offer just a nod to let her know I'm listening. Her hands are bunched together in her lap and her shoulders shake as she tries to talk.

'I was lying on the bed and calling out for someone to help me. No one came. I was bleeding, down there, and shouting for help.' She looks me straight in the eye. 'Why didn't anybody help me?'

'I don't know,' I say, and my voice comes out cold and hard. It's not how I mean it to sound, and I don't know whether she knows I care or not. But I do care. And I do know why. They ignored her because they're exhausted, overworked and underpaid. They ignored her because they're fed up of being spat at, vomited on or hurt by drug addicts and alcoholics. They ignored her because, even though they truly believe that each life is as valuable as the next, they couldn't deal with her while she was high. *Because it's a bloody nightmare.*

'Yeah you fucking do.' As if reading my mind, she says, 'Who gives a fuck about a whore like me?' She lets out a loud cackle, which dies quickly as she looks back to her lap. 'But I was going to change.'

'What happened?' I ask softly, still standing by the door.

'He fell out of me.' She stares straight ahead at the wall.

I suck in a breath as she keeps talking.

'I got up and I felt everything rushing out of me, between my legs.' She squeezes her hands into fists until the knuckles are white, rocking forward on her chair as she talks. 'My jeans were soaked in blood and all this brown shit, and I could feel him pushing out of me.' She clamps her legs together and shoves her hands between them. *I can still see the stains.*

'I was just standing there, screaming for help. I pushed my jeans down and my hands got covered in blood and it felt like my insides were ripping open.' She's panting now and the sweat is beading on her forehead. 'And I looked down and there he was. Just hanging there. And I started screaming, 'He's out, he's out.' and then they gave a shit, didn't they?' Her voice gets louder and louder as she relives it. 'Yeah. Then they all come running over but it's *too fucking late* then, isn't it?'

On her last word she jumps up and runs towards me. I know her shouting is aimed at the staff outside but it's my face it's hitting. I widen my stance and, as she reaches me, I take her by the shoulders and hold her firmly. She's weak – it doesn't take much force to stop her. She's an arm's reach from my face and I hold her there. I can see every vein in her neck and every scab on her mouth as her screams shake my eardrums. I can feel her spit landing on my face and it slaps me into action. *Risk of infection.* I shake her by the shoulders, hard, just once.

'Selina,' I shout into her face. She stops and looks at me. I look right back into her red-rimmed eyes and lower my voice. 'If you want to see your baby you need to calm down. They won't give him to you if you're like this. I'm so sorry this has happened to you, but being like this won't help.'

Her face crumples and once more the rage is gone. I

guide her gently to her chair and sit her down. A knock makes me turn and Cerys puts her head around the door, motioning for me to join her. I step outside of the room, still watching Selina through the window of the door.

'They've got the baby,' whispers Cerys.

I turn around to find the nurse who ushered us into Room 3 standing behind us, holding a small padded bag. I stare at it for a few moments, my brain taking stock of the size of it. Of what it contains.

'She's too unstable,' I say, wiping sweat and spittle from my brow.

'I'll not have that woman kept from her son a moment longer,' says the nurse, puffing out her chest.

'I don't want that either,' I say, raising my hands in surrender as the nurse bears down on me. 'But what if she loses it again? Won't give it back?' *Grabs the baby and legs it?*

The nurse looks me straight in the eye. 'This little one will soothe her. He is precious. She will treat him as so. Trust me.' And I do trust her. I stand aside and she walks into the room.

I turn and look through the window as the nurse approaches Selina. As her eyes rest on the bag, her body goes completely still. The nurse lifts a tiny box from the bag and sets it gently down on the seat beside Selina. The nurse lifts the lid. She nods to the grieving mother, who slowly turns her head to look. As her eyes rest upon her son's tiny body, her face becomes calm. It becomes a mother's face. The sorrow is there, but it's awash with love. She reaches slowly into the box and lifts the tiny bundle out, holding it as if he were the most precious thing she's ever seen. Which, of course, he is.

As she looks down upon him, I finally see the hope that she saw. A dream that I judged as impossible seems, in that moment, just within her grasp. I feel my neck grow hot, ashamed for believing that she couldn't change for her son. Ashamed for wishing his life away. *Wishing another life away*. I turn around and lean my back upon the door. This is Selina's time, not mine. I don't deserve to witness this precious moment between her and her son. Maybe she was right. Maybe things really would have been different. Maybe the love she felt for him would have been the thing that finally got her off the drugs. I nod to the security guard that has just arrived, and turn to Cerys.

'We're not needed any more,' I say as I walk towards the exit. Tears prick in my eyes at the thought that Selina's chance at a happy future has been so cruelly ripped away from her. *Suck it up. Move on.* By the time I get to the car my face is blank, my mind is clear. I change the status on our on-board computer from 'On Scene' to 'Available'. The next call comes through and we're off again.

*　　*　　*

Two weeks later, I drive past and see Selina standing in the red-light district, tummy shrunken flat. I stop and ask if she is OK. She shows no sign of recognition, her eyes glazed and dull. I doubt any quantity of drugs could numb her pain. And I look into her eyes, searching, hoping for a glimpse of that mother's face. I look for the love and the hope that she had when she held him. But it's gone.

9

Baby Blue

It's 4 a.m. and I'm driving slowly through a notorious estate, eyes open for potential burglary suspects, when Ralph's voice breaks the radio silence of the back end of a night shift.

'– BX from 579 – fuck – I need a governor here now – shit –'

I'm jolted rigid by the tone of his voice.

'Did he just say "fuck" on the radio?' Liz looks at me from the operator's seat.

I put my finger to my lips and lean forward to turn up the volume of the car's main set, the radio that's built in to the dash and speakers. My heart thumps against my ribs as I listen to the continuing exchange. I've never heard Ralph sound like this.

'579, from Bravo X-ray, that's all received. We're contacting him now – what's going on down there?'

The static of Control's message dies into silence. I have no idea where he is. I don't know what call he's at or what he's dealing with but I know one thing. Whatever it is, it's bad. I've never heard Ralph's voice break higher than a casual drawl, even when chasing suspects. And nobody says 'fuck' on the radio without a damn good reason. Then his voice again, fading in and out, distant but distinct.

'Jesus – there's blood everywhere – fucking hell.'

'579, receiving Bravo X-ray? Do you need more units? Do you need an ambulance? 579, come in, 579?'

I fight the urge to get on the radio and find out where he is. The control room are trying to get a response and I don't want to block the airwaves. I think of my colleagues around the borough and feel certain that, at this point in time, we are all craning towards our radios, cars quiet, willing Ralph to answer.

'579 – 579, are you receiving Bravo X-ray?'

The Glaswegian tones of the radio controller roll around inside our car and I'm glad that Theresa is on our borough tonight. She's one of the best CAD (computer-aided dispatch) operators I've ever experienced and I know she's got our backs. Always. Even after the local CAD rooms were closed down and the civvies were centralised, torn away from the teams that they were part of. Years of borough experience and local knowledge thrown to the wind. Even after their mandate became more about ticking off calls than it did about protecting their constables, Theresa still has the old-school loyalty to her team. She's one of us. Kind-hearted, with the accent and bite of a Rottweiler, and the ability to drink most of our team under the table, there's no one on the radio that I respect more. You don't mess with her colleagues. I glance across at Liz.

'I give her two seconds before she sends reinforcements.' And as I start to prepare myself for a blue light run to wherever Ralph is, the static breaks once more.

'Bravo X-ray, from 579?' I exhale at the sound of his voice, letting my rigid fingers release slightly from the steering wheel. He still sounds panicked, but I don't think he is in danger.

'579, do you need more units?'

'No – just the skippers and governor. Can you contact CID?' His breath rattles into his personal radio as he speaks, making it sound like he's making a phone call from a windy beach, not standing, surrounded by a bloody mess, in London. 'Terri – this is a Type One – I'll call you direct.'

'All received 579. BX3 and BX1 are on route.'

'What's a Type One?' Liz asks, glancing sideways at me as she swigs from her water bottle.

Ralph is using the CAD codes to disguise what he's really saying. Each call is classified into a code as it's entered onto the computer. Type One is a code that you don't hear that often.

'It's a murder.' I stare straight ahead, imagining blood-splattered walls and splayed limbs. In my peripheral I see

Liz's bottle pause in mid-air. She lowers it slowly and swallows her mouthful of water with an audible gulp.

So the governor and sergeants are nearly there. I sigh at the realisation that my curiosity will have to wait. When you don't want to discuss something on the airwaves, or when something is too serious to discuss on air, then you call the control room direct. *Never say 'murder' on the radio. Or 'bomb'.* Coppers are naturally nosy. Ralph knows that the whole borough will be listening. Plus, there's always the risk of unauthorised users getting into our channels. It's rarer now that our technology is moving with the times, but it's still a risk. The problem is, nosiness is a trait that only gets worse when it's your job to know the precise ins and outs of every situation. You start to expect the full story every time. Makes it all the more frustrating when you have to wait for it.

'God.' Liz rubs her palms up and down the thighs of her job trousers. 'Is it wrong that I'm jealous?'

I smile at the unexpectedness of her question. 'Not at all. I am too. I think we all are – isn't that what we joined for?'

I briefly consider trying to find out where Ralph is. He's told Control that he doesn't need any more units so I'm not about to ask them. My burning curiosity makes me consider sending out some texts, testing the waters, seeing if anyone else knows the address. But professionalism stops me before I've even reached for my phone. The last thing the victim needs, whoever that victim is, is half the Met trudging through their crime scene, potentially destroying evidence, having a good look round, just because they want to stick their noses in. *Have a little respect.*

I feel my eyelids grow heavy as the adrenalin of the murder call starts to wear off. It's warm inside our car and I flick the air con on to try and revive myself. It's that time of night where the calls have stopped and there's no one on the streets. Unoccupied, it's always early in the morning that my body starts to protest at the fact that it's awake.

'I need a cup of tea.' I turn the car towards the nick. A coffee would probably be more effective, but I don't drink coffee. Never have. I flick the fans up to full and aim them at my face as I wind my way through the deserted London streets.

*   *   *

I'm only halfway through my tea when Terri requests my call sign. Tonight I am driving BX21, and this call-sign refers to both myself and my operator. It also tells whoever needs to know that we're driving a marked response vehicle.

'Bravo X-ray Two-One, receiving Bravo X-ray?'

'Go ahead.' I cock my head towards the earpiece of my PR, or personal radio, as I release the transmit button. Liz looks up from the computer, where she's only just logged on. Her coffee sits steaming beside her and I watch the wisps curl up towards the fluorescent strip lights of the PC's writing room. We're the only ones in here.

'Are you available?'

'Sure are.'

**'OK – can you make yourself ready for a call –
Bravo X-ray One will be calling you shortly.'**

The governor. 'Yep, all received.' I raise an eyebrow towards Liz, who's already started logging off the computer. She sits with her hands in her lap as the computer whirrs like a small aircraft, her back as straight as a board, looking at me. Not for the first time I wonder if it's the boxing that gives her such great posture. I unhook my PR from its cradle on my Met vest and hold it in my hand.

'I guess we're going to find out all about that murder now.' I take a few big sips of my tea, enjoying the way it scorches the inside of my throat on its way down, wanting to finish it before the call.

'You think?' Liz looks at me, wide-eyed. Her hands clamp over one another and I wonder whether it's nerves she's tamping down, or excitement.

'What else could it be?' And as I finish the sentence my PR bleeps. Private call.

'This is 215, go ahead.'

'Ah, 215.' The plumminess of the duty inspector's voice fills my ears. 'Bit of a fuck-up. Need you to high-tail it to the hospital to provide continuity for this possible murder victim.'

'Right, Gov.'

'In all of the commotion no one thought to get into the back of the ambulance with the poor thing,' I hear him sigh at the other end. *Poor thing?* I open my mouth to reply but he cuts across me. 'You know the drill, 215, all you have to do is stay with the body for evidential continuity purposes. Who are you posted with?'

'Liz.'

'Excellent. Good experience for her.' A quick muffle of his voice talking to someone else and I imagine his ramrod arms directing the scene. 'Oh, and 215? There's something you should know before you get there. It's a baby. A newborn baby.'

'Okay, gov.' The words are out before my brain catches up with what he's just said.

'Read the CAD as you go – on the hurry up please. Need you there as soon as possible. Make sure you let Control know when you're on scene.' And with that the call cuts out.

I clip my PR back on my vest and toss my polystyrene cup into the bin. 'Hospital, on the hurry-up.'

Liz hops up from her seat and falls in beside me as we march out to the yard. She glances at me twice without speaking and I realise that my face is set in a grimace.

'What is it?' Her voice is soft.

'I'll tell you on the way.'

*　　*　　*

We're sitting outside a small room with a wooden door. Something about it looks odd compared to all its swooshing, plastic and metal-coated counterparts. When we arrived we were brought straight here. Told to wait while someone went and found the keys. We both know what's locked inside. I use the quiet moment to update Control.

'Bravo X-ray, from 215.'

'Go ahead, 215.'

The signal is weak and I turn up my volume. It's common to lose signal entirely in the hospital, so I'm lucky I'm getting through at all.

'We're at the hospital. Currently waiting to see the – *baby baby baby baby* – victim.' My head feels light and I shake it slightly. 'I'll let you know once we've made visual confirmation.'

'All received, 215.'

Terri's voice is muted.

'Hope you're all OK there.'

I smile slightly. You can't get emotional on the radio. Hell, you can hardly get emotional face to face in this job. Not without suffering a massive piss-take. But it's Terri's way of letting me know that she knows what we're dealing with. That she cares.

'Thanks, mate.'

I let my PR swing back to its vertical position on my vest. Force myself to focus on the job instead of the victim. On the way to the hospital, Liz reads the CAD report out loud. The ambulance service had requested that the police attend a flat where a woman had recently given birth. Injuries were reported on the baby and the paramedics were suspicious. The mother and father were present and giving paramedics conflicting accounts. The mother had told paramedics that the baby had cried after it was born. The father had told them it was completely lifeless. Blood all over the house. The baby was dead by the time the paramedics arrived; nothing they could do.

Ralph and his operator, guided by the sergeants and governor, have arrested both parents on suspicion of murder. The father is currently in custody at Bravo X-ray and the mother is under police guard at hospital. Not this one. It's important when dealing with any possible crime scene that suspects and victims are kept completely separate. Where possible, at least. This prevents barristers, way down the line, standing in a crown court room in their fancy wigs, casting aspersions about how DNA evidence came to be transferred from suspect to victim, and vice versa.

I turn to Liz. 'We'll need to find out from the doctors when the autopsy will be done and if they can give us any opinion on a cause of death.' She nods and makes a note in her pocket book. She's been meticulously noting down various details since we got here, and I suspect that she needs something to do with her hands. Suddenly her pen stops moving and she looks at me.

'Have you ever seen a dead kid before?'

No, but I've killed one. My mind answers in a cold drawl. I tell myself to stop being so ridiculous. *I haven't killed anything – it was just an egg – just a –* I shake my head and look at my lap. 'Nope.'

'Shit.' She breathes out long and low. Neither of us has any idea what we will see on the other side of that door. Waxy skin and blue limbs. Staring eyes and bloated faces. My mind cannot connect these images with those of a baby. It's like a CD that keeps skipping past a certain note, jumping and hitching; I'm unable to reconcile the two ideas.

'I'll go in on my own if you like,' I offer. 'There's no need for both of us to see it.'

'It's fine.' She smiles but none of the warmth reaches her cheeks. 'It's my job.'

We both raise our heads at the sound of padding footsteps. Someone is rushing towards us and then a doctor is standing in front of us holding a large bunch of keys. She starts talking at a million miles a minute as we stand up.

'Sorry for the delay. Got here as soon as I could. Thought we'd lock her in here, you know, bearing in mind what's happened.' She starts to rifle through the key ring, 'Although we really need to talk about that. You know, what's actually happened.' She glances at me quickly, pausing her rifling to push her glasses back up her nose. She looks about forty and has thick grey hair, tied back, with multiple strands loose and soft around her face. It gives her a harried look. 'God, such a busy night. Anyway, she's in here. Terrible thing. Poor little mite. You just need to see her, do you?'

I realise she's stopped and open my mouth to respond. But she's off again.

'That's fine. I won't be able to stay for long, I'm afraid. But I can give you the key. Such a busy shift! I haven't stopped.'

She appears to select the right key and it slides easily into the lock. 'I'll give you my thoughts. It's pretty clear cut, as it turns out.' And before I've had a chance to utter a word to her the door is open and we're in a small square room with a table in the middle. The doctor marches round to the other side, keys jangling with her whippish movements.

Liz and I stop about a foot away from the table, just inside the door. The doctor's still talking but then she turns to us and her voice dies in her throat. She takes in our faces and follows our gaze. On the table, there's a box. It's the size of a small, carry-on suitcase, and it's lined with pretty satin. In the box is the baby. Baby girl. She's surprisingly pink, but with a dark purple tinge. There are patches of different coloured skin all over her. She lies on her back, eyes closed, little arms outstretched either side. Her body looks perfectly normal apart from the odd patches of skin. But as I raise my eyes to her head it's easy to see why she hasn't survived.

'God, I'm so sorry.' The doctor's voice has slowed down. 'Insensitive of me. Are you two OK?'

I take out my pocket book and pen. 'We're fine, thank you.' I take down the doctor's name and credentials, contact details and the best times to contact her. After that I think back to the list of questions I had started to form while waiting outside. 'When will the autopsy be held?'

'Autopsy?' The doctor looks puzzled.

'Yes, the autopsy. To establish cause of death?'

She rolls her eyes. 'I know what an autopsy is, thank you, officer. I'm just not sure why we would have one?'

'Well, its – her – parents have been arrested on suspicion of murder. So it's pretty urgent that we establish the cause of death.'

The doctor looks dumbfounded and my pen hovers above my pocket book as she continues, 'Officer – there is no cause of death; this baby died in the womb.'

A frown crosses my face as I think back to the details of the call. 'But the mother says the baby was crying.'

'It can't have been.'

'How can you be so sure?'

'Let me show you.' She reaches into the basket and points a finger towards the baby's forearm. 'Do you see this skin? Here, where it looks as if it's peeling away?'

I bend forwards and take a closer look. I can clearly see that the top layer of skin is whitened and has curled back on itself. It looks like large blisters that have opened, but there's no blood and it's all over her. 'Yes, I see it.'

'This is called skin maceration. It's where the skin starts to break down due to exposure to moisture – in this case, because the baby died inside the womb. This can't have been caused any other way.'

'You're one hundred per cent sure about that?' I catch her eye as I ask.

She nods, a confident, quick movement. 'Absolutely. The skin doesn't start to do this until the baby has been dead for at least eight hours or so. And this is fairly advanced maceration.'

'Right.' I write 'maceration' in my pocket book. 'But what about the head?'

'Again, another sign that a baby has died in the womb. The collapse of the skull with overlapping bones. Babies' heads are very soft. If death occurs in utero then the bones will start to collapse into each other.'

'Right.' *Shit.* 'And you're sure?'

A look of exasperation crosses the doctor's face.

'Sorry,' I rush to explain. 'It's just, I have to be absolutely sure before I tell my superiors.'

The doctor straightens and wipes her palms down the side of her scrubs. 'I'm positive that this baby died in the womb. At a guess – at least twelve hours ago, probably longer.' She starts to shift on her feet as a bleep emits from the pager at her hip. 'Have I given you everything you need? You have my details if you require anything else.'

'Yes. Thank you, doctor.' We back out of the room and the doctor closes the door behind us.

'Do you need the keys?' She starts tugging at the ring of the key that opens the mini-room.

'No, thank you.' I glance at Liz. 'We know that the room is secure and we can sit out here.'

'Great.' The doctor lowers the bunch of keys with visible relief. She goes to leave, then turns back to me. 'Officer, you must release those parents. This wasn't murder. It can't have been. Technically, that baby was never even born.'

'Yes, don't worry, I'll update the officers dealing with it. Thanks again.'

With that she is gone, and only the receding padding of her soft-soled shoes remains. I lower myself into the chair beside Liz. 'Those poor parents,' I mutter.

'That poor baby,' Liz says.

And as we sit in silence, my mind drifts to a novel I read not long ago. In it the protagonist is seven weeks' pregnant and considering having an abortion. She has a counselling session and asks about the development of the baby. I learnt then that at seven weeks a foetus has a heartbeat. A heartbeat and a liver, and tiny arm and leg buds. *You were seven weeks.* What I thought was just a bunch of cells in my womb was already a tiny baby. Nobody told me. *You didn't ask.* If only I'd known. *You'd still have killed it.*

I bolt up from my seat and Liz is startled. 'It's OK.' I put a hand on her shoulder. 'I just need some fresh air. I'll pop outside to update control, too. Better reception.'

Once outside, I lean against the outside wall of the hospital. Unwelcome memories wash over me, strong and painful, and I'm doing my best to push them away when I get a private call on my radio.

'215,' I answer.

'Ah, Boots.' I smile as Terri's Scottish lilt curls around the nickname she has for me. 'How you doing down there?'

'Not too bad thanks, Terri.'

'So, just checking in to make sure you're OK, plus the governor wants an update.'

I tell Terri what the doctor said and she reassures me that she'll pass it on to the relevant people. I don't need to check who she's going to tell. I'm confident she knows what she's doing.

'But what about you?' she insists, 'And Liz. How are you guys dealing with this? Sounds like a tough one.'

I rest my hand across my forehead and lean back against the rough brick of the hospital wall. I want to tell her everything. The guilt of throwing away something that is taken from people who are desperate for it pushes against the inside of my chest. *I don't deserve your sympathy. I can't stop thinking about what I did.* And the hazy image I have of the foetus I terminated gets warped and distorted, overwritten with the form of baby I've just witnessed and I feel lost. Confused.

'Boots? You still receiving?' I realise I've gone silent and force a smile to my lips, gulping down my shame.

'I'm fine thanks, Terri.' I bite my lip. 'It's not nice, but that's the job. Just tired now. I'll be fine.'

A beat of silence and I know she doesn't buy it. 'Well, you know where I am if you need to talk.'

I thank her for always having my back and she tells me to make sure I look after myself. I tell her that we must meet up for drinks soon. She agrees, but we both know it'll never happen. Busy lives.

We end the call and I head back inside to sit with Liz. We'll have to stay until we're officially dismissed, and we both make a concerted effort to make light-hearted small-talk while we wait. But the whole time two words keep running through my head. *No autopsy.* I turn them over in my mind and consider what it means. The baby died in the womb. Does that mean she was never born? No live birth. No autopsy.

I close my eyes as it hits me. *It's like she never even existed.*

10

Weasel

I am smiling as I gun the marked prisoner van up the busy main road. It's 8 p.m., the tail end of a late shift – just two hours left until we clock off. We've had a busy shift, my favourite kind, and I've buzzed up and down the borough on blue lights enough times to get my blood pumping and my cheeks glowing. I grin at Graeme, my operator for the shift. He's more experienced than me and we're both happy to be posted together. He's enjoying a break from driving and it makes a nice change from puppy-walking the probationers.

I love driving the van. I love that the driver's seat is so far from the ground you literally have to clamber up to it. It's a hulking great slag-eating machine with a cage in the back. It's salvation. And to be driving salvation, to see the look in your colleagues' eyes as you scream towards them, racing to reach them because they're struggling with a violent detainee, is pretty high on my 'coolest thing ever' list. I've thought it many a time myself. *Thank fuck the van's here.*

We've just dropped a charming detainee off at the cells. One who insisted on smashing his head off the door of the cage and shouting profanities all the way to the custody suite. I can still smell the reek of stale alcohol and I roll down the driver's window, taking gulps of fresh London air.

'Did you hear about Friday night?' Graeme asks.

'No?'

'Oh my God, have you not heard?' His Irish lilt has a mocking edge to it and I know he's enjoying dragging it out. I groan loudly and decide that there's no use pretending I'm not interested. He's got me right where he wants me.

'You should've been there; missed a cracker of a drink-up.'

I look across at him. He's grinning from ear to ear. I ease the van into fourth and cruise at a steady thirty-five, glancing at passing cars and pedestrians as we talk. This had better be good.

'So, apparently Genna and Liz had a fight.' My mouth drops open.

He laughs. 'I know.'

'Erm, Genna knows Liz is a boxer, right?' I shake my head in disbelief.

'Oh yeah. Apparently it was a very quick fight.'

'I bet.' Still shaking my head, 'What the fuck?'

'You know how Genna gets about Warren. Especially when she's been drinking.'

I know only too well how Genna could get about Warren. I'd been on the receiving end of unfounded flirting accusations many a time. I'm just about to ask for all the gory details as the static of the radio hitches into a different key, and the voice from the control room fills the car.

'I grade call now to suspects on property.'

I hit the blue lights and pull a wide U-turn. I leave it to Graeme to assign us to the call, knowing that he will. There's no question; we're going to this call. A 'suspects on' means that a burglary is in progress and that the suspected burglars are still on scene. It's like a bat-signal for response team drivers. *Come and get us.* After all, it feels pretty good walking through the doors of the custody suite with a burglar who's been caught in the act. I pull the steering wheel firmly, fighting against the weight of the van, and then push the accelerator to the floor. The old girl needs a bit of encouragement, but soon she's roaring beneath me, the vibration of her powerful engine mingling with the pulse of the lights and the scream of the siren. The talk of squabbling nights out is gone. I focus on getting to the location as fast as I can.

'North end of the road.' Graeme is shouting details as they come through. The call operator is still on the line to the informant and the details flash upon our MDT, the in-car computer, as they are added. The van roars towards our destination and I can feel the adrenalin as it starts to flip my stomach. For once the traffic clears quickly and I realise we're going to get there really fast. My excitement builds. We're going to catch them. I kill the sirens but leave the blues on. A silent approach is always recommended for 'suspect on' jobs, and I'm hoping they don't know we've been called. Graeme's head is tipped down as he reads from the MDT. He barks only the information I need, and I think once again how grateful I am that we're posted together tonight.

'Three IC3 males, sixteen to eighteen years old, carrying large pair of bolt cutters, all in dark hoodies. Leaving the front of number 62 now.'

There's no need to look at him. No need for niceties or questions. I am the driver and he is the operator – he gives me what I need to get to the call. We're working as a team and we're doing it well. Graeme unclips his seatbelt as we approach the road where the call has come from, and I reach down and do the same.

I can visualise where the house must be and I slow down slightly to turn the van into the road that will lead us to the address. Both of us are sitting forward now, eyes scanning the dark street. There's a car coming towards us and suddenly it swerves into the path of the van, its lights blinding me as it starts to flash at us. I brake hard and swear as I'm thrown forward, no belt to hold me back. Graeme flails forward, his strong hands smacking against the dash with a loud slap. And then everything is still.

It's the first time I notice the rain. It's weird what you notice in these split-second moments that seem to stretch on forever. The light from the lamp posts dapples and splits into a thousand crystal droplets across the windscreen. And then, through the drizzle, I'm staring into the face of the taxi driver who's sitting at the wheel of the taxi that's skidded to a halt about an inch from my bonnet. His face is alive with panic and he's waving his arms. My first thought is that a taxi dispute has just got in the way of my burglary suspects, and I feel a wave of frustration. *Unbelievable.*

Somewhere in the background I hear the radio again.

'Suspects have left the scene in a taxi. Dark green saloon car – no index seen.'

And it's then, as I compute what I've just heard, that I see the three faces in the back of the car. The taxi is green. *The taxi is green. There are three male youths in the back.* One of them is holding something. *Bolt cutters.* As I look at their wide eyes and mouths, I realise that they are mirroring my expression exactly. We are frozen. Even the taxi driver stops waving and all six of us sit there, gawping at each other. I can feel Graeme static beside me and I feel like a gunslinger in a quick draw, my hands hovering over my holsters, waiting for my opponent to make his move.

Graeme is the first to fire. He pops open the passenger door and the motion of it slams the burglars into action. Suddenly everyone is moving. The taxi's rear door flings open and the bolt cutters fly out, hooded bodies shooting after them like greyhounds from their traps. They dart towards the estate to the right of us, various items of stolen property flying from them as they run. I'm out of the van running before I can even think. I manage a quick shout over my shoulder, towards the taxi driver.

'Stay here. Do not leave!' The last thing we need is our best witness leaving the scene with all of the evidence.

I pump my legs as fast as I can and watch as they get further ahead. The three of them in joggers and trainers and me in my Met vest, kit belt and boots. They've got about ten years on me, and they're fast. I hear Graeme's voice on the radio.

'Assistance required – chasing suspects.'

Four short words that will bring the cavalry.

Then all I can hear is my own ragged breath as they starburst ahead of me: two going left around a block of flats, and one going right. The decision on which way to go is made easier by Graeme racing past me towards the two that went left. Up until that point I had thought I was running quite fast. My legs are already burning, but I don't take my eyes from my suspect. The white soles of his trainers flash like reflectors in the dark as he sprints ahead. I round the corner after him and find myself confronted with a dead end, a flash of the suspect's limbs as he scales a wooden fence like a squirrel up a tree. *Shit.*

It's at that point that I realise I've left the prisoner van abandoned in the busy London street behind us. With the engine running. A movie-like flash of hoodies joy-riding the van across the borough fills me with dread and I swear again. I'd never live that down.

'BX – can we get a unit to Avery Road, junction with Holborn Road, to secure the prisoner van please? On the hurry up.' As I say the words I am praying that the taxi driver has stayed on scene, and has the sense to keep an eye on the van.

'Received, 215.'

I turn my attention back to the fence. It's the type that typically surrounds a building site. It stands at about 2 metres high, sheer sheets of chipboard painted blue and framed into panels that are supported by struts of two by four. I stand looking up at the top, briefly enjoying the cool splatter of rain on my hot cheeks and realise there's no chance of my getting over it. I make a couple of vain attempts to jump, successfully grabbing the top, but my lack of upper body strength prevents me from pulling myself up.

'215 – 215 from Control – update on foot chase please.'

Sighing, I put my radio to my lips.

'This is 215. One suspect has entered the building site to the rear of Pembleton House. Can we get dogs on route, and see if 99 is available please?' As I talk I try and control the shake of adrenalin in my voice. I reign in my panting and clip my words. Calm. Professional. *Not a Doris.*

'Received, 215.'

India 99 is the police helicopter. If my suspect has gone to ground then 99 will find him. I slam my palms into the rough wood of the fence in frustration. It wobbles, ever so slightly. And I'm suddenly certain of what I'm about to do. I take a few steps back, take a deep breath and then throw myself at it. The wood slaps roughly at my forearms and they sting, cold and red from the blow. I step back again and this time I can't feel it as I smash into it again and again. Throwing my upper body, the side and back of my Met vest, into it over and over. I see a split start to form between two of the panels and I reach up and grab a corner, using my full weight to pull it towards me. It's starting to work. I brace a boot on one side of the split and pull on the other. The panels tear about a foot apart and then I'm frenzied, grasping and pushing and pulling and sweat and rain sting my eyes as I force myself through the gap. I wince as the wet timber rips at my fingers, the prickle of each tiny splinter against the pads of my fingertips, the scrape of wood like sandpaper ripping my arms and then I am through. I stand in the pitch black of the building site before turning and assessing the damage. The fence panel gapes like a rotten tooth, flapping slightly in the wind. I turn back into the dark, reaching for my torch. *I'm coming to get you.*

*   *   *

It's forty minutes later and I'm standing on the edge of the building site, which is bordered on one side by a tall brick wall. The wall runs along the bottom of the gardens of a row of terraced houses. I'm standing very still. I've clicked my radio onto silent mode and I'm listening.

During my battle with the blue fence, other units in the area had been speeding towards our location. It goes without saying that if your colleagues are in a foot chase, you want to get to them and get in on the action. I've found out via my personal radio that Genna and Dave went to the road directly parallel to our location and secured the rear of the building site, just minutes after my suspect entered it. It turned out that Graeme had chased the other two around the block of flats and they'd ended up at a similar fence, containing yet another side of the same site. Somewhat gallingly, Graeme had found no trouble vaulting the barricade, and had been securing his side of the site ever since. The site was a square, and it was contained. We knew they were inside. I'd been alone since Graeme and I had split ways on the estate, but I knew my team were nearby. We'd waited fifteen minutes for a dog unit to arrive and when they did they searched the site, guiding their dogs in all the nooks and crannies. I'd watched the dogs slink through the site, wolfish in their desire for a scent, silently searching. It's a little-known fact that police dogs bark only when they're asked. Strong scents had been detected at the base of the garden wall, a wet, muddy spot that I had been standing on ever since.

I stare up at the top of the wall, where wet moss glints in the glow of the city. I strain my ears. I heard a definite rustle a few minutes ago but there's been nothing since. I know they're there. There's nowhere else they could have gone. The dogs couldn't go in and get them because the dogs don't go where a handler can't follow, and the wall is too high, even for them. I look about in the darkness and supress a shiver. Now that the adrenalin has subsided the building site just feels creepy. My body has cooled, leaving me damp, and cold, and slightly fed up of standing in the chunky caterpillar-treaded mud. I decide to give them one last chance to give up. Walking a few metres away from the wall and into the site, I bring my PR to my mouth and talk low into it.

'Dog Unit – Dog Unit, receiving 215?'

My radio is turned right down, so I have to press it to my ear like a phone to hear the response.

'Go ahead.'

'You still on scene at the building site?'

'Just about to head to another call. Whaddya need?'

'Just a bit of noise, please, if you'd be so kind.'

'Always a pleasure, 215.'

I smile as the barking starts. The unit is parked on the other side of the site, but even from here the vicious crack of the dogs' yelping is effective.

I summon my loudest police voice.

'Good news!' I shout. 'The dogs have arrived! And we know you're in there. So why not give yourselves up before I shove a dog over the wall?'

I listen. Was that a noise? It's hard to distinguish where it came from, but I thought I heard a hushed whisper, followed by a low thud.

I've got them thinking. The dogs are still yelping and I reach for my radio once more.

'That's great, thank you, Dog Unit.'

'Received, 215.'

I sigh silently. It was worth a try. Sometimes even the threat of a dog, let alone the barking, has been known to make a suspect break cover. I toe a clump of mud with my boot and, radio still in hand, call Control.

'Control receiving 215?'

'Go ahead, 215.'

'What's the latest on 99?'

'Yeah, they've just updated us, they should be overhead in a couple of minutes.'

I clip my radio back on my vest and look up as the distant chop of propeller starts to echo across the sky. The bird is nearly here. And at the back of my mind I'm worried that there really is no one behind the wall. That I've imagined the scuffles and whispers, that they're actually long gone. That I'm standing here up to my ankles in mud, growing slowly soggy, for nothing. *That I'm wasting everyone's time.* I push the thought to the back of my mind as the radio silence lurches into the heaving static drone of the bird.

'Bravo X-ray, this is India 99, we are now on scene to the west of Pembleton House. Permission to have talk-through with officers on the ground.'

Not for the first time, I wonder if sounding totally cool on the radio is a prerequisite for the job of helicopter operator. His voice is smooth and steady, and would be totally at home over the speakers of a long-haul luxury flight to somewhere exotic. It won't be the pilot speaking, but he damned well sounds like one.

'India 99, please go ahead.'

'Thank-you, BX. Officers on the ground at Pembleton House, receiving India 99.'

A slight beat in my chest as I answer the call. 'This is 215BX. Go ahead, 99.'

'We're overhead. Where do you believe the suspects to be?'

It's a good job that I've spent my time wisely while waiting for them to arrive. Anticipating this very question, I've taken the time to work out where north is. It's pretty lame sounding like you don't know what you're doing on the radio. It's even lamer when there's a crew of highly trained officers sitting in a 3.5-ton bird, hovering 1,000 feet above you, whose very presence is costing the residents of London over a grand an hour, and you don't know your arse from your elbow.

'OK, so there's a row of around ten terraced houses on Avery Road, situated to the west and slightly north of Pembleton House. They're bordering the north side of a rectangular building site. We think the three male suspects are contained in the rear gardens, around the middle of the row. BX, have we got officers on scene to the front of the houses?'

Another unit cuts in, before BX control can reply. 'Yeah, BX, you've got the Motorcycle Squad round the front. India 99, the houses are numbers 54 to 66 Avery Road.'

'All received from India 99. Could all officers maintain their positions while we conduct our area search.'

'All received at BX.'

I stand where I am and gaze up at the blinking lights above me. There's no searchlight, and no indication that the helicopter is doing anything other than hovering above us. The thermal imaging cameras will be seeing the world below in hues of grey and orange. If there's any sense of movement from behind the wall, the sound of the chopper is too loud to hear it.

'All units, all units, from India 99. Could all officers on the ground at Pembleton House, Avery Road, please identify yourselves for purposes of thermal imaging elimination? Thank you.'

I move myself away from the wall and assume the position. The first time I was told to do this, I thought it was a wind-up. But it wasn't. The chopper needs to identify everyone on the ground, and if they're using thermal imaging then all they can see is human-shaped blobs. So, when asked, officers perform a certain manoeuvre with their arms and legs. That way, if any of the human-shaped blobs aren't standing in the right formation then the chopper's got itself a suspect. I stand to attention, awaiting my permission to stand down, from above.

'215 – 215BX, receiving India 99?'

'G'head, 99.'

'We've identified possible suspects in the rear garden of – stand by . . .'

I imagine the camera operator squinting at the land registry map in the sky above me.

'. . . garden of number 60. There's a heat source near the shed at the rear wall.'

I feel a spike in my pulse as I realise that they're just the other side of the wall. But there's no hope of me kicking my way through this.

'BX, from Motorcycle Unit, we're gaining entry to the front of number 60 now.' As I recognise the voice of the motorcycle officer, the inevitability of what's about to happen slaps me in the face. I scramble for my PR, desperately waiting for a clear signal so that I can transmit.

'Alan, they're ours.'

His voice in response is mocking, 'Sorry, 215, you broke – didn't catch that.'

'246 – Alan – our foot chase, our prisoners.'

The next transmission is so soft I almost don't catch it, whispered through the airwaves, sneaking coldly in my ear. 'Finders, keepers.'

A wave of rage grips me at the sound of a back door opening, followed by Alan's cockney drawl. 'Come on then, let's be 'aving yer.'

The creak of leather and jangle of boot buckles as footsteps come closer. All I can do is stare at the blank wall. I hear the squeak of a door, so close to me that it must be the shed. My hands ball into fists. A muffled exchange and then a blast of radio frequency.

'BX, from 246, we've got three suspects detained in the rear of 60 Avery Road.'

'All received, 246BX, well done.'

'Can you check custody space at Bravo X-ray and show three prisoners to the Motorcycle Crew, please?'

I can hear the suspects being cuffed and moved towards the house. I slap my palms impotently against the rough of the brickwork and suck in breath as the sting of the mortar bites into them. I consider shouting something over the wall but decide against an unprofessional show of frustration. Even though Alan has just become my new nemesis, I won't undermine another officer in front of the public. I trudge towards the battered fence and push my way back out into civilisation. Graeme is waiting for me by the van.

'The weasels need transport for their prisoners.' He puts a certain emphasis on the word 'their'.

I shake my head. The 'weasels' is a common nickname for the motorcycle crew, and all of a sudden it makes sense. Up until now, I'd always assumed that it was the tight leather trousers.

'At least they've been caught,' I say to Graeme as we clamber back into the van.

'Fuck that,' he snorts. 'They were ours, fair and square.'

His Gaelic accent gives the word 'fuck' a delicious note and it lifts my mood. 'Now, now,' I grin at him. 'It's a team effort, don't forget.'

'Yeah, and to be fair, they've saved us a shit-load of paperwork.'

I chuckle at this. We both know that we'd rather be the ones to walk those suspects through the custody suite. And as the chance of a burglary arrest disappears over the horizon, so too goes the glory. Still, the rest of our team will know the real story, and if they don't we'll make sure they hear it in the canteen. The thought of getting off on time is already calling to me and, in reality, I don't find it hard to be satisfied with a job well done. *Bad guys in the bin.*

I drive towards 60 Avery Road and collect 246BX and his prisoner with as much grace as I can muster. Once they're safely deposited at Brixley custody suite, Graeme and myself finish up our outstanding reports before heading to the locker rooms.

'Ready to do it all over again tomorrow?' he winks as he pushes the male locker room door open.

'Wouldn't miss it,' I chirp over my shoulder as I dump my kitbag on the floor next to my locker. I look in the mirror at my flushed cheeks and, for the millionth time, think how lucky I am to do this job.

11

Nick

My pen hovers above my pocket book as today's postings are read out. The skipper likes to call them the rollers and riders and I secretly think that's pretty cool. Currently we average around eighteen officers. That means eighteen uniformed officers patrolling our one borough of London, not including the duty inspector (Call sign: Bravo X-ray One) or the sergeants (Call sign: Bravo X-ray Three). Not many. Especially if we have two critical incidents kick off at once – which often happens. We're split into twos and allocated to cars. If there's not enough cars for everyone, then it's the probationers who get to walk the beat. Bravo One, also known as the area car, is the top of the team. It's the most powerful motor in the fleet. A BMW 525D, driven by Level One drivers only. I've been lucky enough to be the operator in it on a number of occasions and can testify to its horse-power. You love to drive – you want to be in that driving seat. It's my goal. Where I want to be in a few years' time. The area car gets to pick and choose its jobs. It's responsible for being the lead cop car in any vehicle chases, and will generally get to the 999 calls first. The ones it fancies, anyway.

It used to be that the area car driver was the most experienced officer on the team, top thief-catcher, and generally awesome copper. It used to be that way. Now the dynamics of the response team are changing. Due to the lack of detectives, newbies come on to response team and are sent up to CID before their two-year probation period is even up. The ever-changing conveyor belt of new officers puts added pressure on those who have to mentor them, and gone are the old days of blatting around the borough with an officer of equal experience. Old sweats are fed up of puppy-walking, and are desperate to get off borough and on to a specialised squad, where the resources, along with the overtime, are plentiful. This means less experienced officers on team. Which, in turn, means that the wait for a driving course for a new copper is shorter than ever. *Not much point being able to get to an emergency call real fast if you don't know what to do when you get there.*

Below the area car are the IRVs (incident response vehicles). Driven by Level Two officers qualified to drive on blue lights, these are the vehicles that are sent to emergency 999 calls. Their call signs begin at Bravo X-ray Two-One and increase numerically, depending on how many response drivers are available. And under the IRVs are the pandas. Originally named because of their black and white markings, these are now essentially the same vehicles as the IRVs, but driven by someone who is not qualified to use the lights and sirens. They're the slow cars. The reporting cars. The cars that poodle round the borough reporting non-emergency crimes, dealing with neighbour disputes and attending sudden deaths. Their call signs begin at Bravo X-ray Eight-One, and again increase numerically depending on how many pandas there are.

Last, but by no means least, you have the prisoner van, loved by all coppers. The sight of a prisoner van screaming down the road towards you can sometimes be the most beautiful sight you'll ever see. Especially if you have a violent suspect struggling underneath you. The van's call sign is Bravo X-ray Two. And it's my favourite posting. Firstly because it's awesome driving a great big hulking piece of metal. Secondly, because you get to drive a lot of blue-light runs, fetching violent prisoners, and thirdly, because the call centre generally tries not to tie you up with any long weary calls. The van needs to be kept as available as possible.

Today we have sixteen police constables on the street. That means the rollers and riders shape up as follows;

Bravo One (area car)
Bravo X-ray Two (prisoner van)
Bravo X-ray Two-One (incident response vehicle)
Bravo X-ray Two-Two (incident response vehicle)
Bravo X-ray Two-Three (incident response vehicle)
Bravo X-ray Eight-One (panda)
Bravo X-ray Eight-Two (panda)

Then we ran out of cars so the last two PCs are walkers. It's really not like it is in the movies or in the USA, where cops use their cars as barriers to block suspect vehicles in or smash them off the road. *Oh look, we've smashed another one! All for a good cause.* Then merrily hop into another car. In the Met, IRVs are precious. There isn't a fleet of hundreds available for us to take and use as we please. There should be eight on our borough. At least two are usually broken or undergoing repairs, one is reserved for the governor and another for the sergeants. So there are usually around five to choose from. You damage it? Pop a tyre? A little scratch? You're walking. *And* you get the pleasure of a talking down from the local garage sergeant, as well as points on your police driving licence.

The clued-up drivers among us don't hang around after parade. We've all got our favourite car. That's why I'm sitting towards the back of the room, closest to the exit. As soon as the skippers finish up I'll be heading to the yard. First out the door, I'll have my pick. I'm not doing a whole shift without air-conditioning again.

I'm twenty-seven years old and just over four years into my police career. My life is a series of unsociable eight-hour shifts that blend into one, topped and tailed with heavy drinking sessions with my team-mates. The term 'binge-drinking' hasn't really been invented yet but it's definitely what I'm doing. Weekends mean nothing to me, seeing as I work three out of every five of them. I regularly say things like 'standby' and 'all received' when talking to friends and family and I never tell my parents about the hairy calls. I'm still young, I'm earning good money and I'm doing one of the coolest jobs in London. And it still hasn't got old.

I've already underlined yesterday's notes and written today's date alongside my shift. Late turn; 1 p.m. to 10 p.m. I wait to hear my number and scrawl down my call sign, Bravo X-ray 21, before noting the shoulder number of my operator for the day; 522BX. I don't recognise it, so I glance up and look around the parade room. The new guy raises his hand as I pass him with my eyes. Then he points to his shoulder and winks at me. I don't think I've ever experienced receiving a wink that didn't come across as sleazy, and this time's no different. Although I think of him as the new guy, he's not a probationer. He transferred onto our team about a week ago from another borough. I've already heard things about him; there are always rumours when somebody transfers boroughs. Whispers of people leaving under a cloud of some kind. Coppers are a suspicious bunch.

I try not to listen to rumours, choosing instead to make up my own mind about people. I don't know how many years he's got in, I guess I'll find out. Once the briefing is done I'm out of my seat and I glance over to the new guy as he stands up.

'Meet you in the yard,' I say. It's a statement, not a question.

I don't wait for a reply. Instead I turn and race down the corridor, pausing briefly to grab my kitbag on the way to the rear yard. I can sense the other drivers on my tail and I burst through the back door, scanning the concrete parking lot for the IRV I want. I spot it at the back, tucked in behind the prisoner van, and smile as I see that it's empty.

Made it. I head over to it and dump my bag in the boot, leaving it open for my operator. It doesn't bother me that my IRV is blocked in. There's always a juggling of cars in the rear yard during shift change, and today is no different. Anyone that has dumped a car outside an official parking space should have left the keys in it so that it can be moved. All of the marked response vehicles should be left with their keys in, and I know I can move them if I need to.

'Ah, fuck, Alice.' It's Ralph. He stands in the middle of the yard with his hands on his hips. 'That's the one I was after.'

'You snooze, you lose,' I smile sweetly as he flicks me the bird before trundling off to the next empty IRV.

I reach into the glove box and pull out the log. Every time you drive a police car you have to sign in and out in the log book. But before I fill out my details, I walk around the car, making a quick visual inspection. I refer to the diagram of existing damage, making sure there's nothing new. Any new damage has to be reported to a garage skipper. Preferably at the scene of where the damage occurred. But there are plenty of coppers who've dinked a car and not reported it. And if I sign into the log book without checking first, I could be held responsible for damage that I didn't cause. It's a way of keeping us accountable. It's pretty good at making us feel untrustworthy too.

Once I'm satisfied that there's no new damage, I sign the book and stow it. I climb into the driver's side and begin adjusting the seat and mirrors. The inside of the car stinks of vinegar and I'm guessing someone's had fish 'n' chips in here last shift. In fact, there's a greasy sheet of chip paper in the passenger foot-well to prove it. I rummage around the car and find two empty plastic bottles, some crumpled statement paper covered in bootprints, and an empty packet of crisps.

'Fucking pigs,' I mutter as I head to the bins, smirking at my turn of phrase. The worst thing I've ever come across is used chewing gum. On the seat. Which stuck to my trousers. It's fair to say that many coppers drive and treat job cars as if they've just nicked them. I sit in the driver's seat for a few moments and watch as the rest of my team begin to leave the yard. Start of the shift; calls will be being sent through to on-board computers, units being allocated to various incidents. I reach over and log on to the MDT. I doubt my operator will have a log-in of his own yet, as he's just arrived on borough, so I use mine. I set our status to 'Available' and a job pings through immediately. Burglary at a local newsagents. We need to take a report.

The yard's now empty and I climb out of the car and look towards the back doors of the nick. He appears just before I have the chance to call his radio, and saunters towards me, steaming cup of tea in one hand, newspaper in the other. I try not to show my frustration as he lights up a fag. *We've got a job on – and the shift's only just started.* He's short and skinny, with brown hair that's slick with gel. He's combed it back and the tooth marks of the comb are still visible, creating grooves between the strands.

'We got a job,' I call over to him.

He nods, changing nothing about the urgency of his

amble. I notice that he hasn't got a kitbag, or any kind of kit, with him. Not even his beat helmet. He takes four or five massive drags of his cigarette before stubbing it out under his boot. I slide into the driver's seat and wait for him to climb in. He chucks the newspaper in the back as he does so, and takes a loud slurp of his tea.

'What we got?' He nods towards the MDT.

'Burglary report.'

A groan.

'You not got a kitbag?' I say it like it's a little thing. Like I'm not instantly irritated by his lack of any apparent preparedness.

'Nah, still gotta sort my kit out.' His voice is South London cockney, and it reminds me of a bad impression of Michael Caine.

I start the engine, no longer having to worry about shuffling the cars around as most of them have gone. 'I'm Alice, by the way.'

'Nick.'

I drive slowly towards the large metal gate that will lead us out into the borough, and wait patiently as it cranks open, before edging out, checking fastidiously for pedestrians. I can't think of anything more mortifying than running someone over right outside the police station.

'How long you got in?' I ask him, glancing in my mirror as I indicate to turn.

'Seven years.' He's pushed the base of his seat as far back as it will go, sits with his foot up on the dashboard. It's an effort to stop myself slapping it down. 'You?'

'Four.' I try not to feel jealous that he has more service than me. It's a pretty nonsensical envy that I often feel. Especially when I sense that length of service doesn't quite match up to the quality of service.

'I was army before that.'

I'm surprised, but figure that maybe he's older than he looks. 'Did you see active service?'

'Oh yeah. Big time.' He looks out of his window, his left hand gripping the Styrofoam cup and his right fidgeting on his thighs. Something about him makes me feel uneasy, and I wonder if he's lying. But why would he be?

I keep my voice light and friendly. 'Didn't want to become a police driver, then?'

'Fuck that,' he snorts. 'I'd never drive for the Met. They'll screw you over faster than you can think.' He chews on a nail as he speaks, and I notice that his fingers are stained yellow, presumably from nicotine. The foul waft of stale smoke hits me every time he moves.

I can't help judging him for his cynicism. Plus, I've heard this response before and it sounds like an excuse. It just sounds lazy. *I don't drive because I'd rather be driven around. I'd rather not share the responsibility. I'd rather not be teamed up with probationers. I don't like puppy-walking.* Or maybe it's more like *I didn't pass.* And I don't believe that the Met wants to screw us over, either.

'So, why the change of boroughs?' We're nearly at the newsagents and I look around for somewhere to park.

There's no reply, and I look over to him to see if he's heard me. All I can see is the back of his head, face towards the window. He's still chewing on a nail, and the sound of it sets my teeth on edge. Then, appearing to have completed the dissection, he buzzes the window down and spits the nail out. This time there's no hiding my revulsion. I stare at him with my mouth open, undisguised horror on my face. He doesn't notice.

'Just fancied a change, you know?' I realise he's answering my previous question, and struggle to remember what it was. And I realise that, no, I don't know. People don't just change boroughs because they fancy a change. I decide he's definitely hiding something. We both step out of the car and walk towards the newsagents. He drops his empty cup into the bin outside the shop and I remember to be grateful for small mercies. Once we've introduced ourselves to the shop-keeper it's time to take down the details of the burglary. We'll need all of the facts to be able to create a crime report once we're back at the station. The number allocated to the crime report will become the victim's crime reference number, which he'll need if he's going to be claiming insurance for the damage done by the burglars. The back door has been forced and the glass is shattered. As the informant starts telling us what's happened, I look to Nick, expecting him to be taking notes. But there's no sign of his pocket book. It's kind of an unwritten rule that the operator takes the first report, but as Nick stands with his hands tucked into the armholes of his Met vest, I realise that he's not going to.

I rip open the Velcro on my vest and pull out my pocket book.

'Sorry, sir,' I interrupt. 'Can we start with your name and date of birth?'

*　　*　　*

It's nearly the end of the shift and it can't come soon enough. I'm driving along the main north/south road in Brixley and relishing a rare moment of silence. If I have to hear one more 'Nick is such a great guy story' I'm going to throw myself out of my moving police car and leave him to his fate.

I've come to the conclusion that he's a pathological liar. That, or it is in fact possible for one man to have been a close protection officer for a high-ranking Iraqi official, a serving soldier in Afghanistan, a heroic marine and a London bobby with seven years' service, all before the age of thirty-five. *As if someone with such a shining military career would chuck it all in to join the Met.* Coupled with the fact that Nick appears to have a serious rage issue, having become incandescent while discussing certain bugbears of his throughout our shift, I'm actually rooting for him to be lying. The thought that he could have been trusted with any kind of automatic weapon leaves me reeling in terror.

We've been back to the station a number of times, Nick claiming to have paperwork to do. I've spent most of my day searching for him, only to find him in the yard with a fag and a coffee. Thoroughly fed up of missing out on calls, I'm determined to at least get a small amount of police work done before we clock off. I drive slowly, scouring the streets with my eyes. Watching for the telltale twitch of suspicion, the movement that stands out from the crowd. And as we approach a busy crossroads I spot it. The quick slip of a green hoody pulled across a face. A turned shoulder. Hands shoved into pockets and a sudden change of course.

'Check him out.' I say to Nick, 'Green hood.'

Nick glances across to the man I've spotted, 'Looks like he doesn't want to talk to us.' He slips off his seatbelt. It's more enthusiasm than he's shown all day and I decide to run with it.

'He doesn't have a choice,' I say, as I pull up to the kerb a few metres ahead of Green Hood.

Nick's out of the car and on the pavement before I've even cut the engine and I start to think that maybe I've judged him unfairly. I clamber out and join him, and we look towards Green Hood, still ambling towards us. I can see now that he's white, with lightly tanned skin and an angular face. There's a moment – a split second – when he considers running. I see it flit across his face. I see it in the way he glances quickly left and right. The way his feet twitch and skitter. *What's he hiding?* But then he's nearly upon us and the temptation disappears, replaced with weary acceptance. He slows his pace and takes his hands from his pockets, turning his palms face up to the sky. He knows exactly who we're here for.

'Keep your hands where I can see them,' Nick barks. 'Hood down.'

'Good day to you, too, officer.' A flash of annoyance flickers on Green Hood's face as he pushes his hood back, revealing a closely shaven head. His voice is clear and he's well-spoken. His skin is healthy-looking. My threat level immediately lowers, but I'm not ready to relax yet.

I glance at Nick. His chest is pushed out and his chin juts forwards. He plants himself about a foot in front of Green Hood. *Far too close.* Nick's hands hover open above his baton and gas, and his cheeks are flushed. The tension in his body makes me tense, and I wonder if I'm missing something. *Can he see something I can't?*

'Against the wall.' Another order from Nick.

'Can I ask why you've stopped me?' Green Hood backs up to the wall, his hands up in front of his chest, palms facing us in a conciliatory manner. I pull my pocket book from my Met vest as Nick and I take our positions slightly in front of him, one on each side. He's the same height as me, around 5 foot 11, but stands around 2 inches taller than Nick.

'No, you fucking can't.' Nick says it with a smirk on his face.

I open my mouth in surprise before closing it again. I'm instantly enraged by Nick's unprofessionalism, but I'm not about to show it in front of an unknown male. I can see a flare of anger in Green Hood's eyes, and his hands snap down to his sides, clenching into balled fists.

'I saw you on the pavement back there as we were passing in our police car,' I point back towards the crossroads, keeping my voice calm and polite. 'You saw our car and quickly pulled up your hood, turning away from us and changing your course as you did so. I thought that this was suspicious, which is the reason we've stopped to talk to you.'

'Thank you, officer.' This is directed very specifically towards me. Green Hood then turns towards Nick. 'At least *some* police officers can be professionals.'

Nick steps forward and puts his face about an inch away from Green Hood's nose. 'You wanna make something of it?' And for a moment they stand there, noses inches apart, panting into each other's faces.

And all of a sudden I'm standing watching pubescent boys face off in the playground. I feel an overwhelming urge to laugh at the absurdity of it. But I don't. Because people are gathering nearby and I can feel eyes upon us. *We are always being watched.* And I know exactly how quickly things can go bad on the streets of Brixley.

I make a last-ditch attempt to break the tension. 'Sir, if I could take your details then I'm sure we can get this wrapped up nice and quickly.'

But Green Hood doesn't even hear me. He's still locked into Nick's gaze.

'Turn around and put your hands on the wall.' Nick is still barking orders like a drill sergeant and I wish he'd lower his voice. For a second I think Green Hood will refuse his request, but then he turns with a disgruntled jerk. He stretches his arms up and out and places his palms on the wall. Nick snaps on a pair of gloves and begins searching Green Hood's pockets. And he's doing it rough.

'What the fuck is your problem?' Green Hood says, still

facing the wall, and it's at such a low volume that I just about hear it.

'Are you swearing at me?' Nick shouts, placing his head right next to Green Hood's ear. 'Are you threatening a police officer?'

I'm not sure how we've got to this point and I shove my pocket book back into my Met vest as Nick keeps shouting. I hang my arms loose by my sides, hands in front, and widen my stance.

'You wanna talk about this down at the station?' Nick keeps raising his voice until nearly everyone around us has stopped to listen. He finishes his search and spins Green Hood back round to face him, pulling his shoulder as a pivot.

'Fucking hell, I haven't done anything!' Green Hood is outraged. And a part of me is too. A part of me wants to grab Nick by his Met vest and shout in his face. But the other part is standing on a busy London street in a police officer's uniform, with a colleague who is being sworn at. I don't know why Nick's flown off the handle. But he's *us*, and Green Hood is *them*. And I know who I have to stand with.

'You're swearing in a public place, causing alarm and distress to all these people.' Nick motions behind him and Green Hood raises his hands to his head in frustration.

'You stop me for no fucking reason.' He's shouting now. 'You get in my face, threaten to nick me, search me with no grounds? I've got nothing! I'm just walking along the fuck-ing street!'

'Stop swearing.' I shout it loud and clear. Let everyone hear the warning.

'He swore at me first!' Green Hood's eyes plead with me, hoping for an ally. *He's got a point.*

'Let's just all calm down,' I say, and no sooner are the words out of my mouth than a flurry of motion erupts. Nick reaches for Green Hood's wrist. Green Hood ducks down and pushes himself backwards, pulling Nick into him. They both hit the wall together and I grab Green Hood's right arm as Nick cuffs his left wrist.

Green Hood immediately starts shouting, 'This is police brutality. I've done nothing!'

'Stop resisting,' I shout as I pull Green Hood's free wrist towards Nick so he can get the cuffs on properly.

'You're under arrest for public order offences,' Nick shouts triumphantly. He chants out the caution and something about the way he does it makes me think he believes he's in a cop movie.

'Fuck you! Fuck the police!' Green Hood is going for it now and part of me is grateful that he is. It makes us look more justified. Nick tightens the cuffs and Green Hood screams in pain. Cuffs rendering him compliant, Green Hood allows Nick to push him over towards our car, where he is promptly folded over the bonnet.

I step back and reach for my personal radio. 'BX, we've got one coming in for public order, can we get a van on the hurry up please.' There's no way I'm putting Green Hood in the back of my car.

'Received, 215, van is on route.'

'Van's on the way.' I shout to Nick over Green Hood's wailing.

He looks at me, leaning over his suspect, and smirks again. Another wink as he pushes down on the handcuffs, eliciting another shriek from Green Hood. I shudder in disgust. *He's loving this.* I turn away and concentrate on making some notes in my pocket book. I write down Green Hood's reply to the caution and then grab some details from witnesses standing nearby. We'll need all we can get if this goes to court.

The van arrives quickly and I let Nick and Graeme get Green Hood into the cage. Nick climbs into the back to keep an eye on his detainee and Graeme hops into the driver's seat.

'What's up?' he says, taking in my thunderous expression.

'Nick's a prick.' I say it low so they can't hear me in the back, although it would be difficult to hear anything over Green Hood's protests.

Graeme laughs at the rhyme. 'Good to know.'

'This is a pile of shit.'

'Isn't everything?' His Irish lilt makes me smile and I feel myself calming down a little.

'See you back at the nick.' I pat the side of the van door as Graeme pulls away.

I sigh as I walk back to the car, trying to process everything that's just happened. Climbing into the driver's seat, I try and imagine how the stop would have gone if I'd taken the lead, instead of Nick. I can pretty much guarantee that Green Hood would still be ambling along Brixley High Street if I had. For the entire drive back I feel conflicted and uncomfortable. *Is what we've just done unlawful arrest?* He was shouting and swearing in the street. But he wouldn't have been if Nick hadn't wound him up. *If he's so easily wound up maybe he deserves to be arrested.* But the situation was created by us. We weren't responding to a call, we put ourselves deliberately in his path. *He should have co-operated with us, the police.* Nick should have been more professional. *Who are you to say that? He's got seven years of experience.* Green Hood posed no real threat to us or the public. *You can't look through another copper's eyes. You can't see the risks they see.*

By the time I get back to the nick my head feels like it's going to explode. I bypass the custody suite and go straight to the skippers' office. I'm pleased to see that my favourite sergeant is in there, alone. She smiles as she sees me, a smile that dies as I shut the door behind me.

'I'm not going out with Nick again. Guy's a psycho.' I cross my arms in front of me.

She rolls her eyes. 'What's he done now?'

I rub my hands across my face and plonk down in a chair opposite her desk. 'God,' I sigh, 'I don't even know. Winding someone up to get a dodgy public order arrest? Using excessive force?'

She looks at me. 'You want to make this official?'

And there it was. The golden question. *Do you want me to do something about this? Do you want to report a fellow officer? Be seen as a grass? Be ostracised and vilified by your team?* And as I looked at her I knew I just didn't have the guts.

'I just don't want to be posted with him again.' I stand up, make to leave the room.

'I can't promise anything, I'm afraid.'

'Yeah, yeah, no worries.' I feel dejected as I walk towards Custody. Disappointed in the job I've come to love. Disappointed in myself. I start to tap the code into the custody door and then stop, changing my mind. Fuck him. *Let Nick deal with his own prisoner.*

I turn towards the canteen, the thought of a nice cup of tea cheering me up already.

12

Dixon

It's as he pushes the door shut behind him that I realise where I've met him before. *Dixon.* I'm immediately transported to that jailer shift early on in my probation, the one I'll never forget. In a flash, I remember Francine's red bloated face, the scarf cutting into her young neck. The pressure of the shift causing me to verbally lash out at another detainee. Suddenly it all comes back to me and I'm standing on that spot, just outside his cell.

> *'You fucking bitch!' His cell explodes with noise and I jump back as his door begins to vibrate with the force of him kicking it. The force of him trying to get to me.*

I step backwards, edging further into the dim living room, further from him, as he takes a slow step towards me. He's wearing a white vest and blue denim jeans, his naked arms bearing a patchwork of prison tattoos and fighting scars.

'Dixon is incredibly violent and known for assault on police. The best bit is – he only assaults female officers.'

'I saw you through the window.' His nicotine-stained fingers drag against stubble as he strokes his huge hands across his chin. 'What? Did you think I wouldn't remember you?'

'What do you mean?' I stall for time, my eyes jumping from the door to the discarded golf club lying beside it, to the heavy-looking glass ashtray in the centre of the carpet. Discarded cutlery and glasses wink at me from nests of empty food wrappers like so many weapons.

He snorts. 'You're not so tough when there's no cell door between us, are you?'

'I think you have me confused with someone else.' I keep my tone light and focus on planting my feet wide. *Ready stance.*

'Oh no,' he winks and shakes his head. 'Nice try, pretty, but I never forget a face. Plus, I recognise your perfume.' A shiver runs down my spine as he meets my gaze and sniffs the air.

How have you managed to trap yourself in here with him? You fucking idiot.

* * *

I grip the sides of my seat as Darryl takes the sharp corner at a speed that will surely roll the van. He glances across at me, the blue lights striping across his smooth brown skin, and laughs.

'Still don't trust my driving, eh, girl?'

I open my mouth to say something but no sound comes out. My eyes are glued to the road and my knuckles are white. I attempt a smile, desperately trying to appear calm, but I can't seem to stop the panic that washes over me when someone else is in the driving seat. *You're a control freak.*

The thing is, I do trust Darryl's driving. He's got about a million years in the job and I love getting posted with him. His easy manner carries years of experience and the respect of his team with grace, but you'd be mistaken for thinking he's past it. At nearly fifty years old he only looks around forty and he's probably fitter than me. The deep gravelly bass of his voice betrays none of his Jamaican ancestry – it's 100 per cent London cockney. Born and bred. He's told me a little about what it was like being a black man in the Metropolitan Police during the 1980s and 1990s, and it only increases my respect for him. As well as igniting a bitter anger at what he's had to endure. I've been told by more than a few people that he has a soft spot for me – in a fatherly manner – and I'd say that the feeling was mutual. I respect him – more than that; I like him. And, even though he drives like a maniac, he's the person I feel safest being driven by.

We're on our way to a well-known address – a hostel for recovering alcoholics who've recently been released from prison.

Informant reports sounds of fighting
coming from the property.

Every address we attend gets run through our intelligence systems. The idea is to warn us of any known officer safety risks before we get there. It's a great idea in practice. In reality, however, you've often arrived before the report has come through. And what copper worth their warrant card is going to sit outside the address of an emergency waiting for an intelligence report to read? I glance at the intelligence we've got and see that the most recent report is over three months ago. It's not even worth reading it. The place is well known to police due to the ever-changing cycle of volatile men who reside there. The residents change so often that a report from as recently as yesterday could already be out of date. I skim the summary and the word 'weapons' jumps out at me multiple times. It's nothing I don't expect from a bail hostel, although there won't be weapons of the kind that are designed and made to inflict injury – no 'made' offensive weapons, as the law would describe them. Instead, there'll be 'collectable' samurai swords hung on the walls of rooms with no other decorative features. There'll be baseball bats and golf clubs propped innocently behind doors belonging to men who've never played sports in their life. Steak knives that haven't quite made their way back to the communal kitchens and screwdrivers discarded from non-existent DIY projects. All noted and recorded by officers gone before us, all with one purpose in mind. *Warn your colleagues. Officer beware.*

We arrive and get out of the car. The house next to the hostel is well maintained and in stark contrast to the bedraggled frontage of our destination. I see the neighbour's curtains twitch and figure we've found our informant. I quickly look away. The last thing I want to do is expose the Good Samaritan who called the police.

We pause on the pavement, in silence; nothing to be heard. Whatever was going on seems to have finished, but we can't leave without checking that everyone's OK. As we walk up to the front door Darryl glances across at me. Gone is the goofy smile from our journey, replaced by a face that means nothing but business.

'You know about this place?' He nods at the door, which bears the scars of a hundred police battering rams.

'Yeah.' I roll my eyes. 'Been here a few times.'

He nods, giving me a look that I know means *On your guard*. It's a larger than average London terrace. Sturdy and not out of place on this street of terraced Georgian houses. The front garden has been completely concreted over and there's nothing that really sets it apart from any other house in the borough. It's a little dilapidated – needs a paint job – but other than that you could walk past it every day and never have a clue that it was a bail hostel. Unless you were unfortunate enough to encounter one of its residents, of course.

We climb up the three concrete steps together. Darryl's knock is firm and heavy. Three loud raps. There's no mistaking it as anything other than a police knock. I glance upwards to the windows above us and take in the greying nets hanging still behind the grubby glass. We stand for a few moments before Darryl knocks again. This time I pace backwards, down the steps and towards the street. From this viewpoint I can see all the windows, and catch a flicker from the top right.

'Movement, top right.' I point up to the window, where the curtain swings almost imperceptibly.

'Good enough for me,' replies Darryl, and he bends down to the letter-box. He lifts the plastic flap and shouts through the gaping hole. 'Police! Open the door now or we'll kick it in.'

The bass of his rich voice echoes across the concrete front garden. It's as I'm walking towards the door again that a shadow passes across the frosted glass and then the door is open, and we're staring at a disgruntled-looking man in his boxer shorts. The stench of stale alcohol smacks me in the face before he even opens his mouth.

'What the feck is it this time?' He yawns widely, giving me an uninvited view of his black teeth and furry tongue.

'We've had calls that there's been a disturbance.' I glance past him into the empty hallway as he rubs his hairy hands across his eyes.

'It's those eejits upstairs.' He crooks a thumb at the stairs behind him. 'They've been fighting again. Woke me up.'

'How many others live here?' Darryl is assessing the risks. The fewer prison-leaving, police-hating drunks, the better.

'Seven, including me.' He nods towards the ceiling. 'Everyone else is out except those two. Numbers 5 and 6. They like to kick seven bells out of each other every now and then. They go way back – best mates.' He cackles loudly before dissolving into violent coughing. I take a discreet step backwards, fighting the urge to slap my hand across my mouth and nose.

Half of his ginger hair is pointing upwards and the rest is flattened to his scalp. He's clearly just got out of bed. But it's better to be safe than sorry. I ask him for his particulars and he provides them with weary acceptance. His name is Mr Aherne. I check his room for any signs of a disturbance and, finding a surprisingly clean and well-ordered bedroom, check myself for judging him so harshly.

'Can I go back to bed now?' he enquires, and I reply with a nod and a smile.

'Thanks for your help, sir.' He grunts a reply as his door slams behind him and I hear the deadbolt slide across inside. *Imagine you would keep your door locked in a place like this.* We continue to the end of the hallway, stepping over take-away flyers and unopened post along the way. There are four closed doors down here, and an open one that leads to the kitchen. Each resident has his own lockable room and they share the bathroom and kitchen. I shake my head as I imagine what the bathrooms in this place are like, and promise myself that I'll do my best not to encounter one on this call.

Darryl's heading up the stairs ahead of me and I hurry to catch up. We emerge into a tiny hallway with three closed doors and one that is wide open, leading to what I presume is the bathroom. I shuffle past it quickly and wedge myself between Darryl and door number 7. Each door has a brass number on it. There's no sound coming from either of doors 5 and 6 and Darryl flicks a pointed finger between both doors before randomly knocking on number 5. I roll my eyes at him, smiling.

A brief shuffling sound followed by a loud bump and slurred cursing.

'Police. Open up.'

I hear the crunch of a key in the lock and then the door creaks open a few inches. First a gnarled hand appears, dry and cracked at the knuckles, followed by one side of a wrinkled face. He's bald and has a teardrop tattooed just under his right eye. He peers round the door at us, eye wide, the picture of innocence. 'Yes, officers?'

The man's cheeks shiver slightly as he talks, and I wonder if it's the withdrawal shakes or the fight he's just been having. Darryl's police boot slides softly into the open crack of the door.

'We've had reports of a disturbance. We're going to need to come in and check everyone's OK.'

The man does his best to look shocked. It's almost comical and I suppress a smirk. 'Oh no, not in here, officer, no.' He looks behind him, as if double-checking that everything's in order, before nodding in a weak attempt at finality. 'We're all fine here. Thanks anyway.'

The pungent odour from this room is different from that of the Irishman downstairs. Just as unpleasant, but fresher. Alcohol consumed recently, and in large quantities, mixed with the stale smell of men. The man turns from us again and attempts to shut the door, but Darryl's boot isn't going anywhere.

'If you're all fine, why is there blood on your fingers?'

And as Darryl says it my eyes light upon the dark red stains under the man's nails. I feel my cheeks warm as I realise I've missed it. *Why didn't I see it?* I'm so close to the door that I can see the faint red swirls of his fingerprints printed onto the white paint.

Without waiting for an answer, Darryl forces the door open, leaning into it hard and shoving it backwards. The bald man staggers backwards.

'I've reason to believe that someone might be hurt at this address and I will be searching it.'

The sight of blood has raised both of our threat assessments and we pile into the room with our hands on the batons at our belts. It's empty. Empty, apart from the detritus of lager cans and flattened plastic cider bottles, littered fag butts and empty takeaway containers. And as he stands swaying in the centre of the room, the utter misery of his existence makes me draw breath. The room smells damp and stale and there's a single bed pressed up against one wall. A small bedside table and two chairs, along with a doorless wardrobe complete the collection of furniture in the room. I glance behind me to the door and am unsurprised to see a wooden baseball bat propped up behind it. *For us or for them?*

The man is staring at his hands and muttering. Now that I can see his whole face I notice a graze under his left eye, with a smudge of blood beneath it. His nose looks swollen and there's a blue tinge across his eyelid. There's no more blood that I can see and I feel myself relax slightly. Darryl clearly feels the same because he's got his pocket book out and is taking down the man's details.

'Who's done that to your eye, then?' Darryl asks. The man mutters something about falling over and Darryl rolls his eyes. The fetid air seems to fill my nostrils and I start breathing through my mouth. I'm desperate to get out of this small, oppressive room.

'I'll check out number 6,' I call over to Darryl, stepping over the piles of rubbish on my way out.

'Call if you need me,' he replies, not taking his eyes from his current ward.

I step out of the room and take a deep breath. The air out here is marginally fresher than that in number 5. A part of me wonders whether I should wait for Darryl. The other part of me, the part that's a woman fighting for equal treatment in a male-dominated profession, tells me that I don't need the presence of a large man to do my job properly. *I can handle myself.* I look at door number 6 and rap my knuckles against it.

I notice the smear of blood at the exact same moment as I realise that the door's not locked. It swings open slowly, propelled by my knuckles, and my eyes are drawn into the dark room before me. I step into the doorway and squint into the gloom. The curtains are thick and block out most of the light, the rest dulled by the thick fug of cigarette smoke that hangs just below the ceiling, circling the bare light-bulb like a giant smoke ring.

'Hello?' I step further into the room, and as my eyes adjust to the haze I can make out a sagging sofa pushed up against one wall. On the carpet next to it, a glass ashtray is cradling a propped-up cigarette. It's glowing. A frown crosses my face as I hear the door swing shut behind me.

* * *

I decide to drop the pretence.

'Mr Dixon.' As I say his name I place my right hand on my CS spray and my left on my baton. I'm not subtle about it. I want him to see. I raise my chin so that it juts towards him and meet his gaze directly. 'What's been happening this morning, then?'

'Ah, so you do remember me.' He seems to take the fact that I know his name as a bizarre compliment and cocks a thick eyebrow, his gaze sliding brazenly from my boots up to my face, lingering as it goes. Revulsion shudders through each part of my body that it touches. I glance at the door behind him. There's no way I can get there without him getting to me first. Fear grips like a giant fist around my chest and squeezes its iron fingers. I swallow it down. *You will not think me weak.*

There's no fooling Dixon. He follows my gaze and he must know what I'm thinking. He places his left fist into his right and cracks his knuckles, and as he does so I see the raw grazes across them, angry and red. A confident smirk cracks on his face and his whole demeanour radiates danger. I know he's the type of sick individual that thrives off the fear of those he deems weaker than himself. Namely women. I've seen his PNC record and know the damage he's done to women in the past. *Weaker women than me.*

Even in the swirling menace of this room I still feel instantly ashamed of my own mind. But there's no room for pity. There's no room for empathy. Because the only thing there's room for is the screaming in my head that's going round and round and round. *I am not a victim.*

In that moment I realise that's he's not going to tell me what the fight was about. I'm not going to get my pocket book out and I'm not going to write down the CAD number, the time and date, or Dixon's date of birth. In that moment I know with everything I've ever learnt as a copper that he wants to hurt me. *Badly.* And as I watch the curl of his lip I realise that, right now, he doesn't care about anything else. He doesn't care that he'll go back to prison. He doesn't care how long he'll stay there. He doesn't even care about his next drink. Because, right now, all he wants to do is inflict pain. All he knows is how good it will feel to teach me a lesson. To show me who's boss. *To make me bleed.* To go back to prison as the legend who fucked up a copper.

As he steps towards me he lowers his brow and the veins in his arms bulge with the throb of intended violence. The part of me that wanted to wait for Darryl is telling me to scream his name. *He can save you.* One shout and he'll be in here in seconds. Dixon would have his face shoved into the filthy carpet before he even had a chance to think. But the other part of me is stubborn as a mule. *I can deal with this.* If I shout for help I'm admitting just how weak I am. If I shout for help, I prove everyone who ever scoffed at the idea of female police officers right. *If I shout for help he'll know how scared I am.*

'Take one more step and I'll gas you.' My CS shoots forward as I straighten my arm and point it directly at his face. *Aim for the chest. Never use in enclosed spaces. Don't spray directly in the eyes.* Fuck that. This fucker is getting a faceful if he comes any closer.

Dixon pauses and I almost cry out with relief. His hands rise and he flashes his open palms at me. 'OK, girly, OK.' He takes a step backwards and looks at the floor. My mind sings with the rush of winning and the adrenalin dump turns my legs to jelly. But I don't move. I know that I need to arrest him for assault. He's clearly the assailant, responsible for the injuries next door, and I am not leaving these two drunks in this house to continue ripping chunks out of each other. But I can't arrest him alone. *Enough posturing.* My left hand still aiming the CS, I reach my right hand across my chest and grab my personal radio. I don't need to look at it to know what buttons to press, and maybe it's just habit, but I glance towards it just before I press the button. And that's when the room explodes in movement.

In my peripheral I see Dixon's head snap upwards. In the millisecond it takes for my brain to register the danger, he's jumped across the space between us and slammed his body into mine. The CS is crushed against my chest as we fall backwards together and I am powerless to break the fall. We smash onto the floor, him on top of me, and his weight slams the breath out of my chest. *I can't breathe.* My arms are pinned to my Met vest and my nostrils are full of the putrid alcohol seeping from Dixon's pores. *He's going to kill me.* He starts to move on top of me, placing his legs over my legs so that every inch of me is crushed against the floor and my mind snaps from blank and reeling to sharp. *Fucking do something*! My radio is still clamped in my right hand and I stretch my fingers up to the top, where the bright orange emergency button sits.

'I'm not going back inside.' Dixon's voice is hot in my ear and full of rage.

I close my eyes and focus on reaching the button. I open my mouth to shout for Darryl but I have no breath and all that comes out is a choked wheeze. Dixon's stinking mass is still crushing my chest and I can't seem to fill my lungs. I can't move. *I can't breathe*. My mouth gapes in silence and I feel a shift in Dixon.

'You fucking bitch.' This time he growls it. And this time his voice is thick with something other than rage. He pushes his groin into my abdomen, hard, and as he does so he shudders a hot breath into my ear. Fear and disgust spike inside my chest. A surge of strength rips through me, from somewhere deep and animal, somewhere I didn't even know existed, and I shove upwards hard, pushing him away from me with all of my might, using my arms and legs at once. I get a few millimetres of space between us. But that's all I need. My fingers curl over the top of the radio and press deep into the emergency button. My radio immediately reacts with a shock of sharp, high-pitched beeps, and the entire handset vibrates against my chest. I have ten seconds of open airtime to send my SOS message. And I shout one word. Feel like I'm screaming it at the top of my lungs, like it will smash windows and burst Dixon's eardrums, but what comes out is little more than a croak.

'Darryl.'

It seems as though it hasn't even fully left my lips before the door to Dixon's room explodes inwards. In an instant the weight is rolled from my chest and Darryl is wrestling Dixon's arms behind his back while pressing a knee into his back. Dixon offers no resistance. *Fucking coward.* I drag myself upright, holding my head against the wave of dizziness that threatens to overcome me.

'215 – 215, come in.'

My radio continues to vibrate and the voice of the control room begins to cut through the daze in my head.

'Urgent assistance required now at 57 Alabaster Drive – all units please.'

I watch mutely, on my knees, arms dangling impotently at my side, as Darryl secures Dixon's cuffs. I listen as unit after unit assigns itself to our location, as my entire team drops what they are doing to run to us. I feel the familiar surge of emotion at hearing a team come together to protect one of their own, then a siren cuts through the silence in the street outside.

'BX21 on scene.'

Then there are boots and shouts in the hallway below and as the fog clears I start to pull myself together. The room comes into focus and my mind snaps back to its usual refrain. *You fucking idiot. Stop acting like a Doris.* I force myself to my feet and grab my radio.

'BX, this is 215. Cancel any more units please.'

I cancel the emergency alarm on my radio as Ben and Cerys stomp into the room. They clock Dixon on the floor, Darryl still holding him down, and nod to me.

'You OK?' Ben asks.

'Never better.' I smile and turn to Dixon.

*　　*　　*

I nick Dixon for one count of assault against his neighbour and one count of assault on police. I have no injuries and Dixon's neighbour almost definitely won't testify against him, so I'm pretty sure that neither case will go anywhere. However, he's on a licence. He's living in a bail hostel and there's a remote chance that his behaviour will get him sent back to prison to serve out the remainder of his sentence. *Instant recall.* The thought makes me smile as I head out through the hallway of the bail hostel. Dixon's already in the van and I'm looking forward to booking him in and shutting the cell door on his evil face.

As I wander past Mr Aherne's door it pops open and his scrunched-up face peers out at me.

'What the feck happened to you?'

I must look confused because he points to the top of his head and gestures at me.

'Your hair.'

I reach up and feel a mess of thick strands that have

come loose from the bun that I neatly wrapped this morning. I start to say thanks but he's already shut the door
again so I head out to the van and peer into the back, where
Darryl sits, keeping an eye on Dixon.

'Were you hoping I'd head back to the nick like this?' I
point to my bird's-nest hair do.

Darryl sniggers. 'Hell, yes.'

I shake my head and hear a click behind me. I turn, and
find myself looking directly into the camera of Ben's phone.

'One for your locker.' He winks.

I roll my eyes and climb into the back of the van. Dixon's
my prisoner and I'll watch him in the cage until we're back
at the nick. Darryl climbs out and heads for our car.

'See you there,' I call after him. Then I slide shut the door
and the van rumbles to life beneath me. I look at Dixon and
find him staring at me. He cocks his head to one side.

'Can I get a fag at the nick?'

I take a deep breath.

'We'll see.'

13
Freddy

I look down at the little white stick. My gaze glancing on and off the blue lines, blue lines that glare at me like double yellows in headlights. A flash-back to the decrepit Hendon toilet block. How the hell has this happened to me? *Again.* I'm sitting in the bathroom at my mum and dad's house. After renting with colleagues for over three years I'm back at home while I search for my next flat-share. A thousand thoughts run through my mind. *We use condoms! How am I going to tell John? We've only been dating for three months.* Not even dating really, more like seeing each other. Seeing each other after drunken team drink-ups. We haven't even had the talk yet. The talk about whether, in fact, we are now boyfriend and girlfriend. I hold my head in my hands and stare down at my ankles. *I don't even know how I feel about John.* I'm twenty-eight, five years into the career of a lifetime. I love every day at work, the team, and the exhilaration. I don't want to sit behind a desk!

But there are other voices too. Happy voices. And, as I listen, they start to clamour more loudly. *A baby.* I look down and realise that my hands are already cupped across my stomach. I imagine myself standing in front of a mirror, running my hands over a large, rounded belly. *A second chance*. I think back to my time at Hendon and wince as I feel the scrape of the speculum. The ache that I had felt for days afterwards. *I can't go through that again.* I think back to just two weeks ago, when John and I were lying on his bed at his flat in Walthamstow and I told him about what I'd gone through during my training at Hendon. He was only the second person I'd ever told, not including the father, and the staff at Hendon who'd needed to know. I could hardly say the words, and when I'd finished, I'd braced myself, waiting to be judged. But all John had done was hug me. I told him then that I could never again put myself through that, and that it was about time I went on the pill. I shake my head. My doctor's appointment is booked for two days' time – I think we might be having a slightly different conversation after this morning's discovery.

I wrap the pregnancy test in tissue paper and tuck it up my sleeve, crossing the landing quickly and into my room. I shove it under my pillow and then stand in the middle of my room with my hands on my hips. It's 10 a.m. on a Saturday and I'm due at work at 2 p.m. for a Saturday late shift. Just what I need after a life-changing discovery. I certainly won't have much time to think. Maybe that's a good thing. I run my hands through my hair and pace the room. Mum and Dad are downstairs. I've made the mistake of not confiding in them before and I've regretted it ever since. I'm not about to do it again. I propel myself out of my room and down the stairs before I have a chance to change my mind. I stand on the laminate floor of the hallway and look into the living room. The door is almost closed but I can see Mum through its rippled glass panels. I pull the door towards me and step into the frame, my heart drumming against my chest. Mum is reading her Kindle – both my parents are avid readers and passed their love of books on to me. Like me, Mum has the ability to disappear into the books she reads; she's engrossed, and doesn't notice me. Tears start to spill down my cheeks and it's not until I give a little involuntary sob that she turns her head.

'Alice! What's wrong?' she reaches out to me, concern etched across her face.

I slide down into the leather sofa beside her. Leaning into her as she wraps her arms around me. I'm properly sobbing now and I feel my nose and mouth swell as I try and get my breathing under control. I don't know how to say it but I know I have to so I just blurt it out.

'I'm pregnant.'

'Oh!' Mum clasps her hands together. I take a second to compute how happy her exclamation sounds as she takes a second to compute my tears. Then she says 'oh' again. Only this time it's an octave lower.

'Whatever you decide, we will support you.' It's the first thing out of her mouth, as I always knew it would be. And I once again curse myself for not confiding in her years before.

'I just don't know what to do.' My words come out in a thick, clotted jumble. 'How can I have a baby? I'm not married, I'm not even in a proper relationship! I love my job . . .' and as I'm talking a darker thought crosses my mind. *What if I'm being punished?* 'What if there's something wrong with the baby? What if it doesn't grow properly?'

My mum takes my hand in hers and I feel the soft, dry crinkle of her skin. 'I think the fact that you're already referring to it as "the baby" tells you a lot about how you're feeling.'

I nod. And then I shake my head. 'God, how am I going to tell John?'

'Don't worry about John. Figure out how you feel first. Make your decision – there's no rush. We'll help you, no matter what you need to do.'

'I've got to leave for work soon.' I reach for the tissues on the coffee table and scrub at my eyes. 'I need to get my face to go down before I leave.'

'Why don't you see if you can get a day off? Surely you'll be too distracted today?' Mum looks at me with a worried expression.

'No, I need to go in – we're short at the moment.' We had two off with injuries sustained on duty, and one off long-term sick. 'Plus, maybe it's better if I'm distracted, I'll drive myself mad at home here all day.'

I head towards the door, but before I head upstairs to the shower, Mum calls me back.

'I know it's early days, and I know you haven't decided

what you're going to do, but . . .' she glances at my stomach. 'Please, just be careful.'

I nod. 'I always am, Mum. Don't worry.'

* * *

I'm not quite sure how I managed to nod and smile my way through the team briefing but suddenly I'm sitting in the driver's seat of the marked police van. I feel my cheeks heat up slightly as I think about John, about the conversation I need to have with him. He had tried to catch my eye in the briefing room but I'd kept my gaze front and centre. I'd shot out of the door as soon as we were dismissed, head down, pausing only to snatch up my kitbag on the way to the yard. And now I'm glancing furtively into the wing mirrors of the van as our team emerges in dribs and drabs from the rear doors. I glance over to Liz, my operator for the day. A basic driver now herself, she's come a long way since I walked her through her first sudden death. A flash of Hilda's corpse in my mind, and I shudder as a wave of unexpected nausea ripples through my stomach. Frowning, I think back to how sensitive I had been at Hendon. *Must be the hormones.*

'Everything OK?' Liz is looking expectantly at me. 'I've logged us on – we're all ready to go.'

'Great.' I flash her a large smile and hope it reaches my eyes. I gun the engine and just as I'm releasing the handbrake I see John behind us. He's ambling towards the van with that white-teeth smile of his that I love. He raises a hand and I know he can see me eyeing him from the mirror. My stomach twists and sweat prickles on my upper lip. I ease the van towards the gate and my fingers dance across the steering wheel as it swings lazily open. John's hand falls as he realises I'm not going to wait to talk to him, and I swallow down the guilt as I steer the lumbering prisoner van out of the station gates. He disappears into the distance behind me, but the snakes in my stomach remain.

A succession of 'I' grades and reporting calls keep me unable to dwell on things until around 7 p.m., when a pause in radio chatter and our rumbling stomachs draw us back to the station. I'm just pulling our response car into the rear yard, trying to ignore the slithers in my belly at the possibility of running into John, when an 'S'-graded call pops onto our on-board computer. We've been working solid since 2 p.m. and were about to head in for our refs.

'God, I'm starving.' Liz pats her tummy hopefully.

'Yeah, me too. Let's mug this one off,' I pull my radio towards my mouth, about to tell control that we're on our refreshment break, when something catches my eye.

'Hang on.' I read the initial text of the call. *Seventy-nine-year-old male not been seen since Monday morning, very out of character. Possible collapse behind locked doors. Welfare check required.* Today is Wednesday. I glance at Liz and see that she has read the call too. I note that the call was made by a concerned neighbour at 5.37 p.m. It's been a busy late turn, full of emergency calls and blue-light runs. This non-emergency call has slipped to the back of the pile.

'Probably a sudden death.' I turn to face her. 'Can it wait?'

She looks at me, considering. 'What if it's not a sudden death – I mean, what if he's not dead?'

She doesn't need to add the word 'yet'. We both hear it. I nod and slot the car into reverse. 'I was hoping you'd say that.'

I back out of the gates. What's the point of conducting a welfare check if it takes you hours to get there? The whole reason we force entry is to protect life and limb, after all. Not because we just assume they're already dead.

'There goes my lunch,' Liz tuts, but she's smiling. She's grown into an excellent copper, and it's nice to work with someone on the same wavelength. We'd both rather make sure this call is answered than stop for refs. 'At least, if he is dead, he'll still be relatively fresh.'

'Yeah, not another Hilda,' I say.

She winces. 'Thank fuck for that.'

We drive the rest of the way in silence. I don't use the lights and sirens because the call has been graded as a non-emergency. I could use them if I wanted; I have that discretion, but in the event of an accident, I would have to justify my decision in court. So, I proceed in normal time. As I drive the image of Hilda's corpse invades my mind despite my efforts to push it out. I wonder if Liz can see her too. I feel my stomach turn at the thought and frown at my squeamishness. Then I remember. *I'm pregnant.* Maybe I should have stopped for refs after all. By the time I pull up to the address I've accepted that this will be another long sudden death call. My belly rumbles and I curse myself and my naive enthusiasm.

As we climb out of the car the front door of the neighbour's flat opens. A concerned woman, around sixty years old, wobbles her way towards us on kitten-heel slippers. She hugs a huge dressing gown to her chest and her hair is taut in bright pink rollers. I like her already.

'Thank goodness,' she breathes and points to the flat next door. 'I am so worried about Henry. I see him every morning, without fail. He comes out to get the milk and he always sits on his little chair.' She waves towards a white plastic garden chair that sits forlornly next to his front door. 'I've knocked and called through the letter-box but no answer. He never goes out!' She clasps her hands to her neck and shivers. 'I just know something bad has happened.'

Liz has her pocket book out. 'Has he got any family nearby?'

'His only son moved back up to Aberdeen a few years ago. He's Scottish, you see – Henry, that is.' She's talking fast and flapping her hands. Liz puts a hand on her shoulder.

'It's OK. You've done the right thing.'

The woman takes a breath. 'Sorry. It's just that I've lived next to him for twenty years. I should have called earlier but I've had the 'flu and I've not really been out of the house and I'm ashamed to say that it only occurred to me this afternoon that I hadn't seen him.' She covers her face with her hands.

'It's OK,' murmurs Liz, patting the woman's back.

'I don't suppose you have a key?' I nod to Henry's front door.

'No, sorry.'

'Have you got his son's contact details?' I ask.

'Oh yes.' Her eyes are moist. 'I've called and left a message on their answer machine.'

I nod to Liz but she's already asking for the number. I leave her taking details and step towards the flat. The door is white PVC plastic with three central frosted windows and a letter-box. I bang loudly on the door. Always best to knock first, just in case. As I expect, there's no reply. The space behind the door is unlit and the frosted glass is black. I step back and bring my PR to my mouth.

'BX receiving 215?

'Go ahead, 215.'

'We're on scene at Parson's Row. Can you please note that we're going to be attempting to force entry as we believe the male here has collapsed behind locked doors.'

'All received, 215. Do you need the enforcer?'

'Yes please, on the hurry-up.'

'Received.'

I clip my radio back onto my Met vest. The radio chatter begins as the control room starts to round up a unit to bring us the bright red battering-ram known as the enforcer. I'm not even going to attempt kicking down a PVC door. I bend down and push open the letter-box. Warm air pushes out onto my face and I take a cautious sniff. The air is stale and there's a tang of something unpleasant, but I'm not entirely sure that it's death. I stand up as Liz appears behind me.

'Well?'

'I'm not sure. Doesn't smell great, though.' I nod towards the neighbour as her fluffy slippers wobble back into her flat. 'Can we get round the back?'

'No, apparently these flats back onto the ones behind; there are no gardens.'

'Great,' I sigh. There are two windows, one either side of the door, both with heavy net curtains masking the interior of the flat. Liz cups her hands against the glass and presses her face to it. I turn my attention to the letter-box again and kneel down so that my face is level with it. I hear Brixley Control confirm that the enforcer is on the way. Liz acknowledges them on her radio as I once again open the letter-box. It's a standard plastic flap with black bristles on the inside. It makes it nearly impossible to see into the hall-way as the bristles are blocking my view. I pull my pocket book out of my Met vest and push it into the gap, shoving it upwards so that the top layer of bristles open. It's too dim inside to see anything. 'Shit.'

The faint sound of sirens reaches my ears and I hope it's our enforcer. One of the best things about working in London is that help is never far away. I should just stand up and wait for them. Smash our way in, find the body and get it over with, but something keeps me on my knees. I twist round and pull my torch from my belt. My knees protest at the concrete floor beneath them as I try and aim the beam of my torch into the gap I've created with my pocket book. My torch illuminates a tiny area of hallway and I squint through the box, trying to make sense of the space. I can see a light coloured floor, possibly Lino, and a brown door directly opposite. To the right of the door is the staircase and at the bottom of the staircase is a pile of beige towels. It's a tiny space and I can only see a thin sliver of it. I am about to pull my torch away when something makes me freeze.

'What is it?' Liz is bending over me.

'I thought I heard something.' I feel a skip in my chest as I hear it again. A faint shuffling sound. Something close by. I press my ear to the gap in the letter-box and wait.

'What was it?'

'I don't know. Something moving, maybe.' I put my finger to my lips and we both hold our breaths, our ears straining. I hear nothing except the sudden blast of sirens from behind us. The enforcer has arrived.

Andy and Darryl climb out of the car, Darryl swinging the red lump of brute metal like it's an empty shopping bag.

'Right.' He stops behind me and takes the battering-ram by both its handles. 'Out the way, then.'

I can tell he is raring to do some damage. My eyes run briefly over his bulging muscles and I consider the fact that I can barely lift the enforcer myself. He holds it with such ease. I hold my hand up to him, palm out.

'Hang on there.' I just want to take another look before we do the door. 'I thought I heard something.'

He shrugs and lowers the enforcer to the ground. It makes a heavy *thunk* against the concrete as he places it down. I turn back to the door and push my pocket book back into the letter-box, aiming my torch as far right as I can go. I peer at the bottom of the stairs. *There's something about that pile of towels.* And then I see it. It's not a pile of towels at all. It's a dressing gown, dropped in a pile on the bottom step. The cord of the gown has been mostly pulled off and it snakes towards the corner just inside the door, on the right side. I strain as I try and peer into the space, pressing my face hard into the plastic of the front door. There's something tangled in the cord. Again a skip in my chest as I realise what I'm looking at. It's a foot. A pale, perfectly still, foot.

'Jesus, he's right behind the door.' I turn to glance at the others. Darryl looks a bit pale. No doubt he's thinking the same thing I am. *Thank fuck we didn't smash the door in.* I press my face to the letter-box again and call through to Henry. 'Henry! Henry, it's the police. We're here to help you. Henry, can you hear me?' Absolute silence.

I press the talk button on my personal radio. 'BX, receiving 215?'

'Go ahead, 215.'

'Can we get an ambulance running to this address, please, along with the London Fire Brigade. I can confirm that this is a collapse behind locked doors. The male has collapsed just inside the front door. He's showing no signs of life. We can't use the enforcer because of his position. We'll need the assistance of LFB to gain entry.'

'That's all received, 215.'

An idea comes to me and I start to push my fingers into the letter-box.

'Careful,' Darryl says from behind me. It's generally advised that, as a copper, you should never put your hand through a letter-box. Mainly because there are lots of nasty people out there that want to do us harm. And sometimes they put booby traps in letter-boxes in the hope that they'll do some damage. That's not even considering the possibility of what someone could do to your hand while it's in there. I hesitate. Briefly my gaze falls to my lap and the thought that it's no longer just me I have to worry about crosses my mind.

I push my arm through the letter-box. Twisting it around, I try and reach up towards the door handle. My arm wedges stuck abruptly a couple of inches below my forearm, and my hand clasps around impotently. I swear and pull it out.

'Is he dead?' Andy asks.

'Looks it.' I wipe my brow and rub at my arm. 'Skin on the foot is very pale.'

'What about the noise?'

'I don't know.' _Maybe I imagined it._ I press my ear to the letter-box once again. My three colleagues still behind me. I feel as if we're all holding our breaths. There it is again. I tense as I press my ear harder against the cold plastic casing. A low groan, almost inaudible, reaches my ears. My arm is back through the letter-box before I can even consider what I'm doing. 'He's alive!'

'Holy fuck,' Darryl mutters. Andy begins updating control, asking them to expedite the LAS and LFB as much as they can.

I am frantic. I shove my arm as hard as it will go. Henry's been on the cold hard floor for at least two days and he doesn't have much time left. Of that I am certain. *If I can just reach the damned handle.* I push my hand upwards until the pain makes me drop it limp. It lowers and I start at the touch of cold skin. I feel leathery fingers, far too cold, dry and crepe-like against the soft of my fingertips. As I wrap Henry's hand in mine I feel a squeeze of response.

'It's OK, Henry,' I push my mouth to the gap. 'We're here to help. We're going to get you off that floor'. I'm panting with the effort of maintaining my position, cramped against the door, arm wrenched up into the box. But the small warmth left in Henry's hand pushes me on. I reluctantly let go of his hand and take a deep breath. Shoving my upper body forward as hard as I can, I force my arm into the letter-box. The metal casing scrapes at my skin as my elbow wrenches through the gap, allowing me to bend my arm upwards towards the handle.

I can hear my colleagues behind me, offering support, making suggestions. I can feel the warmth of Liz's hand on my shoulder, the grit digging into my kneecaps and the burn of my grazed arm. But all of a sudden it's just me and Henry, and if I can just reach the handle I can get to him. Rescue him. I'm begging an extra millimetre from my outstretched fingers as they fumble for the handle, my arm screams at the strain and I'm about to give up when I feel it. The cold edge of the door handle, just at the end of my fingertips. I use all my concentration to push onto the top of it, inching it downwards. *Please be unlocked. Please.* I shut my eyes as I feel the clunk of the lock as it releases. The door swings inwards slightly and I try and pull my weight away from it, conscious of Henry's position.

A murmur of excitement from behind me as they realise that I've done it. I loll my head against the door for a second but now I'm the one in the way and I need to get my arm out of the door. It's wedged nearly up to my armpit.

'We need to get in there,' I call back to Liz and the boys. 'You're going to have to pull me.' I immediately feel hands on my Met vest as they begin to pull me backwards. An involuntary yelp escapes me as my arm burns in agony.

'Shit. Careful.' Andy levels his face with mine. 'You OK?'

'Yeah.' I try a smile but I'm pretty sure I'm just grimacing. 'I can take it.'

'OK.' He nods to the others. They pull again and my arm shoots backwards out of the letter-box. The metal rips at the skin around my elbow as I fall backwards onto the concrete floor. I watch as Liz gently pushes the door open and takes Henry's hand. I pull myself up from the floor and start to try and bend my arm. I look over the grazes and decide that I'll have some nasty bruises tomorrow. But I can't feel any pain right now. Because right now, all I feel is euphoria. *I did it.* Henry's still alive and I've done what a police officer joins up to do. *I've rescued someone.*

Later on I sit in the hospital and begrudgingly allow a nurse to apply some antiseptic cream to my grazes. Henry's son has shaken my hand with tears in his eyes and I've smiled and nodded and brushed off his praise. I sit and watch as he holds his dad's hands, as he places a soft kiss on his forehead. And for a brief moment I believe I witness the point of all these happenings we call life. And although I knew, deep down, that I'd already made my decision, I cup my hand across my stomach and I smile. *I'm going to have a baby.*

*   *   *

My hands shake as I pick up the phone and select John's number. I've shut myself in my bedroom to make the call. He picks up on the second ring.

'Hi. Everything OK?'

There's an edge in his voice. I wade straight in without any preamble. 'Look, I know you thought I was avoiding you yesterday, and – well, erm . . . we need to talk. I'd come to you but the trains are a nightmare on a Sunday; engineering works.' I pace up and down my small box-bedroom. 'Can you drive here?'

John blows out a long sigh. 'What do you want to talk about?'

'It's not something I can discuss on the phone. Please, John, don't ask any questions. Please just come?'

'Alice. If you want to split up with me please just do it. I really don't want to drive from Walthamstow to Cheshunt just for the pleasure of being dumped.'

I rub my hand across my forehead in frustration. 'John – I'm not going to – please. Please just get in your car.'

A long pause. 'Are your parents in?'

He's never even met my parents.

'Yes, don't worry, I'll meet you outside. Park in the turning circle at the end of the street. We can talk in your car.'

'Very romantic.' A pause, and then, 'OK. See you soon.'

'Thank you.' I close my eyes. 'See you soon.'

It takes him around forty-five minutes to arrive and I spend the entire time flitting between my room and the bathroom, feeling queasy with nerves. I've never before experienced to such a degree the literal motion of hand-wringing. I always thought 'hand-wringing' was just a term that writers used to convey anxiety. But it's very real. And my hands are wringing, from clammy to dry then tingling – never still, gripping and grabbing at each other, patting and stroking at my thighs as I wipe down my palms. I haven't thought about what I'm going to say, because every time I try to work out how I'm going to phrase it, it all jumbles up again. There's nothing to do but wait until he gets here. Wait until he's in front of me. And let the words spill out.

I'm looking out of my bedroom window as his red Seat Ibiza turns into the street. Immediately I can see that something is wrong. Thick black smoke is billowing out of the bonnet. I run down the stairs and pop my head into the living room.

'John's here.'

Mum and Dad look up from the TV. 'Good luck.' Mum smiles at me.

'Right,' says Dad. 'Where's my shotgun?' Mum has updated him overnight and this is his particular brand of Dad humour. Or his way of coping with the news.

'Very funny, Dad.' I roll my eyes and head out of the door.

The smell of burning hits my nostrils as I slide the porch door shut behind me. I live in a quiet close on the edge of a commuter town. A light patter of drizzle lands on my forehead as I head towards the turning circle at the end of the close, where John's Ibiza sits smoking in the dusk. John climbs out as I approach, unfolding his 6 foot 2 inch frame from the small hatchback.

'What's happened?'

He already looks stressed and I feel a stab of sympathy for him. *Am I about to ruin his life?* He scrapes his fingers through his close-cropped hair and wrenches open the bonnet. Smoke billows around him and he starts to cough. I step forward to help but something stops me. My hand instinctively covers my nose and mouth and I think about the toxins in that black cloud.

John starts talking between coughs. 'The bloody engine light went on about halfway to yours, then the temperature needle shot up.' He motions towards the bonnet, attempting to fan the smoke away with his long arms. 'At least there's no flames. Hopefully the rain will help cool it down.'

'Excellent timing.' I attempt a laugh.

'The smoke started about ten minutes from here. I should have pulled over, but I couldn't, could I?'

He looks at me. The question lingers between us. *Why did you bring me here?* We're standing about 2 metres apart. Him at the front of his bonnet, me on the smooth tar of the circle. I know he won't close the gap between us – he doesn't even know why he's here. It's up to me. I walk towards him until I'm only a few inches away. I'd quite like to kiss him but I can't because I don't know what's about to happen.

I open my mouth to speak. I hesitate. 'You need to call the AA.'

'I'll sort the car out in a minute. What did you want to talk about?' He looks down at me as the rain falls around us. The drizzle has grown into cold, icy drops and I shiver as they tendril their way under my collar. He swipes at the drips that have gathered at his hairline. 'I would suggest we sit in the car, but it's full of smoke.'

I glance towards the red car, away from the intensity of his gaze, and the words finally come. 'I'm pregnant.'

A beat of silence in which I dare to look at him. He's looking towards his feet, chewing his lip. 'I thought it might be that.'

'Really?' I look at him in astonishment.

'Well,' he grins. 'I was really hoping you weren't going to dump me, and after that, what else could it be?'

I'm glad he's smiling. 'I can't believe that we're standing in the rain having this discussion.'

'Yeah,' he chuckles. 'Next to my smoking car.'

'You really do need to call the AA.'

While he makes the phone call I open the windows of his car to let out some of the remaining fumes. Heat radiates from the engine but the smoke has all but stopped.

John disconnects the call and I step towards him. He wraps me in his arms. The damp of his jacket feels cold and rough against my cheek.

'They'll be about an hour.'

I look back to the house. 'Do you want to come in and warm up?'

'Are you kidding?' he laughs. 'Hell, no.'

I nod and, thinking back to Dad's shotgun comment, decide that maybe he has a point.

'Well, now the smoke has cleared we can probably sit in the car. How about I grab us a cup of tea?'

He's waiting in the driver's seat when I return with the tea. We sit in silence for a few moments before he speaks.

'Whatever you decide, I'll stand by you.'

I smile into my mug, the hot steam blurring my glasses. 'I've already decided. You know what I went through at Hendon. I can't go through that again.' He turns to look at me. 'Plus, I want this baby.'

'Wow.' He puffs out his cheeks. 'That's the first time you've used that word.'

I nod and wait.

'So we're having a baby, then.' He stares at his fingers in his lap.

'Look,' I begin, staring ahead. 'I don't know how this is going to work – I don't know *if* this is going to work. I just –'

His warm hand cups mine and I stop talking, turning to look into his eyes. They're glinting. 'We'll be fine. We can do this.'

'How do you know?'

'Because I think I'm in love with you.'

I stare at him. My first instinct is to say it back. But my head is so full of questions and doubts and hopes and fears that my mouth stays closed.

He laughs softly and looks down. 'I had hoped for a more romantic setting.'

I squeeze his hands and smile. 'You know what? I think we're going to be fine.'

14

Mrs Mowbray

I lie in bed and I think about the boy. I think about the crop of new stubble on the tip of his chin. The patches of acne on his cheeks and the way he had tried to fold his gangly limbs in on themselves. I think about the thin horizontal lines that laddered up his arms, varying in colour from shiny white to deep purple, and I wonder what other scars he was hiding. I try to push his face away – *I need to sleep* – but he sits stubbornly on those stairs, staring at me. I can still smell the carpet. Stale smoke and acrid urine. I bury my head in my pillow and breathe in the fresh smell of my fabric conditioner. I hold my hands over my ears but I can still hear the squeak that his dirty trainers made as he pushed the tips of his toes together. There was a hole in the toe of the left one and I wonder if he was wearing socks; if his big toe was cold.

I think of him as a boy because that's what he was. Fifteen years old. But his eyes told a different story. In his eyes was the weary acceptance of a thousand disappointments. The weary acceptance of me, a police officer, standing in front of him. Questioning his presence in the communal hallway that led to the flat where he lived. We'd been called to the address by a concerned neighbour. Apparently he'd been sitting on the stairs, smoking, for hours and she was too scared of his hoody to walk past him. I'd taken his details and chatted to him. He was distant, depressed. But polite. I felt no threat. I stood there casually, with my hands tucked into the sides of my Met vest. He was sat on a small landing at the top of five steps. So, although he was sitting, his face was almost level with mine. And at the end of the conversation, he had looked me in the eye.

'You're one of the good ones,' he had said.

'I hope so.' I had smiled.

'I knew that bitch upstairs would call the cops. You know what I was thinking?' He clasped his fuzzy chin in both hands and breathed into his palms. 'I was thinking – if the cops come – I'm gonna fuck them up.'

An instant chill had snaked its way around my neck. I wrap my warm hands around it now as the memory courses through me.

'But – you're so nice, I've changed my mind.' He had reached both hands behind him. And still I stood there, hands in my vest. Even when I heard the chink of metal on metal. *Stupid!* Something froze me to the spot as both of his hands came back into view, each holding a large knife. One had been a cleaver, wide blade, moulded from a singular piece of metal. The other was long and thin, serrated blade with a black handle. That's the one that snagged my gaze.

He placed them gently on the carpet before him. Stood up and raised his hands. I still hadn't moved. And as I lie staring at my ceiling, listening to the tiny breaths of Freddy, my baby son, in his bassinet next to me, I replay the image of those knives over and over and over again. And I can't sleep, even though I've never been so exhausted. And I can't get the images out of my head.

What if things had been different?

What if?

*   *   *

I twist and twist my engagement ring around my finger as the doctor waits. His middle-aged face is open and patient. I feel a stab of anger at John for making me come here. But then he reaches across and puts a hand on top of mine. I look at him and he nods at me. *You can do this.* He was true to his word and has stood by me throughout my pregnancy. Freddy is one now and John asked me to marry him a couple of months ago. We live together in a rented two-bedroom flat and I've been back at work for around three months. And I'm not coping.

The words run through my head, tumbling over each other like toddlers at a soft play centre, jostling at the edges of my mouth. There are so many ways to say it. I've rehearsed a million different versions in my head. But my lips remain clamped. I can feel the cold film of sweat as it gathers on my forehead and my mind chastises me for being so weak. It's been drilled into me for so long. *Be* strong. *Don't show fear. Nothing can break you.* But I'm not the person I was before. *Just say it.*

'I think I have post-natal depression.' The voice must be mine, but I don't recognise it.

The doctor nods and looks at his screen, tapping lightly at the keyboard. John squeezes my hand. The tears flow freely down my cheeks and I feel the light splatter of them as they break against my chest.

'You gave birth over a year ago?' He raises an eyebrow and faces me once more.

'Yes – I know – I should have come before.' *But I don't believe in depression. It's just laziness. It's just failure. I'm just not a good enough mother.* 'I guess I thought I could get through it on my own.'

The doctor nods again. 'I'm glad you're here now. There's nothing wrong with asking for help, and lots of women go through this.'

'Thank you.' I smile through my tears at the blurry outline of his jowly face. I can feel my lips and nose swelling as my sinuses begin to fill up, and I lick my dry lips. I've always been an ugly crier. But birth and motherhood has a way of stripping your dignity and I'm so far past caring.

'Can you tell me some of your symptoms?' The GP's hands are poised at his keyboard as he waits for me to elaborate.

'I – um – I'm always crying. Feel like I can't cope.' My voice comes out in staccato bullet points. 'I'm exhausted but I can't sleep. My mind races. I have chest pains, palpita-tions—' I drift off mid-sentence. Another symptom. I'm just about to add it when John joins in.

'She's really angry all the time.' I glance at him and my cheeks burn.

'I can't turn off my mind – at night – I can't forget things at work like I used to be able to.'

'What do you do?'

'I'm a police officer.'

I take a breath and reach for a tissue from the box that the GP has delicately slid towards me.

'I keep imagining awful things happening to Freddy.' The vivid colours of violent death streak through my mind, my son superimposed onto the victims I've seen.

The doctor nods. 'I think you need to consider medication.'

I nod. I push down all the concerns I have about the stigma of taking antidepressants. The bad rep they've had in the past. I tell myself that they're different now – not as damaging, not as addictive. I'm not sure I really believe the doctor when he tells me that it's not my fault. He tells me that sometimes the brain needs a 'little pick-me-up' to get itself back on an even keel. And as he's talking I'm watching his mouth move and I'm nodding my head but the only thing that's going through my mind is *I'm just not a good enough mother and no amount of drugs* are going to change that. But I wrap my hand around the little green and white slip he hands me and clutch it all the way to the pharmacy. Because, right now, I'll try anything.

* * *

I sit in the briefing room as the runners and riders are called out and feel the familiar excitement of a whole shift ahead of me. Wide open and full of opportunities. But now there's something else. It's something I never felt before becoming a mother. Something in the back of my mind that dampens the excitement like a cold rain. *Fear.* And as I sit staring at the floor in-between my boots Freddy pops into my mind. I have a tiny person at home who relies on me. And I don't feel quite so invincible any more.

I'm working part-time – I do 60 per cent of the hours a full-time constable would work. It's taken a lot of juggling but I've finally found a way that I can fit my hours to the D Team shifts, meaning that I can stay with the team I've been with since the beginning. However, since I've been back I've realised that so much has changed in the nine months that I've been away, that it wouldn't really have mattered which team I joined. There are so many new faces and sadly, a lot of the old ones have moved on to new boroughs or new squads.

I've been on the antidepressants for around two weeks now. I'm crying a lot less so I'd say they were working, although in many ways I don't really feel any different. The same crippling thoughts and fears run through my head every night, it's just that now I feel a little more numb. And when I say I'm crying less, I actually mean I don't think I could cry even if I wanted to. It's like the tears have been bricked up inside me. The pressure's still there as they push up against the inside of my chest, but there's no way to release them.

The doctor has advised me to tell my supervisors, so that they can support me through the transition back from new mother to serving police officer. But every time I open my mouth to try the words just stick in my throat. I have post-natal depression. *Depression.* That word that's bandied about by my team members with a roll of the eye. The word that, until about a year ago, I had thought meant plain old *lazy.* The word that we hear day in, day out, at nearly every call we go to. And now I'm grouped in with all of them. *Just another loser who's too weak to cope.*

I feel a nudge on my shoulder and look up at Graeme. 'You're miles away,' he smiles down at me. 'You ready then, partner?'

I've been so lost in thought that I haven't even realised we've been posted together. But it cheers me right up and I jump upright and clap Graeme on the back of the Met vest.

'So, who's driving?' I ask with a grin.

'You. Obviously.' He picks up his kitbag and lugs it up onto his shoulder. 'I fancy a break from driving today.'

We head down to the yard together and start loading up our chosen IRV. I feel like my old self again and it fills me with hope. Then comes the familiar stab of guilt for enjoying time away from my baby. It's so nice to feel like something more than just a mother. To have adult conversations, to swear, banter with the team; to be me again. I fill out the log book and give the car a quick once-over before we climb in. It's as I'm easing our vehicle out of the back gate and onto the streets beyond that he asks the question. The question that everyone asks.

'So, how are you finding motherhood?'

I pause. I'm used to answering the question by now and am about to roll out the perfunctory answer. But this is Graeme. He's got a son of his own and we've been working together for a long time. He's one of my closest friends at work. So, instead, I open my mouth as the hundred million feelings I have about motherhood swarm in my head. The best and the worst. *The hardest thing I've ever done. The most wonderful thing I've ever done. The thing that makes me feel totally inadequate. The thing that makes me feel totally complete. An exhausting, never-ending, boring, frustrating, guilt-inducing groundhog day of responsibility.* But all that comes out is a deep sigh.

'Yeah.' He stares straight ahead. 'I get it.'

We lapse into silence as I wind my way around the busy Brixley roads. I weave through an estate notorious for anti-social behaviour and home to some of Brixley's most prolific criminals. I cruise slowly, pausing at nooks and alleyways. We're both looking out of our respective windows, both aware of what we're looking for without having to communicate it. The ones who walk without purpose. The loiterers. Those that amble slowly past parked cars, peeking sideways into windows, hunting out the opportunity to break the law. But before we can spot anyone of interest the radio lights up and an emergency call is announced.

'Officers to respond to an "I" graded call now to 19 Brinkley Villas, informant stating that she has a knife and is going to kill herself.'

Graeme groans as I assign us to the call. He leans forward and starts to read the full incident report on the on-board computer.

'Unsurprisingly, we've been here many times before.' By 'we', he means the police. I push the big red 999 button in the centre of the dashboard and the lights and sirens blast into life. As I make progress through the traffic, Graeme keeps calling out relevant details from the CAD.

'Mrs Mowbray. An obese fifty-four-year-old. She's threatened police officers before, been nicked for police assault. Schizophrenic and has a fascination with knives. Bloody brilliant.'

'She sounds lovely,' I joke.

'Multiple attempted suicides and threats of suicide.' He sighs and reaches behind his seat for his Met vest, pulling it through the gap between our seats and shrugging it on. 'She obviously hasn't seen the presentation.'

My laugh dies in my throat and I pray that he doesn't notice my sense of humour failure. The 'presentation' refers to a group of memes that flew around the nick, from phone to phone, about a year ago. It was a mock presentation entitled, 'Suicide: Getting it right the first time'. It went the police equivalent of viral, meaning nearly everyone saw it at some point or another. Downloaded and deleted from phones in the same few minutes, it was not something that should be found on a constable's handset. At the time I'd told myself it was harmless. Just a bit of a joke, a way of releasing the tension that built up from dealing with people with serious mental health problems on a day-to-day basis. If you didn't laugh you'd cry, right? The infamous dark humour of the police officer. We'd all thought it was hilarious.

But thinking about it now, I struggle to see the funny side. I'd never tried to kill myself but I'd certainly thought about suicide in the last few months. Not necessarily *considered* doing it, but the idea of it had run through my head. I'd thought about getting in my car and just driving away. Just leaving and never coming back. I hadn't thought about what would happen when I stopped driving. I'd had long nights when I couldn't sleep and my head was so full of screaming doubts that it felt like it would burst. On those nights I'd imagined slamming my head against a wall, imagined the pressure whooshing out of it like steam from a kettle, imagined the release of oblivion. And the strongest voice, the one that stood shouting the loudest on the tallest podium, was the voice that told me that I just wasn't good enough. *You're a terrible mother. He'd be better off without you.*

So, I'd never actually hurt myself. Or even seriously thought about it. But nonetheless, the possibility was there. The idea was in my head. And until you've felt like you're truly out of control, you'll never understand how terrifying it is to not know what your brain is capable of doing next. What if I had tried to end it? Would I be the one that two coppers were discussing? Shaking their heads and wondering if I had seen the 'presentation'?

It's only three minutes until we arrive at the address and

we climb out of the car, my train of thought broken. The flats are tall and brown, the poster child of all run-down London tower blocks – bikes and washing and discarded items of furniture litter the open walkways that front the flats. Luckily for us, the communal door is broken, and we step unchallenged onto the concrete steps that lead up to the first floor. The familiar stench of urine prickles in my nostrils and I wonder what it is that's so temping about pissing in stairwells. Brixley Control call us on the radio as we approach number 19.

'Bravo X-ray Two-One, receiving Bravo X-ray?'

'Go ahead,' Graeme whispers into his radio. We're close to the front door and we don't want Mrs Mowbray knowing we're here.

'Update from your informant. Apparently she's now said that she'll stab any police officers that try and stop her killing herself.'

'Received.'

Graeme glances back at me, a grin tugging at the side of his mouth. 'This just keeps getting better and better.'

'Does make you wonder why she bothered calling us in the first place?' I muse as we round upon her door.

It's red and covered in circular dents that have chipped the wood and cracked the paint. I recognise the circular print of the enforcer, and feel no surprise that it's been used here before. It's obvious she's a frequent customer of ours. Today the door lies open, gaping into the gloom of the hallway beyond, and I'm relieved that we won't have to break it down.

Graeme raps loudly on the door.

'Mrs Mowbray?' He shouts into the small landing, slowly pushing the door open. 'It's the police.'

No reply as we move into the hallway. The familiar smell of council flats meets my nostrils. Damp air and sickly-sweet air fresheners. Even in the nicest flats in this block you can't disguise the seeping smell of damp. It's as much a part of the block as the piss-stained corridors. I go to push the door closed behind me before hesitating. The mother at the back of my mind tells me I may need a quick exit, and I feel a quiver of apprehension as I turn back towards Graeme.

There are two doors that open off the little lobby we're standing in, and a flight of stairs that lead downwards. Both doors are open and it's easy to see that the rooms up here are empty. The furniture is topped with doilies and ornaments, everything neatly in place. The carpets are red and covered in a busy floral pattern that's faded after years of use. And the layer of dust that covers every tiny china figurine makes me think that these rooms are never used.

'Where is she?' I hiss to Graeme.

'Fuck knows,' he whispers back, before shouting again, 'Mrs Mowbray? It's the police! You called us?'

And I realise that down is the only way we can go.

'We're coming down.' I shout, and Graeme steps down first. There was a time when I would have been the one in the lead, desperate to get down there and sort Mrs Mowbray out. I feel my cheeks redden as I realise that I am purposely letting Graeme go first. *What's wrong with me?* And suddenly all I can think about is the boy with the kitchen knives, and the huge pile of knives in the property store at the nick and the knife that Mrs Mowbray is probably holding now. I grip onto the plastic banister as we edge down the stairs. They're steep and tight and boxed in so that we turn into the second flight without really being able to see what we're heading into. The notes of a song reach my ears and I realise that music is being played downstairs. *Maybe that's why she hasn't answered.*

We step out from the claustrophobic stairwell into another tiny lobby. The music is louder now, and it's coming from behind a closed door. It sounds tinny and old, and I picture an old gramophone in a black and white movie, the notes sounding wavy and thin. Or maybe that's in my head. I step up to the door, pushing away the instincts that are telling me to turn and run back up the stairs, and knock firmly on the door. The last thing I want to be doing is bursting in and surprising a potentially suicidal someone with a knife.

'Mrs Mowbray?'

'Who dat?' Her voice is thick and loud. I roll my eyes at Graeme. *Finally.*

'It's the police, Mrs Mowbray. You called us?'

'Nah, nah, I don't want the police. Don't come in here, now.' She sounds like she's turning away an irritating salesman, positive that we'll just leave her in peace.

'Mrs Mowbray, you called to say that you were going to

kill yourself.' I look at Graeme again. He's shaking his head. 'Now that we're here, I'm afraid that we can't leave without making sure you're OK. I'm going to open the door now.'

I put my hand on the round brass doorknob, but something makes me pause. I can hear the music through the door and I realise that I recognise it.

Jeepers, creepers, where'd ya get those peepers . . .

A shudder runs through me as I recognise the song that was the soundtrack for a horror movie, *Jeepers Creepers*. In the movie, a monster hunted people for their eyes. I look at Graeme, who seems oblivious.

'Jesus, can you hear that?' I ask him, keeping my voice low.

'Yeah,' he shrugs, 'some old music. What's wrong?'

There's something about the cramped space of the flat, the disembodied voice of Mrs Mowbray and the creepy song that is making me feel a little freaked out. I feel a trickle of sweat run down the small of my back.

'I don't know. Got a bad feeling.' Then I shake my head, feeling foolish, 'It's nothing. Don't worry.'

'What you two whisp'rin about out there?' Mrs Mowbray's voice is high and wheedling. 'Why don't you just get on and let me get on with killin' myself?'

'Mrs Mowbray,' I tighten my grip on the doorknob. 'We're going to open the door now.'

'I wouldn't do that if I were you!' she sing-songs like a child teasing its playmate.

Jeepers, creepers, where'd ya get those eyes?

'I've got a mighty big knife in here, and if you open that door, I'm going to cut you up into teeny tiny pieces.' She cackles maniacally, her voice cracking and catching before dissolving into hacking coughs.

'She sounds like she's at death's door,' whispers Graeme. He slides his gravity auto-lock baton out of its holster and racks it downwards, so that it extends to its full length. He nods for me to open the door.

Oh, those weepers, how they hypnotize!

A flash of the eyeless corpses, dripping blood.

Mrs Mowbray's voice again. 'Come then, little lady, come and get it!' A shiver runs down the back of my neck as I imagine Mrs Mowbray sharpening a knife like a wicked witch in a Disney movie.

'Do you think we should get the shield from the car?' I ask Graeme, knowing that, even with a shield, I still won't want to open the door to this room.

'Seriously? She's fifty-four and fat. She sounds like she just coughed up a lung. I bet she hasn't even got a knife. Plus, what if she tops herself while were standing out here deliberating?'

Jeepers, creepers, where'd ya get those peepers?

I realise he's right. *Stop being such a wimp.* I rack my baton and grip the doorknob for the last time.

'Do you want me to do it?' Graeme asks, looking concerned.

'No, I've got this.' And I set my jaw. Push all the horrifying thoughts from my mind and turn the handle. I shove the door backwards hard and wait as it swings backwards and slams off the bedroom wall.

The room opens up before us. Dead ahead of us, smack bang in the centre of the room is a single bed. In it sits Mrs Mowbray. She's propped up with pink pillows and a lacy pink valence ruffles around the edge of her bed. Her grey hair is tightly set in pink rollers and her pink nightdress appears pressed and clean. She is nearly as wide as the single bed she lies upon. As soon as she sees us, she tries to push herself up in the bed. She starts shouting and waving a large machete in the air.

I watch as it arches and swoops and I feel like laughing. I drop my baton to my side and Graeme approaches the bed. The machete looks like it's been left outside in the rain for about one hundred years. It's so rusty that nearly the entire length of it is deep orange.

'I'll cut you!' Mrs Mowbray shouts, her fat arms wobbling wildly as she pokes towards Graeme with her orange blade.

He steps up to the bed and swiftly grabs her arm, holding the knife by the dulled bade and yanking it from her grasp. I stand in the doorway and run a clammy hand over my damp forehead.

Jesus Christ.

*   *   *

I'm staring at the ceiling again. My body begging for sleep but my mind refusing to quiet, processing in minute detail every call I've dealt with today. Every time I felt I wasn't good enough. Every time Freddy cried and I didn't know why. Every time I couldn't settle him. Every time I turned away from something because I was scared.

And as I close my eyes it's Mrs Mowbray that I see. Except this time she's not in bed. This time she's standing just the other side of her bedroom door. Her slippers press into the thick green carpet as she curls her toes, her thick hand tight around the handle of the machete. It's not rusty any more. Its blade glints, its sharp edge caught by the chink of light slicing through the heavy curtains. I see her tombstone teeth as a wide smile splits her face, as she raises the blade high above her head. My hand grips the doorknob in the other side. It starts to turn. Mrs Mowbray slashes the blade downwards as I step into the room. And then I'm sitting up in bed and panting, my heart beating against the inside of my chest like a pedal drum. And no matter how many times I tell myself it didn't happen, that it won't ever happen, that I'm going to be fine, I still see Mrs Mowbray grinning from the other side of the door. And in her face is every violent criminal who wants to hurt a police officer. Every mental health patient who wants to lash out. And I know, for certain, that one day she's going to get me.

15

Trevor

His eyes are glassy, but clear.

It's not too late.

As I look down at him I realise that this is it. This is what all the Emergency Life Saving training is for. The taste of the antiseptic wipes, the cool plastic of the resuscitation dummies. The sore knees, bending over the prone dummies, hoping my knickers aren't sticking out of the top of my jeans. All this flashes in my mind. Along with the doubts. What if I do it wrong? What if I make him worse? *Where are the fucking paramedics?*

There's no chance for my brain to respond because I'm already on my knees. This time I can't feel the pain as they grind against rough pavement. His skin is still a rich brown but his lips are turning from red to purple. Kara is shouting into her radio behind me. It's the first time I've been posted with her and she's got about six months' experience. There are so many new members of the team since I came back from maternity leave that it's easy to lose track. I don't know what she's like, don't know if I can rely on her. The only person I know I can rely on is myself. A circle of feet has closed in around us. The noise of the crowd dulls and suddenly we're in an empty tunnel. Just me and him. And I'm pulling at the latex of my gloves but my hands are sweaty and they're not going on. *You're running out of time.*

He is not breathing. I don't need to put my ear to his lips or feel his chest because his perfect stillness is screaming at me. *He's running out of time.* I reach for the face mask that we're told to use when giving CPR. Miraculously my fingers find it first time and pull it out of the small pouch of my kit belt. I rip at the paper sachet and tug out the plastic sheet, seeing immediately that it has fallen to pieces within its wrapping. How long has it been in there? Half of it drops from my hand and is carried away on the breeze. The other half dangles impotently from my frozen fingers. *Risk of infection.* Always use a mask.

Fuck it.

I drop the mask and reach into his mouth to check for obstructions. His tongue is soft and warm and his teeth catch slightly on my fingers as I sweep them around his gums. I pull down his chin with my right hand and place my other palm on his forehead. I look down his throat; all clear. This is it.

Pushing on his forehead, I lift his chin and tilt his head back. I expect it to slide perfectly into place like Resusci Anne, the mannequin we use in training school, does. But this isn't training school. And my stooge isn't helping me by lifting his head. Instead I fight against the weight of it, the muscles in his neck pulling against me as it tries to flop to the side.

I hear Kara talking to Control. 'PC Hearn is starting life support.'

A brief look up at the crowd. Gaping faces, waving phones. A flash of anger at the thought of people recording this. *What is their problem?* And then I'm leaning over, my mouth lowering closer and closer to his, until the heat of his skin radiates onto my lips. I open my mouth as wide as I can, stretching to cover his slack mouth, and as my lips squash onto his face the bristle of his three o'clock shadow prickles at their edges. There is no movement of breath from within him, no warm air fills my mouth. *How long has his brain been without oxygen?* I push my face into his, trying to create a seal over his mouth. His bones grind into my lips and his skin becomes slick with my saliva. I'm still clutching his chin with my right hand, stretching his airway straight. As I push the air from me into him his body resists it. It doesn't seem to go in, so I blow harder. There's no chance of me hearing the breath in his chest. The crowd brays and the road roars as my ears strain to catch it. *Two rescue breaths then start compressions.*

Again I make a seal with my mouth and blow out force-fully, looking sideways, down his body, hoping for a rise of the chest. *How do I know if it's working?* I rise from the rescue breaths and place my hands, one on top of the other, in the centre of his chest. I lock my elbows so that my arms are straight and my shoulders are above the man's chest. I know that the oxygen I just gave him is useless without the heart pumping it round his body. I lean forward and push the weight of my upper body down into his chest. I've seen this done before by paramedics. It's not like it is on the telly. It's brutal. I know that I have to use all of my force to get his heart to pump, and so I pump up and down on his chest, as hard as I can, my own breath coming in short gasps as I push and push and push. *Thirty chest compressions, then two rescue breaths. Continue until help arrives.* Down again for breaths and this time I see a definite rise in his chest. The sheer relief of knowing that I'm doing it right makes me soar inside. *You can do this!*

I keep going and lose count of how many times I repeat the process. My head begins to swim as I rise from countless rescue breaths. I glance around quickly for Kara and see that she's trying to move the crowd back. My head is light and my vision is darkening around the edges. It feels like I've been doing this forever and my knees are suddenly screaming at me and my arms are shaking as I pump. Sweat runs down the sides of my face, and I feel it trickle down my neck and under my collar. I want to shout to Kara for help but I'm so out of breath I can't speak. And I can't stop, because if I stop I'll lose count and if I lose count he could die. I don't want him to die. And as I'm begging my arms to keep going and gasping to regain the breath I've given away, I at last hear the beautiful sound of sirens. *They're here. It's nearly over. Just keep going, not long now.* All these phrases swim through my head as I pump and rock and blow.

And finally I see Kara and the paramedic racing towards me. He is on his own but he's still the best thing I've seen all day. Kara is weighed down by two huge first-aid kits and rushes to keep up with him as his green trousers kneel beside me.

'You're doing an excellent job, constable.' He has an Australian accent. His voice is loud and steady and I instantly have full confidence in him. And I'm so glad he is here. 'Keep doing those chest compressions, nice and hard. I'll take the breathing.'

'He was like this when we got here,' Kara is kneeling with us, imparting the information she must have got from the crowd. 'Apparently he was just walking along with his friends and collapsed. He's twenty-five, normally fit and healthy. His cousins are in the crowd – somebody called them.' I catch her eye. The rest of the family will be on their way.

The paramedic puts a clear plastic mask over the man's nose and mouth. It is attached to a large bag.

'Hold this, make sure it's tight.' Kara takes hold of the mask as the paramedic begins to pump the bag. 'See how I'm doing it? Nice big pumps, not too fast.' Kara nods and reaches her other hand for the bag. The paramedic looks to me. 'OK, hold on the compressions.' He leans towards the man, feeling along his wrist for a pulse.

I sit back onto my feet, my arms red and patchy with exertion, and clasp my hands between my legs to hide the shaking. It's the first time since we got pulled over that I haven't been moving, or pumping, or doing something. A wave of fatigue hits me with the force of a ten-ton truck and I try to control my breathing so that I don't sound how I feel: like a fat dog who's just run too fast at the scent of biscuits.

As I'm sitting there, watching the paramedic complete his preliminary checks, I hear the sound of more sirens and see an ambulance arrive, followed quickly by a patrol car. The ambulance crew jump out of the front and head straight round the back, opening up the tall double doors and gathering equipment. I see Darryl striding towards me from the patrol car, his operator following behind.

'Whaddya need?' Darryl nods at me. 'You OK?' I manage a nod in return.

'Crowd control.'

And as they wander off, shouting and herding away the growing crowd of onlookers, I feel myself calm slightly. But the adrenalin is nowhere near done with me and I suppress a shudder as I focus again on the paramedic.

A frown creases across his forehead. 'Strange – his pulse is strong.'

'Is that unusual?' I ask.

We surround the man on three sides, Kara at his head, holding the mask firm across his face, hand monotonously squeezing a steady rhythm. The paramedic kneels on his left side, the busy street at his back, and I am on his right, kneeling next to him at chest height, behind me about a foot of pavement before the solid wall of a building.

'How long's he been down for?'

I shake my head, look to Kara. I have no idea. It feels like I have been resuscitating him forever.

'We got here at ten past one. He'd already been on the ground for about a minute at that point.' She answers without looking away from the oxygen bag, all of her concentration focused on pumping precious oxygen into our ward.

I glance at my watch. It's cheap plastic, scuffed and digital. Practical. 'So it's been about fifteen minutes.'

The paramedic continues his primary survey as he talks. 'Usually if someone stops breathing, it's only minutes until you'll lose a pulse as well.'

'So it's a good sign that he's got a pulse?' I'm desperate to hear good news.

'It's hard to tell right now. Depends what's caused him to collapse in the first place. It's unlikely that he's had a pulse this whole time, although it is possible. It's more likely that his heart has stopped at some point, and that you've managed to start it again with CPR.' A small thrill flips in my stomach at the thought that I may have actually saved him.

'But he's critical. Very unstable. His heart could stop again at any time.'

The newly arrived paramedics rattle towards us with a trolley, the wide pavement made clear by Darryl and Joseph, who have contained the crowd at either side of us with cordon tape. Kara and I help lift and load the man onto the trolley. One of the crew takes the breathing bag from Kara and I feel her sigh with relief at the release of pressure.

'You go in the back with them,' I say. 'You'll have to be the continuity officer. I'll follow in the car.' She nods and trots after them. Whenever police attend a seriously injured or collapsed person in the street we always have to accompany them to hospital. There's always the possibility that foul play could be involved, and the continuity of the victim and any possible evidence is crucial to any future court case.

I look over to Darryl, who jerks his head towards a group of people who are just within the cordon, huddled together. *Family*. I am about to go over to them when a thought pops into my head. I turn and jog over to the ambulance, where the man is already inside and hooked up to numerous monitors. Kara sits in the back and tries to keep out of the way, scribbling furiously in her pocket book.

'What hospital you going to?' I shout it at their backs as they all busy leaning over their patient.

'UCH.' The answer is shouted over their shoulders and I know immediately that they are referring to University College Hospital, Euston.

The Australian turns and begins to pull the doors shut.

'Wait – what do I tell the family?'

The paramedic looks at me, and suddenly it's as if I can see every job he's ever been to in the lines of his face. It's a look of bitter resignation. 'Tell them he's critical. It's not looking good. Prepare them for the worst. A young, healthy guy like this doesn't usually collapse without having suffered a major medical event.'

I step backwards to allow the door to swing closed, but before it does, the Australian's face pops out.

'Good job, constable.'

I smile as the fluorescent door of the ambulance swings shut in my face. As I watch it pull away from the kerb I stand for a minute, watching it disappear into the distance, my mind blank and swimming, the smile slipping from my face. Then a voice behind me catches my attention. She has the same rich, brown complexion as the man on the floor and I even imagine that I see a likeness in the shape of their cheekbones. Her voice has a deep Jamaican twang.

'Please, he's my cousin.' She is clutching a phone to her chest. I can see a tremble flit across the skin of her collarbone as she visibly shivers. 'Where is he going?'

I reach out a hand and place it gently on her shoulder. Now that the ambulance has left, the crowd is starting to disperse. She stands within the group of people I noticed just a few minutes ago. Too anxious to wait for me to come to them, they have approached me instead. I talk directly to her, and the others hunch closer, their heads closing together, straining to hear me over the busy road.

'They're taking him to the UCH. It's on Euston Road, not far from Euston Station.'

'Thank you.' She instantly begins to tap into her phone.

I pull out my pocket book and flip to my last entry. 'Can I take his details? Do you know who his next of kin are?'

'Yes,' she nods. 'His mum. I've called her and she's waiting to hear which hospital to go to.'

'Where does she live?'

'Just up the road, Reynault Park. But she's disabled, and she doesn't drive.'

'OK, hang on.' I look over to Darryl and see that he's pulling the thin plastic cordon tape down. He looks up and I signal him to come over.

I write down the man's name, address and date of birth

in my pocket book as Darryl approaches. I learn that the man's name is Trevor, and that he's only twenty-four years old.

'Can you go and collect Trevor's mother, get her to the UCH on the hurry-up?'

'No probs.' He grabs his pocket book and opens it. I tell him the address and give him the details of what's happened, so that he can properly inform Trevor's mother. Once he's heading for his car, I ask Sandra, Trevor's cousin, to call his mother and let her know that we're on our way. I take her details, making sure to also note down the time and my location. And then, as I fold my pocket book and slide it back into the top right pocket of my Met vest, I realise that I've put off the inevitable for far too long.

I place my hand on her shoulder once more, and look at the small group of anxious faces. It's true that the more you deliver bad news the better you get at it. But it's never something I want to do.

'Trevor is seriously ill. He's in a critical condition.'

And then comes the question. 'Is he going to die?'

Her eyes are glossy and bloodshot. The only thing I can tell her is the truth. Because, although I may not remember this moment in years to come, after years of delivering death messages, she will never forget my response. And I will not dish out false hope.

'I'm sorry, I don't know. All I know is he's very seriously ill. They'll be able to tell you more at the hospital.'

She is nodding now, and fat tears scatter from her eyes

onto her cheeks. The people around her rally and form a tight unit of comfort.

'Can you get to the hospital OK?'

More nodding as I turn to leave. I start walking towards my car.

'Officer!'

As I turn back I see that she's broken from the group and is a few steps behind me.

'Thank you.' Her breath comes in wobbled gasps. 'I saw how hard you were trying. Thank you.'

I feel humbled that someone so distraught could think to thank me, just for doing my job. But you get little thanks in my role and I cling on to every bit of gratitude I can get. 'That's fine,' I say, trying not to shrug off her praise. It's a habit I have when receiving any kind of compliment, but I'm determined not to belittle her grace with a shrug. 'I just hope it helped. I'll see you at the hospital.'

I climb into my car and sit staring through the windscreen. Now that most of the emergency vehicles have left the spectators have dispersed and the public mill to and fro like nothing ever happened. Just another busy London street, save for one discarded rubber glove that's crumpled at the side of the road. I consider getting out of the car and picking it up, but I'm stuck to my seat with the heaviness of exhaustion. I pull out my phone and check that there are no messages from the childminder. I flick to the most recent photo of Freddy and realise that I haven't thought about him once throughout the whole incident. Familiar Mum guilt washes over me, but this time I fight it. *You've done nothing wrong*. Because back there on the pavement I wasn't a mother. I was just a copper trying to save someone's life.

* * *

Turns out there was nothing I could have done to save Trevor. He'd been totally unaware of the large aneurysm in his brain. According to family members, he'd suffered no symptoms and was a very upbeat, active man. The sac of blood had ruptured violently and his brain had rapidly started to die. By the time his mother got to the hospital the doctors were ready to break the news that Trevor probably wouldn't survive.

He died the next day, surrounded by loved ones.

16

Lily

It's around 4 p.m. when we get the call. Sitting in our car, we hear the voice of Brixley's controller pipe up on the radio. The speakers blare the message out and it echoes in unison through our personal radios.

> **'Anyone free for an "I" grade, just come in, domestic in progress.'**

My hand is grabbing my radio before I even realise it.

'Show BX21,' I say, twisting the radio towards my mouth. As I let go, it swings back into place, clipped securely to my Met vest. I nod to my operator, Andy, who smiles in reply and clicks in his seatbelt. Experience tells me that it's best to get to domestic incidents as quickly as possible. I've seen too many battered women to even consider not taking this call seriously. Plus, it'll probably result in a 'body' – meaning an arrest, not a corpse. You get used to the lingo fast in this job.

Shifting in my seat, I square my shoulders and tighten my grip on the wheel. It's rush hour and in this traffic the address is a twenty-minute drive away. If I was in a normal

car. But I'm not. I'm in a marked police car, and I'm not planning on worrying about the traffic. I've been a response
driver for nearly four years now and I still love every minute
of a blue-light run. I reach forward and push hard onto the
big red button in the centre of the dashboard. I feel that
familiar surge of adrenalin as the button lights up, bright
red, and I hear the sirens scream into life. I pull away from
the kerb, but there is no squealing of tyres, no loud revving
of the engine. I am trained to make progress through the
traffic safely, to get to the incident in one piece, as quickly as
possible. Yes, I drive fast when it is safe to do so, but I'm not
interested in spinning wheels and burning rubber. In fact, I
see these things as a loss of control, something that I am
determined will not happen. I drive smooth and fast, taking
the path of least resistance, keeping my eyes on all of my
mirrors and watching for pedestrians with headphones.
They have a nasty habit of stepping out in front of you.

As we get closer to the address, Andy is giving me more
information. We've worked together many times since my
first shift with him back in our probation; guarding a bomb
at Wormwood Scrubs. I'm thirty next year and we've both
got the benefit of experience behind us as we head to the
call. He's reading from the on-board computer and listening to his radio, which is pressed against his ear. He shouts
above the sirens, 'Previous domestics at the address, male
flashes violent, weapons and mental health.' I nod and
continue to concentrate on my driving.

We pull up to the scene about five minutes after receiving the call. The front door is open and the street is silent.

Dusk is falling across the city and the streetlamps glow pink, warming up in the cold air of early winter. I snap my radio from my Met vest with a practised twisting motion.

'On scene,' I say quietly into the receiver. If the suspect is still around, I don't want to alert him to our presence by shouting.

'Received.'

The muted reply from BX Control.

We walk up the three or four steps to the open door, its splintered appearance telling me that we've been here before. I can feel the adrenalin starting to kick in and a buzz of fear spikes in my chest. *It's too quiet. Why?* I move into the hallway of the flat. Andy's right behind me. The hallway opens long and straight ahead of us, stairs at the end. The carpet is stained and I can feel it peeling from the soles of my boots as I walk across it.

'Police,' I shout, as loudly as I can. I hear running steps across the floor above. A door slams and muffled crying reaches my ears. The training that's been drummed into us disappears in that moment; *hold back, assess the scene, don't rush.* The crying slaps it out of us and we run up the stairs, forgetting everything but reaching the person who's hurt, stopping the person who's hurting them. *We're coming.* Our loud steps ring out across the flat and the crying stops momentarily as we burst into the kitchen. It takes only a split-second of looking at the woman to know that we need an ambulance, and fast. Andy's already on it.

'BX, ambulance message, female approximately forty years, multiple wounds and blood loss, breathing, conscious.' Andy speaks smoothly into his radio – nothing of the scene in front of us is betrayed in his voice. *Remain calm.* I walk towards the woman, careful not to tread on the blood spots that are staining her kitchen floor, and kneel down in front of her. She is curled in a corner of the room, back against the cold wall, knees held to her chest by her tightly wrapped arms.

'Where is he?' I ask, looking into her one good eye.

She shakes her head.

'I'll check the flat,' Andy walks out of the kitchen.

'It's OK,' I say, voice low and reassuring. 'You're safe now, the ambulance is on its way.'

I take her hand in mine and we sit for a moment in silence, two women together. Before I can help it, a thought runs through my mind. *I would never let a man do this to me.* I look at the floor, feeling guilty for judging her.

'What's your name, sweetheart?' I ask, glancing towards the door, constantly aware of the possibility the suspect might return.

'Joanne.' Her voice trembles as she talks, and she winces. I can smell the sour tang of alcohol on her breath. A lot of alcohol.

'OK, Joanne, tell me where it hurts.'

'My head.' Her voice slurring, she reaches up to touch her forehead with her free hand. I can see that her nails are torn and bloody. Her fingers shake as she gingerly touches her cut and bleeding lip.

'Did he hit you with anything, or just his fists?'

'Just his fists,' she mumbles, and then she gives a short hacking laugh. 'Only his fists, as usual.' She coughs, leaning her head back on the wall behind her, staring up at the ceiling.

'He'll be nicked for this, Joanne. You know that, right? Will you support us?'

She points her good eye at me and gives me a look that says she's heard it all before. 'What's the fucking point?' She wheezes, blood spitting across the room as she curses. A warning flash flares in my mind. *Risk of infection.* I reach for the gloves in my pocket. Her breath is ragged and tight as she sighs, 'He always gets me back, in the end.'

Andy walks back into the room.

'Flat's empty, he's gone,' he says, pulling out his notebook, relaxed now that the suspect is out of the way. *We should be out there catching him.* Snapping on my gloves, I get a description from Joanne and circulate it via my radio. Other units are on the way to conduct an area search. He'll be arrested. We know who he is and where he lives. He'll not escape for long.

Still kneeling on the floor, I concentrate on Joanne and her injuries, keeping a watchful eye out for any deterioration in her condition. Her nose has been broken. It's swollen, and purple welts are slowly appearing under both of her eyes. One eye is already swelled shut, and from the way she is breathing I would say that he's fractured her ribs as well. I can hear sirens in the distance as my radio once again crackles to life.

'21, the ambulance should be with you shortly.'

'Received,' I say, then to Joanne. 'You'll get some pain relief soon, sweetheart, you're doing really well.'

Joanne looks up at me. The confused fug of concussion or booze lifts momentarily and she pulls her hand from mine. She starts trying to push herself up.

'Whoah, Joanne, stay there,' I say, holding her shoulder gently. 'What's wrong?'

'Where are the girls?' she slurs, still making a weak attempt to get up.

I pause, instantly understanding what she means. *The girls.* I look at her and she suddenly becomes something different in my eyes, something other than just a victim. Something more responsible. *And not so innocent.*

'You've got kids here?' My blood runs cold. Joanne is nodding weakly as I push myself up off the floor and storm towards the kitchen door. Freddy's face is in my mind and the thought of him being anywhere near this kind of shit fills me with horror. It's not him. But there are children here.

'Andy, you see any kids?'

His jaw tightens. 'None.'

'They'll be hiding . . .' comes Joanne's shaky voice from behind me. 'Top room . . .'

I leave the kitchen and take the stairs in front of me, two at a time, up to the highest room in the small maisonette. *Has he taken them? Are they hurt too?* Although I'm rushing, I'm trying not to stamp my feet, aware of small ears. I walk into the top room. The wallpaper that isn't torn off is pink, there's a single bed shoved against one wall. A battered travel cot sits against the other, with a space of only 2 feet between them. Most of the floor is covered in clothes. I can't tell if they're clean or dirty, but from the smell of the room I know which I'd guess. I frown. There is nowhere to hide in this room. Apart from the bed and the cot, it is empty of furniture except for a dresser, the drawers of which are mostly pulled out or broken, gaping, like empty teeth, without their drawer fronts. There's a pair of makeshift curtains pegged up at the window. They have fallen down at one side, allowing the last of the winter sun to cast a pallid shaft of light across the bed. The sheet has been dragged partially off the mattress and hangs over the side, flowing onto the floor. As I turn to leave the room, I catch a tiny flickering movement across the sheet. I move closer to the bed, my footsteps soft.

'Hello?' I say gently. 'I'm a police lady. Is there anybody in here?'

I hear a faint sniff from beneath the bed. *Thank God.* I kneel in front of the sheet and reach out to slowly pull it aside. Bending forward, so that my head is just inches from the floor, I look under the bed. And I smile. I see two little faces looking back at me. *They're OK.* My initial relief fades quickly as I note the wide eyes and pale faces. Two girls, messy blond mops framing their round faces, one bigger than the other.

'Hey, I found you.' In that moment I forget that my nose is just inches from the fetid carpet. 'You guys OK?'

The little one looks to her big sister. Her sister nods at me, eyes saucers in the low light. Before I can say anything else, she opens her mouth to speak. 'I saw Daddy hitting Mummy and now I'm panicking.'

I reach out to the girls and they slowly crawl from under the bed and sit up on the floor in front of me, until we face each other. The older one must be around five years old, the younger one barely three. They each have a small thin summer dress on, in matching patterns.

'I love your dresses,' I say, smiling at them. As I look at them both, I hear the paramedics arrive downstairs, Andy talking to them as he leads them into the kitchen.

'What are your names?'

'I'm Lily.' The older girl takes charge. Points to her sister, 'She's Faye.' She looks down at her pale knees, then back at me, 'I need a cuddle.' As I watch her eyes dart away again, I realise that she's scared I might say no. She is small with scrawny arms and a grubby face. White tracks of clean skin shine underneath her eyes. Surprised, I hold out my arms and she hops onto my lap, wrapping both her legs and arms around me. The little one just watches. I smile at her as I cuddle her big sister.

'It's OK, honey,' I say, as I wrap my arms around her. And in that moment, in the moment where I should just be a woman, comforting a child, a thousand thoughts rush through my head. *Should I be touching another person's child? Am I allowed to do this? What would Joanne think? What have these girls seen? I want to take them away from this.*

The girl shifts in my arms. 'You're too hard,' she says. For a second I'm confused, until I realise that she means my vest and belt.

'Sorry, honey,' I say. 'You want to sit with your sister again?'

She nods and climbs off of my lap.

'It's OK now, girls. Your daddy's gone to calm down and your mummy's going to be looked after by the doctor. She's going to be fine.' I try my best to sound reassuring.

I hear a door slam downstairs. Someone's shouting.

'Stay up here, girls.' I hold my hand out to them as I walk to the bedroom door. They nod their heads together as I leave the room. I close the door softly behind me.

As I start down the stairs I can hear a male voice in the kitchen; whoever it is sounds agitated. *Got to get to Andy.* I rush down the stairs and swing open the door to the kitchen. Andy is standing in the centre of the room, facing a young man. The man is shouting and swearing. Andy has his hands out in front of him, palms facing the man, trying to calm him down.

'Who's this?' I ask. Joanne squawks a reply from the corner of the room, over the heads of the paramedics now treating her wounds.

'My eldest.' I can barely hear her over the shouting.

'Calm down, Jason!' Andy shouts, as the man continues to rant.

'I fucking told him. I fucking told him if he ever touches her again I'd fucking kill him.' Jason is red in the face and pacing up and down across the kitchen. He's around 6 feet tall and very broad. I'm not thrilled at the prospect of restraining him. We need to calm him down, fast. We also need to get him out of the kitchen. One of the first things you're taught about domestics, get everyone out of the kitchen. *Too many sharp things.*

'Jason,' I have to shout to get his attention, but I don't continue that way. I lower my voice, hoping he will follow suit with his. 'Jason. I know why you're upset, I would be too, mate, but let's let the paramedics look after your mum, eh? They can't concentrate with all this noise. Shall we go outside?'

Jason looks at me. For a second, I think I've got through to him. But that thought is very quickly pushed out of my mind when he suddenly flings himself towards the kitchen counter and pulls a large butcher's knife out of a block.

'I told him,' he says, enunciating each word slowly, so that I am left in no doubt of his intentions. He is panting loudly, shoulders bunched, tendons in his thick neck straining with the sheer force of his anger. He looks me straight in the eyes and he brings the knife up in front of him. For a short moment there is complete silence. *Knife, knife, knife.* We stand like that and milliseconds stretch out until they seem like hours.

Andy's shout erupts into the room.

'DROP THE KNIFE.'

There is no time for batons or CS gas. The kitchen is small and there are already six people in it. In a flash, Jason has piled into Andy in an attempt to get to the door. Andy falls backwards, his head banging off the wall, and Jason gets to the doorway before I can reach him. I lunge forward and grab his arm, using both hands, pulling him back with all my might. I'm not strong enough.

'Jason, stop. You can't go out looking for him. Jason, stop now.' I am shouting at him as I try to pull him back.

Jason's spittle flies out across my face as he shouts at me, and I can smell cigarettes on his breath and the heat of his rage burns in my face. 'Fucking let me go. I'll fucking kill him.'

Somehow, through the madness, I hear my radio as it crackles into the room. It's one of my colleagues.

'We've got the suspect stopped outside the house.'

I know Jason's heard it as his brows knit together in a look of sheer determination. I know what's going to happen a split-second before it does. *Oh shit.* He grunts loudly as he shoves into me hard, pushing me backwards into the kitchen table. I can see the knife glinting in the air as his arms swing wildly. But it's not meant for me. The force of him causes me to lose my grip for only a moment, but it's enough to allow him to run through the kitchen door.

I'm up in an instant and I'm running down the steps after Jason. *Got to warn them.*

'Get the suspect away from the house. Male with knife. BX, more units.' I shout into my radio as I jump the last four steps and manage to knock Jason sideways into the wall. *Watch the knife.* Andy is less than a second behind me and then we're wrestling with Jason and the knife. Me,

241

Andy and Jason bashing against the walls, the knife glinting between us.

'Drop the knife.' We shout again and again. *Andy hasn't got his Met vest on.* We manage to push Jason to the floor but he's fighting us with everything he's got. His knife arm is lashing dangerously close to Andy's white shirt. I lean my whole weight on his arm and Andy manages to get a boot on it. Jason drops the knife as Andy crushes his arm into the floor beneath his Magnums. The same boot kicks the knife away and it bumps off of the foot of the stairs, impotent. *I hope the girls can't hear.* Jason lies on the carpet of his filthy hallway and cries, his face pushed into his balled fists.

Andy handcuffs him and props him up against the wall of the hallway. It's all we can do for now, to contain him. I can hear more sirens approaching, cops from all around, answering the call for more units. *One for all and all for one.* I lean against the wall, panting.

'Cancel any more units, male in cuffs,' I breathe into my radio. I push myself up and walk through the front door and onto the street. The suspect stands by the kerb, swaying, drunk, contained by two of my team-mates.

'You fucking slag,' he shouts up at the windows of the flat. 'She fucking deserves it, the fucking whore.' He spits at the ground in front of him.

'Take him away, for God's sake,' I say, sitting momentarily on the front steps of the building, still catching my breath. Andy sits next to me, one eye still on Jason in the hall.

'I haven't got my Met vest on,' he mutters.

'I know,' I smile at him out of the corner of my mouth. *You fucking idiot.*

The suspect is dragged to the police van, shouting and swearing the entire way. I get up and walk to the pavement, standing where his odour still lingers. Something makes me look up, and as I do, I see the small face of a girl at the window. She's seen it all. Her hand is pressed up against the pane and I feel like she's calling out to me, like I've been punched in the chest. *You're too hard.* I take a deep breath and walk back up the stairs to finish my job.

*   *   *

I'm lying in bed later that evening with the girls' faces in my mind. I thought about them on the train on the way home. Thought about their filthy hair as I bathed Freddy and tucked him into his freshly laundered Babygro. I imagined their eyes widening as they watched their mum being struck across the face, their tears as they hid under their bed. And now, as I lie in bed, my tired eyes stinging and desperate to close, I can't get them out of my head. *There's nothing you can do.* I stare at the ceiling and mentally check off the paperwork I've completed after the incident. I've written my report and completed a child 'come to notice' form which will be sent to social services. I've detailed their living conditions, their mum's alcoholism and their father's violence. I've completed a crime report and a criminal intelligence report, each stressing that there are young children exposed to violence at the property. But I still feel like I've done absolutely nothing. *It's all you can do.* But it's not good enough. Since becoming a mother myself I just can't forget the children I see. They clamour at me at bedtime. They pop up in my mind, my own child's face sometimes superimposed across their faces, so that I am forced to see them again and again. I roll over and rummage in the bedside drawer for the sleeping tablets the doctor has prescribed me. Diazepam. I text John, who is still downstairs watching TV, and let him know I'm taking a pill. I worry that I may not hear Freddy when he wakes in the night and I need John to know to listen out for him. Then I lie back against my pillow and breathe deeply until my thoughts start to haze and the drug lulls me to sleep.

17

David

It's the call everyone's been waiting for since 7/7.

> **'Immediate graded call now to Brixley Central tube station – IC4 male acting suspiciously outside station – chanting in Arabic – wearing a rucksack with visible wires hanging out.'**

I'm in the rear of the area car, Brixley One, and am immediately pressed backwards into the upholstery as Trevor flicks on the blues and twos and puts his foot down. I've worked with Trev for a few years now, and I'm totally at ease in the back of his car. It's just after 1 p.m., the second half of a Friday early turn, and we've just finished our refs. I'd been driving Brixley X-ray Two-One earlier in my shift, but my operator for the day had left after two hours, complaining of a migraine. Single-crewed, I have attended a few low-risk reporting calls, clearing up some of the outstanding calls on the borough, before hopping in the back of the area car for the rest of my shift. It's a welcome novelty to be driven, instead of being the one doing the driving. Especially in the area car, the most powerful car in the fleet. Cerys is Trevor's operator for the day, and she keeps an eye on the on-board computer in the centre of the dashboard as we weave through the afternoon traffic.

I estimate that we have about four minutes before we get there. Four minutes to come up with a strategy for dealing with a potential suicide bomber. My mind is blank. I look to Trev, his face set in concentration as he makes progress on the road. Cerys sits rigid in her seat.

A minute shake of her head and she jerks into action, sitting up and reading from the MDT, 'Description coming in now – IC4 male, thick black beard, white T-shirt, black tracksuit bottoms, wearing a black and red rucksack with visible red wires dangling from his collar.'

Our eyes meet as she turns to look at me and I clip off my seatbelt, moving into the middle of the rear seats and leaning in so that my head sits between theirs. My eyes flick across the MDT and back to Cerys. 'A hoax call, maybe?' Her eyes are hopeful at the suggestion.

'Update from Brixley Control – this is now the third call we've had about this suspect at Brixley – apparently loudly chanting now – your CAD is being updated.'

The chances of it being a hoax just disappeared. Multiple calls usually means something big. Cerys and I look at the display again and catch the screen flicker as more intelligence is added by control.

Cerys continues to read aloud for Trevor's benefit. His reply is a terse nod and I find myself wishing that he'd say something. I've always looked to him for advice and I want to know what he thinks. I stare at the side of his face, questions on the tip of my tongue, but my mouth remains closed. I won't distract him. His focus should be on the road. The questions I want to ask bounce like balls around my head. Is this for real? What if it is? *What are we going to do?* We're getting close quickly. And there's a feeling of utter dread in the pit of my stomach. I grip onto the back of the seats in front of me as my mind starts to try and normalise my situation. *It's one o'clock on a Friday afternoon. It's not peak time. Why would a suicide bomber choose Brixley Central? It's just a small station. It's not a real bomb. It can't be.*

And then Freddy's in my mind and I'm drifting down the path of *if anything happens to me then Freddy will grow up without a mother* and I shut that shit down. I sit on my hands to stop them from shaking. *You're a copper. This is what you joined for. This call. Do what you always do. Turn up, protect the public; get through it.*

We're less than a minute out and there's just time to enquire after the armed response teams. I lift my radio to my mouth, 'Brixley, from Bravo One?'

'Go ahead, Bravo One.'

'We're nearly on scene at Brixley Central. Are there any armed response on route?'

'That's affirmative, Bravo One, armed response on route from the city. ETA fifteen minutes.'

'Received.' I click my radio back onto my Met vest.

We're on our own.

*   *   *

We step out of the car onto the pavement outside the station. It's completely empty. No chanting suspect, no concerned members of the public. We rush into the entrance to find a cluster of station guards and members of the public, hurriedly talking over each other.

Trevor cuts through the noise with a loud question. 'Where did he go?'

Everyone points towards the escalators. And I know that I should take some details. Get the witnesses' names and addresses. I know I should find out in more detail what's actually happened, I should let Control know that we're on scene and I should certainly let them know before I head down the escalators and out of radio range. But I don't do any of those things. Instead I just run.

'How long ago?' It's the only question I have time to shout backwards as I sprint.

'Just now.' It's one of the guards who answers, but there's no time to thank him.

Without a word between us we each take the same course of action. We reach the rumbling stairs within seconds of each other and then the three of us are running downwards, our boots striking the metal steps, shaking the handrails. And my mind is blank. There's no strategy or fear or doubt or hesitation. There's just the knowledge that we need to stop him.

We're halfway down when I hear the familiar rumble of a train. I can't tell if it's coming or going but I up my speed from full-tilt to breakneck. We slam off the escalators and onto the tiled floor of the platforms. Three pairs of black Magnums echoing through the tunnel like bullets. Trevor goes left and I go right. Westbound. As I run onto the platform itself I hear Cerys behind me. I slow my pace as I see the back end of the train slip away into the tunnel.

'Shit!' The word echoes about the platform, which is now deserted.

'Maybe he's on the other side.' pants Cerys, and we jog through to the Eastbound side of the tracks. Trevor is about halfway down, walking calmly through the twenty or so passengers who stand waiting for their train. I immediately slow my pace and motion for Cerys to do the same. There's nothing that'll cause a panic as much as a running copper. Especially on the underground. And I really don't want to start a stampede in such an enclosed, dangerous space. *Not unless we have to.* I scan the travellers and see no one that meets the man's description.

'He must have got on the Westbound train,' I nod to Cerys. 'We need to let everyone know where he's heading.' I go to grab my radio before realising that it's going to be dead. Sure enough, as I lift it up to view the display, I see the *no signal* symbol. 'Fuck,' I say, spitting out the word in frustration. A silver-haired man nearby raises his eyebrows in shock and I feel momentarily chastened by his expression. But there's no time to apologise.

Trevor has made a lap of the platform and reaches us once more, slightly out of breath.

'He must've gone Westbound.' he says, and I nod in agreement.

We walk calmly back to the stairs, only picking up the pace once we've turned the corner and are off the platform. Taking the escalators two at a time, my thighs start to burn halfway up and a woman on the way down gives us a concerned glare. I open my mouth to reassure her, before realising that I can't. We simply don't know where he's gone. So I look away and carry on.

Trevor is already at the guards when Cerys and I reach the top of the escalators. 'Next Westbound station is Holywell,' he shouts back to us and there's no time to pause as we head to the car.

Once we're in Trevor guns the engine and I update Control.

'Brixley, receiving Bravo One?' Still out of breath, I try not to pant too hard into the radio.

'Go ahead, Bravo One.'

'Suspect lost at Brixley Central, we think he's boarded a Westbound tube towards Holywell. We're heading there now. Please make sure that BX1 is aware, as well as the British Transport Police and the tube network.'

'That's all received, Bravo One, BX1 is aware and monitoring, liaising with Transport for London and Gold command. Do you want me to re-route the armed response vehicle to Holywell?'

'Yes please, we're two minutes away.'

'All received, 215 – their ETA is now nine minutes.'

I sit back in my seat as we weave through the busy streets and tuck the loose strands of hair that have escaped from my tight bun behind my ears. The habit of fastening my seatbelt is so ingrained in me that I have to physically stop myself from doing it. *We'll be there in less than two minutes.* The risk of being thrown through the front window at high speed doesn't seem to register quite so much, now that we're chasing a potential suicide bomber. The vibration of the siren pulses through the back of my seat, through my Met vest into my chest so that I can't tell the adrenalin from the sound.

As we speed towards Holywell, it occurs to me that some London tube stations are just a few minutes' walk from each other, and even as I question the randomness of my thought process, I'm still wondering why more people choose to sit in roasting tin bullets, fervently avoiding the gaze of other human beings, than choose to walk in the fresh air. As my mind lingers in the wired tunnels below, the images that were published after 7/7 flash across my mind. Warped doorframes and windows. Mangled metal, torn seats. Brightly coloured wires hanging from gutted compartments like the tangled guts of a wounded beast. Dark blood on metal grilles. A bolt of fear throbs in my chest. *What must it have felt like?* I lean forward in my seat.

I had been working a jailer shift on 7 July 2005. Stuck in the windowless depths of the custody suite, I had been desperate to be released, to run to the scenes to help, in any way I could. I had begged the skipper to let me go. But he'd stood fast. I was needed in Custody to monitor the prisoners. I've always felt guilty for not being there when London needed me most. As I crane forward I can just make out the red and blue of the tube sign. The curved road opens up ahead of us, the limit point stretching into the distance, me willing it forward with my mind, as if it might get us there a millisecond faster. I think of their faces. All those who lost their lives that day. *I'll do anything to stop that happening again.*

Trevor has killed the sirens and we glide to the kerb outside the station in silence. There are around six or seven people milling around the concourse, in various commuter stances. Man looking at phone, white: no rucksack, lady with a small girl *nope*, three young adults laughing together *students: casual and relaxed*, a man sweeping the street in a high-visibility jacket *road worker*. My gaze flicks from one to the other, eliminating each in turn. None of them is our suspect. My mind has made these assessments in the fraction of a second that it takes for us to climb out of the vehicle. We pause by the car as Trevor speaks low into his radio.

'Bravo One on scene.'

'Received, Bravo One.'

It's as Trevor is clipping his personal radio back onto his Met vest that we see him. And I know that each of us has clocked him at the same time because I feel Trevor tense and Cerys freeze as the breath sticks in my throat. He steps out of the station entrance and onto the neat brickwork of the concourse. The only thick thing about him is his dark beard. The rest of his frame is gnarled and twig-like. His cheekbones are sharp but his eyes have the watery look of madness as they jump from my face to Trevor's and Cerys's and back again. He wears the black and red rucksack on his front. Which, on its own, looks weird enough.

More concerning is the thick red wire that runs from the base of the rucksack, on his right, up and over his left shoulder. It reappears on the right side of his neck and seems to tuck into his collar, a couple of inches below. I'm just grateful it's not running into one of his hands. *No dead-man's trigger* (a switch sometimes used by terrorists to ensure that, if they get shot, the bomb will still detonate; once the trigger is compressed the bomb is primed to explode. Any release of pressure and it detonates immediately.) My eyes flick back to the rucksack. It's full and pendulous, the criss-cross laces at the front pulled tight against the bulging canvas. The shoulder straps dig into his bony shoulders, the material taut, stretching in the middle and rolling in at the edges. I wonder if his shoulders are aching under the strain. I wonder what's in the rucksack and think back to the discarded bomb at Wormwood Scrubs. I imagine the black and red canvas of his rucksack packed with soft yellow explosive, dotted with nails and screws.

There are around 4 metres between us. The public continue to move around us like lazy bees circling a hive. I am aware of them in my peripheral but my entire focus is on the man with the rucksack. Time stretches and warps as an invisible tunnel opens up between us, everything outside it fading to grey. Like a slipstream of current under the ocean, the only people in it us and him, the world's detritus separated from us by an invisible wall of water, we are perfectly still as we regard each other. I am aware that it is less than a second before we act. Less than a second before we are forced to act. But something in me wishes that this second could last forever. That we could all stay frozen this way, unharmed. *Whole.*

Moving slow *no sudden movements* I twist my head to the right and slide my right arm up to my PR. I press the transmit button and the muted bleep tells me I am on the air.

'Bravo X-ray, from 215, suspect in sight at entrance to Holywell tube. We are switching radios to safe mode.' I twist the volume down so that my radio is silent. I don't hear the reply. I don't need to hear it. The only thing I need to focus on is the man with the rucksack. I nod to Cerys as Trevor switches off his radio, and she fumbles to do the same. It's been drummed into us since day one that you don't use your radio when dealing with explosives. There's a risk that the transmission of radio signals near an explosive device could trigger the detonator. I also don't want the noise of the radio chatter to interfere with whatever negotiations we are about to embark upon. *If he gives us a chance to negotiate.*

He hasn't moved since we arrived. His hands still hang

limp by his sides, his legs slightly parted, feet firmly planted on the ground. We move forward as three, slowly closing the gap between us and him. And then the little girl runs through the slipstream between him and us and her tiny form ignites me from within. My mind fumbles for the right words as she teeters towards the doors. How to convey urgency without setting off the tinderbox? Aware that any sudden actions could worsen the situation, but desperate to get the girl and her mother out of there. And the phrase that's been drilled into me at officer safety training every six months, year in year out, the phrase that I've shouted too many times to remember, the phrase that gets to the point and grabs their attention fires from my mouth and cuts through the concourse like a bullet.

'Get back!' A jolt runs through the mother and her face turns from me to her daughter, to the man with the ruck-sack. Like an electric current her shock runs through the commuters and I feel the atmosphere around me thicken as realisation hits them one by one. Movement explodes all around me. The girl is whisked up into her mother's arms and she runs past us away from the station. The people around us starburst away from the entrance. Somebody shouts and the man with the rucksack raises his arms. Trevor has closed the gap and is standing directly in front of him. Cerys and I stand either side of Trevor, so that we surround the man on each side. A glance at her shows me pale skin and wide eyes.

It takes me a moment to register that his arms in the air are not a sign of surrender. I follow the glaring red wire as it snakes up the inside of his arm and up into his closed fist. He is breathing so hard that his nostrils flare with each breath. His eyes are bulging and almost rolling back in his head. From where I am standing I can see each bead of sweat on his forehead. A strong musk wafts from his exposed armpits as I feel my own sweat gather on my top lip. A beat of silence before Trevor speaks.

'Do you want to talk about it?' A flicker of confusion crosses the man's face. He glances from Trevor to me and back again. His lips twitch. In the distance a siren starts to wail. His eyebrows knit at the sound and he straightens his arms above his head, shutting his eyes and tilting back his head. A wave of fear hits me. *This is it. He's going to press the button.* The air around me seems to contract as I wait for the blast. At close proximity it's not the fire that kills you when a bomb explodes, nor the shrapnel, although both can do it. It's the pressure. The rapid expansion and compression of the air surrounding the detonation causes your internal organs to rupture. I wonder whether they'll find parts of the bomber's bones embedded in parts of my soft tissue. If parts of us will become inseparable, indistinguishable. I wonder whether the tiny parts of me will be laid out in a lab somewhere, labelled and catalogued and then shoved in a bag for my coffin. *Please let it be quick.*

I glance at Trevor and wonder how he's so calm. He is gazing up at the man's hand. 'I don't think you have a bomb at all, do you?'

The man's shoulders sag. Trevor flicks his hand forward,

and before the man can stop him he's tugged on the red wire at the bottom of the rucksack. It unravels with no resistance. Trevor lets it go and it hangs there, swaying slightly, its rubber end torn to expose copper strands. Connected to nothing. I release a breath I didn't realise I was holding and shake my head.

The man stares blankly at us, his mouth chewing on words that won't come out. Trevor leans forward and unzips the rucksack. A balled up pair of socks fall out. He reaches into the sack and pulls out a pile of stuffed-up clothes. My legs feel like jelly as I watch them tumble to the floor. I feel like laughing. Like screaming. *Like punching him in the face.* Just another mental health patient receiving care in the community. It's as the sirens grow closer that the fleeting relief I feel is replaced with a gnawing urgency.

'Put your hands down,' I plead, glancing backwards along the road to see if the armed response unit is in view. 'If they get here and see you like this, they're going to shoot you.'

Trevor laughs. 'That's what he wants. Suicide by police. Fucking coward.'

The man continues to stare into the middle distance as a bolt of anger courses through me. *All this because he hasn't got the guts to do it himself.* And then I look at him. His wasted frame, his liquid eyes. The stains across his T-shirt and the shake of his arms as he struggles to keep them up. His eyes slide to mine and he suddenly looks so childlike. He's not in his right mind. He's begging for help. *I've been there*. I grab my radio as the armed response screech into view at the end of the street. I push on the transmit button but it makes a low error sound as I begin to speak. *Shit*. It's still on safe mode and I can't transmit. *There's no time*. I hear the roar of the engine as the ARV draws closer. I reach forward and grab the straps of the rucksack with both hands.

'Trevor, we need to get this off him.' I start to pull at the straps but the man's hands shoot down and close around them. He starts to mumble under his breath in a low, slurred drawl. We shove into him and then we're on the floor, he on his back and Trevor pulling the straps off one side while I work on the other. I grasp at the red wire and tug it away from his fist, throwing it backwards. As I hear the ARV pull up to the kerb behind me I finally tug the rucksack free and immediately tip it upside down, spilling more clothes onto the pavement. I hold one of the suspect's arms and Trevor holds the other, so that he is pinned to the ground with his arms out to the sides. And then I freeze as four doors slam behind me and the concourse erupts in noise.

The armed officers are shouting 'Armed police' at the top of their lungs. Four guns point directly at the suspect. And even though these guns are on my side, it's still a sobering experience to be looking down four barrels.

'No explosives found!' I shout. 'No explosives. Suspect under control.'

The guns lower slightly and I look at the officer closest to me. He nods in our direction. 'Good job, guys.'

A little candle of pride lights in my tummy. I feel Trevor relax next to me and I loll back onto my haunches slightly, careful not to release the man's hand. I can already feel my calves cramping up. I smile over at Cerys, who finally has some colour back in her cheeks. And as we stand there on the concourse we all share in the relief of a disaster averted. All of us, that is, except the man who is pressed to the floor, his body racked with silent sobs, his pleading eyes turned to the sky.

After the detainee is loaded into the van and carted off towards Brixley nick we stand and talk to the armed officers for a few moments. I try not to gawp at their guns. Nearly seven years in the police and I'm still like a schoolgirl around armed officers. There's one female out of the team of four and I'm desperate to talk to her without appearing too much of a groupie. I sidle up to her as casually as I can and decide to be direct.

'So what's it like then?' I nod at her MP5. 'Being armed response?'

She smiles. 'I love it.'

I just grin moronically until she asks, 'You interested? We're always looking for more females.'

I puff out my cheeks like I've never considered the possibility. 'Yeah, I mean – you know – maybe.'

She hands me her card. 'I'd be happy to chat about it if you are interested. We do a mentoring scheme so anything you want to know, just give me a shout.'

Just then their radios pipe up and they jump into the car before pulling off, on their way to another job. I stand by the side of the road clutching her card like a teenager who's just got Justin Bieber's autograph.

*　　*　　*

His name is David. Diagnosed with schizophrenia at a young age, he is also a drug addict. He's spent most of his younger years in psychiatric care homes but was kicked out when he turned eighteen. He's spent most of his adult life trying to get back in.

Schizophrenia can be managed. But not by someone who would rather smoke skunk than take his meds. And who could blame him? If his reality was mine I'd want to escape it too. There is no one to remind him to take his pills. No one to keep him on track. And every time he reached out for help he was misunderstood. The community turned their backs on him. His most regular interaction with other human beings was with the police and mental health workers. In and out of cells and hospitals, what he really needed was long term, 24-hour care. But that's a rare commodity these days. Multiple attempted suicides noted on his PNC record.

He has nothing to do except keep on trying. Keep crying out for help and attention until one day there's nobody there to stop him. Nobody there to save him.

18

Darryl

It's a lazy Sunday evening in Brixley as Darryl weaves our marked police car through the labyrinth that is the Pemberton Estate. It's just gone 7 p.m, our call-sign is Bravo X-ray Two-Two and we're about halfway through our late-turn shift. I don't bother to stifle my yawn as I gaze out at the groups of youths gathered on corners, hoods pulled up and backs turned as we crawl by. I was up five times with Freddy last night. He's two-and-a-half but has never been a good sleeper. At the moment he has a cold, and his stuffed-up nose bothers him. It also makes it hard for him to suck on his dummy, which, in turn, wakes him up. A lot. John's voice echoes in my mind as I turn up the air-conditioning and aim the vents directly at my face. *We need to get him off the dummy. He should never have had one in the first place.* He often likes to make these helpful comments in the middle of the night, while I'm shuffling towards Freddy's room and he's turning over to go back to sleep. I chew my lip as the familiar twist of Mum guilt flips in my stomach. I think back to that desperate dash to the super-market. Sick on my top and cotton wool wrapped around my brain. So sleep-deprived that I was willing to do anything to get Freddy to settle. I'd thrown seven different types of dummies into my basket and barely stopped to sterilise them before I shoved one in his mouth. I remember the tears rolling down my face as I watched him suckle, watched his tiny eyelids close. The first time he'd slept without my holding him. *Fuck you, John, I love the fucking dummies.*

I roll my eyes at Darryl as a skinny youth squares his shoulders and stares into our car. He looks past me and straight at Darryl, narrowing his eyes. Their eyes lock, but I know Darryl won't rise to it. This kid wants trouble, wants to look like the big man in front of all his mates. Wants them to think that we're interested in him. I chuckle to myself. I couldn't be less interested. He'd love nothing more than to be pressed across our bonnet, screaming about police brutality. As we crawl past I roll down my window. I feel the thick London air on my face as I smile up at the youth.

'Good evening, sir.' I smile wide, adopting my best English plum. 'I do hope you're enjoying this fine weather we're having.'

The youth's mouth drops open a touch and his brows cross. For a moment he looks so gormless that I can't help but feel sorry for him. He recovers himself and folds his arms across his chest. He makes a slurping sound with his mouth and I assume that he's trying to kiss his teeth at me. Darryl guffaws beside me and I nearly lose my straight face.

'Well, we must be off now – you know, doughnuts to eat and all that.' I wink at him. 'Good day to you!'

I watch him stare after us as we glide away.

'They never expect you to be nice.' Darryl grins at me from the driver's seat.

'I know,' I mock with an affronted expression, palms to the sky. 'I've no idea why. I'm a genuinely nice person.'

Darryl is chortling as we pull out of the estate and onto the main road. His voice is so full of bass that I feel like it's vibrating my eardrums. I revel in the sound. I love being posted with Darryl, and as much as I hate to admit it, I feel safe with him. I think back to Dixon's bedsit, his weight crushing my chest, to the moment where he seemed to fly backwards as Darryl wrenched him from me. I try not to think about what could have happened if he hadn't been there. And I try not to feel the familiar sense of shame that comes from knowing I couldn't protect myself.

I glance across at him as he drives, his powerful frame relaxed behind the wheel, his face placid. The affection I feel towards him is powerful. When you're in a car with someone for eight hours a day, when you face the things we do together, when you're all they've got and vice versa, it gets intense fast. And although I feel no sexual attraction to Darryl, I find myself wondering, as I have done many times, if that is the reason why there are so many illicit relationships on response teams. *Everyone seems to be sleeping with everybody else.* My train of thought is broken as I notice the black BMW X5 in front of us. I reach for the rubber-covered keyboard on my lap. Tapping the touch screen of the MDT, our on-board computer, I tug on the curled cord of the keyboard, tutting to myself as it lazily unfurls.

'Did you know that they're one of the most stolen to order vehicles at the moment?' I jerk my head towards the BMW.

'Yeah,' Darryl nods. 'In the paper, wasn't it?'

I select 'PNC' from the options on screen and then 'Vehicle', before tapping the registration into the keyboard. Nothing happens on the screen.

'Fuck's sake.' I lob the keyboard into my foot-well in frustration. 'Piece of shit.'

I start typing the registration into the MDT, using the touch screen, but each time I touch a number it enters the number next to it instead. 'Jesus! When is the last time this screen was calibrated?'

I glance up at the BMW just as the driver clocks us in his rear-view mirror. Immediately there's a flash of brake lights, but just for a millisecond.

'He's noticed us.' Darryl keeps a level speed, matching the SUV in front of us.

'What's the flash of brakes about? Nerves?' I sit up straight as I consider the BMW. The driver glances at his rear-view mirror again and the vehicle slows. Another touch on the brakes.

'It's three-up.' Darryl is speaking low, almost as if the occupants of the car in front might be able to hear us. He's referring to the fact that the car has three passengers. Two in the front and one in the back, on the offside, directly behind the driver. I watch as the front-seat passenger leans forwards and tries to see us in the nearside mirror. From what I can see of the backs of their heads, they're all male.

'They're definitely shifty.' I reach for my personal radio.

'Gotta do all checks on channel two now.' Darryl glances across at me.

'Shit, I'd forgotten.' I twist my PR so that it unlocks from its cradle on my Met vest. Changing the frequency to channel two, I immediately hear the voice of an operator reading out the results of a vehicle check. I jump in as soon as she stops transmitting, to get myself in the queue.

'BX, from 215, vehicle check please.'

'215, you're now in the queue.'

I sigh and start to tap my knee with my free hand. I'm still looking at the vehicle in front and all three heads are now perfectly still. Facing forward.

'Now they try and play it cool.' Darryl rolls his eyes and chuckles. It sounds forced. We're both on edge for some reason.

I can almost hear the conversation in the BMW. The driver telling his passengers to sit still, face forward, act normal. Hands in their laps. Sweat on their brows. If only he could take his own advice. Three times now he's hit the brakes, as if to make a turn, before continuing along his original route.

'They don't seem to know where they're going,' Darryl observes.

A familiar phrase enters my mind. *Driving without purpose.* It can also be applied to walking. It's a sign you

learn to look for, something tangible you can tell probationers to seek out. There's a whole list of 'suspicious' behav-
iours we can tell them to look out for. Someone who hides
their face. Someone who loiters. Someone who changes
direction upon seeing police. But they're the obvious ones.
It's much more difficult to explain the feeling you get about
someone. The almost imperceptible signals that people give
off upon seeing police officers. The behaviour of an addict,
or of someone looking to steal. The way someone's hands
will move subconsciously towards the very thing they're
trying to hide. The way someone looking to run will move
from one foot to the other and look behind you for an exit.
The copper's nose. You can't teach it. Some police officers
will never get it. The ones that do get it one way, and one
way only. It's not instinct. At least, it doesn't become instinct
until you've been on the streets day in day out, week after
week, until it *clicks*. And once it clicks, you can never turn it
off. It's looking up when you're walking. It's looking people
in the eye. It's stepping towards the person who gives you
the jitters instead of walking away from them.

My eyes are still glued to the car as I press my radio to
my ear. Two PNC name checks and a vehicle check and it's
still not my turn. The BMW has turned left now three
times, and Darryl is shifting in his seat.

'We can't keep following them for much longer, we're
going to have to put the stop in.'

I nod in agreement. 'I just hate doing it without the intel
first.'

It's standard practice to conduct vehicle checks before

you stop a vehicle, if possible. Sure, it's nice to know if the car is insured and who owns it, but most importantly, it means that you're aware of any warning signs connected to the car. As I keep watching the occupants I notice that the rear-seat passenger is bending forwards. His head keeps going out of sight as he bends over in his seat, and his shoulders start to shrug in rapid movement.

'The rear-seat passenger's up to something.' The urgency to stop the vehicle in front increases dramatically and I flick the frequency of my radio back to channel 1, the main frequency. 'Fuck channel two,' I mutter to myself before pressing the button to speak.

'BX, from Bravo X-ray Two-Two.'

'G'head, Bravo X-ray Two-Two.'

'We're about to stop a vehicle on Braeburn Way, three up, occupants acting very suspiciously. Channel two is busy and I need a vehicle check urgently please.'

'215, vehicle checks are to be carried out on channel two.'

I wonder if the operator, a male voice that I don't recognise, has actually heard a word I just said.

Darryl thumps the steering wheel. 'Fucking morons!'

I watch as the front-seat passenger turns to the rear of the car and dips his head down so that it's almost touching that of the male in the back.

'We need to stop them now, they're up to something; they could be hiding stuff.' I feel a flutter of adrenalin as

Darryl nods and powers up the blues and twos, flashing his headlights at the BMW. The driver immediately signals to pull in, and we start to move over to the kerb.

It's as I'm taking off my seatbelt that Terri's Scottish lilt pipes up over the airwaves.

'215, you still looking for that vehicle check?'

I silently thank a lord that I don't believe in that Terri is working tonight. She's one of the old school. She was around when the control rooms used to be positioned in police stations. When you could walk in to the CAD room and see the faces of the people that backed you up every day over the air. We used to go for drinks together; form relationships. They were part of the team. They knew us by number, they knew the borough back to front, they knew the shirkers from the workers and they knew who to send to what. Most of all, their number one priority was the safety of *their* officers. Then the Met centralised all control rooms. Now we deal with disembodied voices of people we've never met. Voices whose number one priority is to clear the jobs from their screens and meet the targets set for responding to calls. Needless to say the love that once existed between officer and operator has been lost, which is a desperate shame, because we should all be working towards the same thing.

'Yes, Terri. Thanks, mate. We're on Braeburn Way, index is HG10 EVG. Vehicle is stopped.' I climb out of car still talking, 'I'm approaching it now.'

'Received.'

I hear Darryl's door slam behind me and continue to approach the nearside of the vehicle, from the pavement. I can see Darryl in my peripheral, before he levels with me. He is in the road, approaching the driver's door. I peer into the car as I draw level with it, my hands hovering at my sides. All the windows are rolled down and the men are sitting facing forwards. Now that I'm level with them I can see that they're all middle-aged, Asian males. The driver turns to Darryl and his front-seat passenger cranes around to look at me. The male in the back stays facing forwards and I think how odd it is that he hasn't moved at all. The height of the SUV is preventing me from seeing the men's hands, and I step closer in an effort to get a visual on them. Terri's voice cuts across my thoughts.

'215, 215, receiving BX?'

'Go ahead.' My voice is calm and I'm grateful that it doesn't portray the uneasiness I'm feeling. Through the open windows I see Darryl tilt his head towards his PR. He holds out a palm to the driver. A clear signal to wait.

'Are you free to speak?'

My eyes meet Darryl's as we both hear the question that usually precedes sensitive information. Operators are supposed to ask you to make yourself 'free to speak' before they transmit any intelligence likely to affect the result of the stop. This is to prevent the information being overheard. Most operators do this. Some don't. And I've been on the receiving end of the consequences when a violent suspect overhears that they're wanted by police and are about to be arrested. They're not fun.

I take a step back from the car and turn my radio down to its lowest setting, releasing it from my vest and pressing it to my ear. I glance across to make sure Darryl has done the same.

'Go ahead, Terri.'

'Right. The vehicle is known on PNC as being linked to some intelligence regarding firearms and terrorism.'

My blood runs cold.

'I'm trying to get more details now. PNC states that the vehicle should only be stopped with the assistance of armed officers.'

A bolt of fear rips through me as I digest what Terri has just told me. Noise explodes in my ears and I realise that Darryl is shouting, and it's only a millisecond before I'm shouting the same as him.

'SHOW ME YOUR HANDS!' I bellow as loud as I can. 'Show me your hands, now!' The males react instantly by reaching for the roof as I rack my baton out to its full length and raise it in the air. My eardrums thrum at the volume of my voice. I have a moment to consider how useless my baton will be if they pull out revolvers, but it's all I've got. And I need them to take me seriously.

I can hear Terri calling my number on the radio but there's no way I can answer now. Not until the men are cuffed and under our control. Time slows as we consider each other and my one free hand hovers above my canister of CS gas. I need to be able to react quickly if things go wrong. *Can I make it to cover if they pull a gun?* There's nothing around me on the pavement and behind me looms a tall brick wall. I'm a sitting duck. My only hope would be a dash to the police car but even that wouldn't provide much safety. It's not like it is in the movies. Bullets go right through car doors.

The males seem to be co-operating, but we need them out of the car. We need them searched and cuffed, preferably prone on the floor and unable to reach for anything. We're two and they're three and I wonder how we'll keep them under watch closely enough to do this safely. I look to Darryl and he shouts through the car.

'One at a time.' His baton is high and he points his free hand to the driver. 'Driver! Keep your hands up where I can see them.' He's still shouting, but he's decreased the volume slightly. Darryl leans forwards and pops open the driver's door. 'Get out of the car slowly.' I watch as the driver starts to shuffle out of the car, my eyes flicking between the hands of the two passengers. Darryl pulls the keys from the ignition and slips them into his trouser pocket. A shift from the male in the back seat as his hands lower an inch or so.

'Keep your hands up!' I shout directly at him and raise my baton. 'Keep your hands up or I will strike you in the head!' His eyes widen and his hands shoot upwards. I've never struck anyone in the head with my baton before but, at this moment, I'm convinced that I would do it. I think of Sharon Beshenivsky, the mother of three shot dead in the course of her duties in Bradford in 2005. She had been murdered on her youngest daughter's birthday; a fact I couldn't forget. *I will not let you shoot me.*

As the driver stands up Darryl quickly cuffs him in a rear-stack, a tactical handcuff position used to immobilise the suspect as much as possible. Once the driver's hands are twisted up his back, Darryl walks him around the front of the car and out of my view. Tempted as I am to follow them with my gaze, I keep my eyes fixed on the two passengers in front of me. I can feel the pulse of my heart throbbing against my chest but my baton is steady. The men are co-operating but I'm not about to drop my guard. One thing you learn early on in this job is that things can change in the blink of an eye, and they very often do.

My radio buzzes with activity and I know that Terri, having not received an answer to her calls to us, will be sending units to our location. I feel the familiar conflict between wanting the world and his wife to arrive and help us, and not being seen as 'making a fuss'. Then I hear Darryl's voice in stereo as he transmits from behind me.

'BX, from Bravo X-ray Two-Two, we have the vehicle stopped, request one other unit on the hurry-up please, to assist with search.'

'Bravo X-ray Two-Two, from BX, that is all received. We have a unit en route.'

'Received. Thanks, Terri.'

'Do you want me to get an armed-response unit on its way to you?'

'Nah, mate, it's a bit late for that.' Darryl tuts as he ends his transmission and appears beside me. 'Who's next?'

'Him,' I nod towards the rear-seat passenger who still won't meet my eye. Of all of the males in the car, he's the one I'm most concerned about.

They still sit with their hands in the air and my baton is still raised. Darryl points to the back-seat male and directs him out of the car, handcuffing him as soon as he is standing. As they retreat behind me I nod to the front-seat passenger.

'Keep your hands raised and get out of the car, nice and slowly.' I pull open the door as he turns towards me. He struggles out of the car keeping his hands high and I reach for my cuffs with my free hand. Slipping my baton back into its holster, still at full length, I take hold of his right wrist and slap the handcuff across the bare skin. I tighten it before twisting his arm up his back and securing his other wrist in the free cuff. Taking a firm hold of the cuffs by the solid plastic bridge between the metal, I pull him backwards and away from the car. It's only at this point in the stop that I release some of the breath that I seem to have been holding for hours. With the three males in cuffs, it's unlikely that they will be able to use any weapon against us. I look to Darryl, who is patting down the rear-seat passenger. The driver has already been searched and is standing facing the wall, his hands secured high up his back. I hear sirens in the distance and know that they're for us.

'OK.' I talk to the front-seat passenger from the side, still holding his cuffs. 'We've stopped this vehicle because of the suspicious actions of the driver upon seeing a police car. After conducting a police check on the vehicle I suspect that you might be concealing weapons upon your person, therefore for my immediate safety I am going to search you.' The male looks at me blankly. 'Do you speak English?' He nods. 'Do you have any weapons on you? Anything that might harm me or you?' He shakes his head. Sweat beads on his lower lip. 'Turn to face the wall, please.'

It's standard practice in the Met for male officers to search male suspects, and female officers to search female suspects. And as I begin to feel along the male's arms, I wonder whether I'll get in trouble for searching him. It briefly occurs to me to wait until Darryl is finished with male number two and ask him to search my detainee instead. I shake my head in frustration and feel around the male's collar. I'm a copper and this guy could have a gun. I'll be damned if I'm going to put my safety on the line for red tape. I set my jaw as I begin to run my hands up along his legs, from his ankles to his crotch. I turn my hand over so that the back of it runs up in between his inseam and back down the other side. *Fuck it, let him sue me if he wants.* I'm sure my actions are justified.

Once I'm satisfied that he's not concealing a weapon I let go of the cuffs and tell him to stay where he is, facing the wall. If necessary he can be searched in more depth by a male colleague or even back at the station. I've ensured our safety and that's as far as I'm prepared to go for now. As Darren and I step back from the three males a marked unit pulls up next to us. It's Ralph and Ben. With the three males in cuffs and back-up on scene, I feel myself relax. Darryl gives me a wink and I realise he feels the same. It can't have been much more than five minutes since we received the warning that the males might be involved in firearms, just five minutes since my heart jumped into my mouth, but it seemed much longer. I can feel a layer of sweat on the back of my neck and my shirt is stuck to my back beneath my Met vest. The adrenalin that coursed through my veins has nowhere to go and I can almost feel it brimming behind my eyes. I fist my hands to erase the possibility of them shaking.

'Right then.' Darryl is snapping on a rubber glove. 'Let's get this beast searched.'

I nod and turn to the BMW. Tugging on my own gloves, I realise that this is the first time since we stopped the SUV that I've turned my back to the males. But they're hemmed against the wall by Ben and Ralph. I grin as I relish the prospect of searching every nook and cranny inside the spacious interior of the SUV. But there's an area I want to get to straight away. An area that's been burning away in my mind since we observed the men from our police car. I think of the rear-seat passenger shuffling in his seat, of his head bobbing up and down as he seemed to reach down into the foot well.

I climb onto the rear seats from the kerb side, and flick on the central passenger lights above me. The smell of leather fills my nostrils as I run my gloved hands across the plush interior. The foot well illuminates. It's empty. I stare at the clean, bare carpet and a vision of my own car pops into my head. Biscuit crumbs, plastic toys and crisp wrappers. Undeterred, I reach a gloved hand down and underneath the driver's seat. I hear the crumple of a plastic bag as my fingers make contact with something hard. The coolness of the object seeps through the thin rubber of my gloves and I can tell that I'm touching something metal. And I know what it is. Even before I curl my fingers round it, the plastic bag crunching as it moves under my grasp, and pull it towards me. Even as I sit up and look down at the Tesco bag in my lap, pulling the top open and peering inside.

'Gun.' The word is out of my mouth before my brain has caught up with the item in front of it. Darryl is there in a second, his face next to mine as we stare at the revolver in my lap. Then he's squeezing my shoulder, grinning.

'Awesome fucking stop.' He's laughing. He's heading over to Ben and Ralph and I hear their palms slap against the Kevlar on the rear of his Met vest. I hear him asking the males whose gun it is. I hear him arresting them on suspicion of possessing a firearm, calling for a van and requesting that a firearms unit attend the scene to make the weapon safe.

And I sit there with a gun in my lap. A gun in my lap and my son's face in my mind. A funeral procession. White gloves, helmets glinting in the sun. John holding Freddy as he cries for his mummy. My tongue sticks to the roof of my mouth and for the first time in my police career, I just don't want to do this any more.

*   *   *

It's 2.30 a.m. and the cool air of the early morning hits my face as I leave the stuffy police station. After a full search of the BMW, we found a briefcase containing a large amount of cash in sterling and euros, fraudulent credit cards, and bank statements in many different names. The Anti-Terrorism branch called me on my personal mobile phone before we even left the scene. We were met at the nick by three of them and I led a debrief in which we described every detail of the stop. My heart has been banging like a drum since I found the gun and it still is as I quick-step through Church Market towards the bus stop. Each piece of evidence has had to be packaged and exhibited for court. There were sixty-three items in total, including the firearm, which was confirmed by a firearms expert as real, but unloaded. My hands sting from paper cuts and my fingers ache from writing my signature over a hundred times. I can still hear the squeak of the thick tape used for packaging exhibits.

John will be leaving the house for an early shift in three hours and I'll be taking over the childcare. I sigh as I realise that Freddy will be awake in less than four hours, and I've got at least an hour and a half until I will be in bed. It hardly seems worth going to sleep. It occurs to me that I'm so wired I couldn't even sleep if I tried. My eyes sting and I curse as I remember my contact lenses. I pull them out at the bus stop and slip on my glasses. The night bus rolls up and I'm relieved to see that it's almost empty. I flash the driver my warrant card as I get on and he nods as I pass. I finger the card of the female firearms officer that I've kept in my pocket for the last four months. I shake my head in disbelief. *As if you could ever be an armed officer.* I can barely cope with the shifts as it is. I walk to the back seats and collapse in the corner. Pushing the earbuds of my headphones into my ears, I surrender to my heavy eyelids.

As the bus pulls away I smile to myself. It was an awesome stop.

19

Arnie

'What the hell is wrong with you?' Andy looks at me from the passenger seat. His voice is light and jovial. It's a question formed of genuine concern, not chastisement.

'Shit,' I mutter as I rub my hands across my face, leaning forwards to place my forehead gently on the steering wheel. 'I don't know.'

But I've got an idea.

We're late turn. The busiest of shifts. Just two hours into our eight-hour beat and we've just left a domestic. No offences alleged, just a loud argument between a couple at breaking point. It still needs to be logged and reported. Even when there's no crime committed, no assault or threats, domestic incidents always get logged because they're so high-risk. *Because so many women get beaten to death.*

The man was leaving and the woman was trying to stop him. They were about my age. She was in tears and literally begging him not to go. Apart from our similar ages, there was absolutely nothing about the call that touched upon my own life. Nothing to make me emotional, nothing that connected me to them. It's a call that would usually make me roll my eyes. Yet I had found myself welling up. Andy had noticed it and suggested I 'check the car.' I'd gratefully fled outside and was sitting alone in our police car until he just climbed in.

'I'm not feeling great,' I say, turning the key and clearing our status on the on-board computer.

'I'll say,' Andy laughed. 'Let's go back to the nick. You're white as a sheet and you've been avoiding calls all morning.'

'Ah, you noticed that,' I look sideways at him.

'Yeah, I noticed that.'

'Sorry, mate. Maybe a cuppa will sort me out.' I indicate and pull out from the kerb. A posh London street where flats are priced at a premium. As usual, when we're called to affluent areas, I find myself thinking that domestic abuse is one of the few crimes that isn't contained by class.

'Maybe you've picked a bug up from Freddy?' he suggests. 'Wasn't he ill last week?'

I smile involuntarily at the mention of my son's name. Then I sigh.

'He's always picking up something or other from nursery,' I say, shaking my head. 'He seems to deal with it fairly well, whereas if I catch it, it nearly kills me.'

Andy chuckles at my exaggeration.

'That must be it then. You should get home.' He twists in his seat and forms a cross with his fingers, pushing it towards my face. 'Plus, I don't want the lurgy.'

I try a chuckle but it falls flat. He's right, of course. We've been working together long enough for him to know when something's up. I have been avoiding calls, but I don't think it's a bug that's making me feel rough. My nausea and inappropriate tears have only confirmed my worries.

The last time I felt this emotional, I was pregnant with Freddy.

The thought that I may be pregnant again worries me. Not because I don't want another baby, because I do. In fact, John and I have already discussed it, and I've stopped taking the pill; we're letting nature take its course. I just didn't think nature would be so bloody quick. The possibility of pregnancy number two worries me because I'm sitting in a police car. It worries me because I love my job, and as soon as I tell anyone that I might be pregnant then, well, I won't be allowed to do it for at least a year, possibly longer if I can't work out the nightmarish childcare arrangements that shift-workers face. Of course, I won't actually lose my job. I'll still be a copper. But I'll be tied to a desk. Or stuck in the station office. Kept away from prisoners and the front line. And I joined this job because I love the front line. I joined because I couldn't stand to work in an office every day. I joined for the action. For the challenge. But with action comes risk. I glance briefly down at my lap as I weave slowly through the heavy London traffic.

'Do you mind if I pop into the chemist's on our way back?' I ask, trying to think of one on the way.

'Course not.' Andy points ahead. 'Isn't there one just up here?'

He's right again. I search for a spot before pulling up on

a double yellow. It's not something I normally do but this isn't a normal situation. I need to know. Right at this moment it's the only thing I care about. I may not want to get stuck behind a desk, but if I'm pregnant I'll do it. I'll do whatever it takes to protect my unborn child. I'll suck up the months of mind-numbing paperwork and form filling and reporting. It's just not worth the risk not to.

I hop out of the car and in through the chemist's doors. There are two old ladies browsing and three members of staff behind the counter, chatting. As soon as my boot hits the lino all eyes are on me, and the chatter dies away. My mind toys between trying to browse casually and just being direct. I walk up to the counter.

'Pregnancy test?' I say. There's no point talking in hushed tones as the old ladies have already paused and pointed their ears in my direction. *Hopefully they're deaf.*

An almost imperceptible pause as the three staff members digest my request, before the most senior-looking one nods and reaches behind the counter.

'Do you need an early one or just normal?' she asks.

'Whatever's cheapest.' I stick with the blunt approach.

A faint smile crosses her face as she pulls out the test. She slides it smoothly into a paper bag, crisply folds down the top and places it on the counter. I hand her the money and wait for my change. The shop is silent. But I've been wearing this uniform for a long time, and I'm used to being stared at. *And eavesdropped on.* To be honest, I usually don't mind. Today, however, my cheeks warm slightly as I wait.

Eventually she hands it over and I thank her before turning to leave. One of the grannies has snuck up behind me while I waited for change. She's standing close. Her mouth is open and she's staring. I can see large hearing aids poking up from behind her ears on each side. *Aw shit.* I stride towards the door as fast as I can without causing a panic. Running coppers tend to do that to people.

As I slide into the driver's seat I throw the paper bag casually into the back.

'Strepsils,' I say.

Andy nods. He's busy filling in the twenty-page booklet that we have to complete at each domestic we attend. There are questions we have to ask at each call, questions that sometimes seem ridiculous, especially when it's a minor argument with no violence. Neighbours call the police when they hear shouting, and so they should. I'd rather go to a hundred 'no crime' domestics if it meant preventing that one domestic murder. Sometimes people apologise for calling us. They think they're wasting our time. I won't hear of it. If in doubt, call us. It's what I always say. So much domestic abuse gets hidden away, and so many women can't ask for help themselves.

We're nearing the station as Andy flips his report closed.

'You go to the canteen, I'll get the tea.'

'Thanks, Andy.' I pull into a free spot in the back yard and turn off the engine. Andy hops out and nips into the custody suite, where the tea is free if you ask the right jailer. I quickly reach into the back and grab the paper packet from the chemist's. Stuffing it into my pocket, I step out of the car. The closest ladies' toilet is on the ground floor, but I'm not going in there. It's only got one cubicle and I need room to hide. I take the stairs two at a time, up to the second floor. A short walk from the stairwell and into the larger ladies' loos. I try to catch my breath as I walk into the middle cubicle and sit on the closed toilet. I shut my eyes and wait until my breathing slows. I feel a slight pang of guilt about doing the test before telling John, but I know that he'll understand. He's a copper too.

I unzip my Met vest and hang it on the hook on the back of the cubicle door, along with my kit belt. I pull my damp shirt away from my skin and make myself comfortable. Ripping open the kit, I take the stick straight out and dump the packaging and instructions on the floor. Once the dipstick is saturated I put the plastic lid back on and hold the test up in front of my face. It makes me laugh when you see people do pregnancy tests on telly. The way they pace about and agonise over the 'two-minute wait' for their results. It's all bollocks. As the moisture spreads through the stick, the 'test' window displays a cross. That tells me that the test is working. Then, the 'result' window displays a cross. That tells me that I'm pregnant. *Oh right.*

There's no agonising wait, no drama. It's just me in a smelly Met toilet with a positive pregnancy test in my hand. I have the presence of mind to realise that this is the second time I've done this in a smelly Met toilet. I look up at my Met vest and belt. I look at my handcuffs, CS spray and baton, and hear the muted radio chatter from my PR. And then I smile. A little brother or sister for Freddy.

Perhaps a girl? I try and push the thought away. A healthy baby will be enough. A thousand thoughts start running through my mind as I stand up and lift my personal safety equipment from the hook. I need to start taking folic acid. *How many weeks am I? How many drinks did I have last Saturday?* I unlock the door and walk to the mirrors. Splashing cold water on my face, I wipe my smudged mascara from under my eyes. A quick slick of lip-gloss and I'm halfway normal. I run my hands across my stomach and smile again. *Hello down there.*

I'm delighted. There was no question really of me being anything else. But as I walk through the canteen to my locker room I start to consider the hurdles ahead. I had a difficult pregnancy with Freddy and ended up on crutches due to serious pelvic pain. Then there was the post-natal depression. The thought of going through it again is a sobering one. But, I got through it. In fact, it has made me a better police officer. *I who once naively thought mental health disorders were reserved for the weak and lazy.* I shake my head slightly, ashamed that I ever thought such a thing. I now know, first hand, that it can happen to anyone. I shoulder open the locker room door and take the six or so steps over to my locker. Swing open the door and throw in my belt. I hang my Met vest on a hanger and zip it up. I've become rather attached to it. Knowing that it's going to sit in my locker, unattended, for more than a year makes me pause and stare at it a little longer than I usually do. It's my shell. My literal protection against harm, and my metaphorical armour against the world. In my vest I am unshakable. I know what to do.

Now I stand in trousers and shirt. I stare in the full-length mirror on the wall. Unmarked apart from my epaulettes, which display the metal numbers and letters that identify me: 215BX. A number I have answered to for nearly seven years. Now I must be kept away from crime scenes, suspects and the public in general. Time to talk to my governor. But, before I leave the room I pull out my phone. John's number is the first that comes up and I select call. I wait as the dial tone rumbles in my ear before clicking to voicemail. Oh well, I tried. I can't delay it any more.

I walk from the changing rooms back across the canteen and along the hallways of the top brass. As if positioned to remind us of their authority, all of the senior police officers reside on the top floor. Many times have I taken the long climb up the echoing stairwells with a feeling of dread in my chest, words arranging and rearranging themselves in my head. Responsible for explaining actions or non-actions at some crime scene or other. But not today. Today I have no care about what I'm going to say. I'm just going to say it. I find the duty inspector's office and knock lightly.

'Come,' barks the voice from within.

I push the door inwards and step into the musty room.

'Ah, 215.' Inspector Green is sitting behind his desk with a pile of papers spread out in front of him. 'How can I be of service?' He smiles and points to a chair. He's the best duty inspector our team has had for years and I'm thankful it's him that I'm telling first.

I plonk down on the offered chair and lean forwards, elbows resting on my parted knees, hands clasped together.

I don't think I've bothered sitting in a ladylike manner since I started the job.

'I'm pregnant.'

The second slight pause of the day. Then the governor recovers the decorum that he has in spades, and nods his head.

'Congratulations.' He smiles.

'I've just found out. Needless to say it's early days, so . . .' I spread my hands before him, palms facing up.

'So . . . you don't want the rest of the team to find out?'

Relieved, I nod. It's far too early to be telling everyone just yet.

He stands from behind his desk and wanders around it, pacing in a gently military fashion. I get the opinion that he enjoys a bit of subterfuge.

'So, what shall it be, 215?' He strokes his smooth chin. 'Minor back injury good for you?'

'Sounds fine.'

'Excellent. Take over from the station officer today and we'll find you something more permanent as time goes on.'

'Thanks, Gov.' I get up to leave, then a thought stops me.

'Gov, I haven't been able to get hold of John yet, so please don't say anything if you see him?'

'Discretion is my middle name, 215,' he says as he sits back behind his desk. 'Close the door on your way out.'

I walk away from the office and down one flight of stairs. I poke my head into the CID office to see if John is around, but I can't see him anywhere. He's probably in the custody suite. But the idea of going in there causes another wave of nausea to seize my stomach. I'll tell him tonight. The thought of sharing the news with him and Freddy brings another smile to my face. I head towards the station office as Andy rounds the corner in front of me.

'Where have you been?' he laughs, pushing a polystyrene cup into my hand. 'It's probably cold now.'

'Sorry, Andy, been to the loo.'

'Sounds like too much information to me,' he quips, holding his hands to his ears.

'Listen, I'm going to finish out the shift in the front office. I just can't face going back out there today.' I rummage in my pocket and pull out the car keys. They're warm as I place them into Andy's hand.

'No worries, mate,' he pats me on the back and we walk round together.

As soon as I walk into the station office my heart sinks. I can see right through to the reception area and there's a queue of around twenty irate-looking people lining up before the Perspex box that separates us from them. *Bloody hell.* Both of the phones are ringing and the probationer PC is standing in the middle of the office looking faint. He's got a penalty ticket in one hand and a bag of evidence in the other. He looks at us with hope in his eyes. Today his prayers have been answered.

'It's your lucky day,' I say to him, arms crossed. 'We're swapping, right now.'

His face lights up and his eyes flick between me and Andy, waiting for the punch line.

'I'm serious.' I nod to the door. 'Get out of here.' I can't help smiling at the look of delight on his face. He looks like he might pinch himself at any moment as he grabs his coat and radio and bounds towards the rear yard like a puppy on the way to the park.

Sighing, I walk slowly towards the reception desk and take a deep breath as I step out in front of the crowd.

'Who's next?' I shout.

A little old woman pushes away from the front of the queue. She's about 5 feet high with a grey top-knot and lipstick on her teeth. She shuffles towards me. I feel a little relieved as I lean onto the counter and duck my head towards her. A gentle one to start me off.

'How can I help you, madam?' I ask in a loud, clear voice.

Her head whips up and she looks me in the eye.

'I'm not bloody deaf.' She curses with a strong cockney accent. 'And I've been waiting in that sodding queue for twenty minutes.' A waft of stale cigarettes permeates the screen between us and I feel my stomach turn again.

I take a small step back.

'I'm sorry you've had a long wait, this is the busiest time of the day here in the police station. How can we help you?'

I wait as she sizes me up, one eye squinting as she gives me a good look over. Apparently deciding that I am qualified enough to deal with her complaint, she points outside towards the park.

'I want to know what you're going to do about those 'effing squirrels.'

I pause as a sense of hopeless weariness washes over me.

'Squirrels?' I enquire cautiously.

'Yes. Those sodding beasts are vicious. They're always fighting in the park and scaring my little Laddie.' She points outside again and as I look past her I can just make out a tiny, bedraggled-looking dog sitting outside.

'I want them reported.' She slams her fist on the desk and sets her jaw. I doubt she's going anywhere without a crime reference number.

The team will love this. I imagine telling them all about it later as I reach for a memo pad and biro. I instantly have a suggestion that I think will please the old lady, and also mean I don't have to create an intelligence report about squirrels.

'Thank you for letting us know, madam.' I take her particulars and note them down. 'The council caretakers are always grateful to receive intelligence like this. I'll pass on all of your details.'

She stands slightly straighter as I utter the word 'intelligence' and seems satisfied. I'm not about to tell a ninety-year-old that she's wasting our time.

'Thank you, officer.' Her top-knot shakes as she turns and walks towards the exit. I push the memo note to one side and call over the next impatient customer. Something about the look on his face tells me that he may also be here to report violent squirrels. He starts gesticulating and mumbling before he even reaches the counter. I take a deep breath and pull out my pen again.

It's going to be a long nine months.

20

Faith and Fury

They walk into court like chalk and cheese. I recognise them immediately and nudge John, who has his nose in a book beside me. He glances up.

'Jesus,' he murmurs. I take it that he's referring to the minuscule skirt and 6-inch heels that Fury has chosen as her 'court outfit'. Faith, in stark contrast, wears a tracksuit and trainers.

Without a close inspection of their faces I doubt anyone in the courthouse would suspect that they'd shared a womb. They'd come into this world only a year apart, and from what I had learnt about their lives so far, had pretty much only had each other to rely on ever since. I feel the familiar wave of sadness as I look at them. They haven't seen us yet, and I use the few minutes I have before they clock us to observe them. Faith is a large girl. Not fat, but solid; athletic and tall. Fury is smaller, but has adopted the essence of her name with a vengeance. She stands now, one manicured hand on a cocked hip, stilettoed feet planted wide, chin high as her eyes move around the room. She meets the gaze of anyone who looks her way with a defiant *and what*? Her legs are long, dark and shiny. My mind boggles at the fact that she's only thirteen years old. *Thirteen*. She could easily pass for twenty-five.

The laces on Faith's Nike trainers are tied in an unfathomable pattern that I'm guessing is incredibly cool. Her hair is scraped back, oiled and tight against her scalp, secured in a bun on top of her head. Her shoulders are bunched and she curls in on herself, hands shoved into the pockets of her tracksuit bottoms. For a moment I wonder if she's the shy one. But then I meet her gaze and realise that, when it comes to these girls, there is no shy one. She locks her eyes into mine. She's not hunching to make herself smaller. She's trying to control her rage. She stares out at me from under her brow, before cocking her head to the side and nudging her sister. Fury's gaze turns to mine and for a moment her face is blank. Then, slowly, a wide smile appears across her face. And she winks at me.

*   *   *

Five weeks earlier John and I shove through the back door of the nick, bursting gratefully into the fresh air. We've got exactly twenty minutes until our train leaves and it takes at least fifteen to get there on the underground. That's if we're lucky and hit the platforms at the right time. We're quick-stepping like speed walkers on, well, speed, as we turn into the busy market street that will take us down to the tube. Now that I've left the station my mind immediately switches to Mum mode. I've been back at work for just over three weeks, after taking nine months' maternity leave with our second son, Arnie. I suffered a second bout of post-natal depression and am back on the anti-depressants. I feel the familiar tightening across my chest at the thought that we might miss our train. If we miss the train, we miss the childminder's 'cut-off' and, if we miss that, we pay extra. Never mind the side order of guilt that Freddy and Arnie will be the last to be collected – again.

I swallow down the guilt and keep walking, ignoring the thought that now plagues me most days while I'm at work. *I can't do this any more.* I hate that I work an hour and a half away from my babies. I hate that I struggle with the shift-work, meaning I'm always tired. I hate that they get the brunt of my exhaustion. I hate the London I see through a copper's eyes and I hate that I can't forget the difficult jobs. I feel like a completely different person to the wide-eyed 23-year-old that walked into Hendon nine years ago. I'm thirty-two and the glamour of my job has most definitely worn off.

We weave quickly through crowds, heads down. It's in stark contrast to the way a police officer usually conducts themselves. *Always be aware of who's around you.* When I'm not rushing for a train I walk deliberately, looking at the people around me, clocking faces. It's amazing how many people never look up.

It's as I'm squeezing in between a fruit and veg stall and a slow fat man that my gaze is dragged from the ground by a scream. I look across to John and can tell he's heard it too. We keep walking but now we're straining our necks to try and see what's going on ahead of us. I weave into the middle of the road, where there are no cars due to its being market day, and the usually car-filled street is filled with stalls and shoppers. I can see a small clearing in the crowd ahead. In the clearing are about five or six schoolgirls. I breathe a sigh of relief.

'It's just school kids messing about, keep going,' I shout across to John as we keep fighting our way through the crowds towards the station. But as we draw level with the kids I can see that it's a little more than that. Two girls are fighting. Shoving and pulling hair. There's a flurry of violent movement as they shove each other around. They look around sixteen years old, one in a blue blazer and the other in a white shirt. White Shirt seems to be coming off worse. I pause, stopping just outside the circle of onlookers that has surrounded the fight. Immediately someone shoves into my back and I hear the frustrated grunt of someone behind me. I look ahead to John, who's turned to see why I've stopped. He shakes his head at me and jerks it in the direction of the train. I know exactly what he's trying to say. *It's just a silly school fight. Not worth it. We're going to be late.* And I'm about to do just that. I turn away from the brawling girls and step towards him. Just as a loud shout rings out and a splatter of blood squirts across the pavement, narrowly missing the toe of my left trainer.

I watch John's shoulders sag. I turn to see White Shirt sprawled across the pavement, clutching her face. *Fuck's sake.* And I realise that there's no walking away from this now. I look up at the CCTV cameras above us. If I walk away I could lose my job. *I want to go home and see my baby.* What if she's seriously hurt? I don't want to split up a fight without any kit. I look at the older males on the edges of the fight, shouting support for the aggressor that has knocked the girl to the floor. I look at the tattoos on their faces, the low-slung tracksuit bottoms and bandanas. *What if they have knives?* But my decision is already made and I find myself pushing forcefully through the crowds. Blue Blazer seems happy with her performance and is fist-bumping her supporters, sticking out her chest and grabbing her crotch. They mimic her and for a moment they look like a troop of demented Michael Jackson fans. I've nearly reached them when, to my amazement, White Shirt drags herself off of the floor and throws herself back into the fray. *Victim, my arse.* She tears ferociously at Blue Blazer's hair and starts dragging her to the ground.

I clear the last few feet or so in a run and shout 'Police' at the top of my voice. I lace a foot in between the two girls and use the flat of my palm to shove White Shirt in the centre of the chest. She stumbles backwards, creating the distance I need to put myself between them, but Blue Blazer is already up and gunning for her again. I place an arm across her chest to stop her from reaching her target. Her face is inches from mine and I can see just how young she is, her skin unmarred by wrinkles or flaws. She smells like cigarettes and coconut. She pushes against me and I have to plant my feet wide to stop her from pushing me over. *Shit, she's strong.* John steps into the clearing from the other side and holds out his warrant card, shouting 'Police!

Stop fighting!' and instantly I feel the crowd change around me. The Blue Blazer supporters shrink back and I hear whispers of words like 'feds' and 'po-pos' murmur around the group.

I glance up at the CCTV cameras again and silently pray that they've seen us. I wonder if anyone in the crowd has thought to call the police. We're literally metres away from our colleagues, just around the corner from the nick, yet completely alone. I feel a keen vulnerability as I stand in the centre of the group in my ballet pumps and leggings, handbag strewn across my chest, hair loose and streaking across my face. Usually Blue Blazer would be in cuffs by now. *I'm lost without them.* I wonder whether I can get to my phone but the thought is rendered ridiculous as Blue Blazer continues to push against me. Suddenly White Shirt is at my back and they're going at it again, this time with me sandwiched in the middle.

'Police! Stop fighting or you will all get arrested!' I push my arms out in front of me in an effort to separate them. I look round to see where John is, wondering why he's not helping me, but I can't see him anywhere. I'm starting to wonder how we will ever get this fight under control when Blue Blazer's double steps up beside her and starts shoving White Shirt in the chest. I am momentarily stunned by the appearance of a clone. They are dressed exactly the same, even down to the way they've knotted their school ties. My eyes flick from one to the other and I am hit by the realisation of who I'm looking at. *The Sisters.* I've seen their faces staring out at me from countless briefings. *Violence. Weapons. Gang connections.* I don't know much about them, except for one thing. They're notorious. And, in this borough, you don't get to be notorious for nothing.

The pressure of White Shirt pressing onto my back is suddenly released and I hear John behind me, shouting at her to calm down. Now I can concentrate fully on the sisters. I stand in front of them and push them back, one hand in the centre of each of their chests. They're all shouting about who started it, each blaming the other, and I can see bruising on one of the sisters' faces. *Cross-allegations*. I sigh inwardly and realise that we'll have to arrest all three. But how? The sisters' friends have started pulling them away from us. Now that it has become common knowledge that we're police officers they seem keen to leave.

I can hear White Shirt crying behind me. 'They just jumped me, they're fucking psychos.'

A man from the sidelines. 'No, she started it! The one in the white shirt!'

A stall owner shouts back. 'They're trouble-makers, those two, I've seen them before.'

The crowd explodes into pointing and noise and everybody's shouting at once. I can hear John trying to restore order and I reach into my bag for my phone, keeping my eyes on the sisters as they start to back away. I press triple 9 and hold the receiver to my ear.

'999 emergency, what service do you require?'

'Police, please.'

'Connecting you now.'

I wait while the controller reads my mobile number to the police call handler.

'Caller, you are now connected to the police. What is your emergency?'

'Off-duty police officer in need of assistance.' I raise my voice to be heard above the shouting and the words come out of my mouth in a calm, automated voice. '215BX, requiring assistance on the hurry-up to Church Market, Brixley, dealing with a fight.'

'All received, 215BX, we have units on the way to you. Can you give me any more information about what's going on there?'

'Fight between schoolgirls, injuries received—'
I pause as sirens pierce the air. And the girls start to run.

Hesitation freezes me. I take a couple of steps after them as they jog away from me. Glancing back to John, I see he is dealing with a wildly gesticulating shopkeeper and White Shirt, who has dissolved from world-class prize fighter to wailing toddler. I press the phone to my cheek and glance at the faces surrounding me. I feel, rather than hear, their judgements. *She's letting them get away.* I pause, and the pressure to act stretches each second into hours. The mother in me has her say. *Let them run. You have no kit. It's not safe to chase them on your own.* White Shirt can identify them anyway. But the copper's not so easy to talk down. My adrenalin is pumping. I'm breathing heavily through my nose and my gaze is locked to the girls' backs. *They're getting away. They can't just fight in the street and get away with it. You're a copper – act like it.*

'215BX, are you still there? Update please?'

The operator's voice buzzes in my ear and I realise that my phone is still pressed to my face. I begin to jog after the girls. My large handbag immediately starts slapping into my stomach and I clamp it to my side with one arm, careful to hold my phone tightly in the other.

'Chasing suspects—' and I am about to describe the girls when a large man steps into my path. I screech to a halt, narrowly avoiding slamming into him. He's taller than me and skinny. He's wearing a bright red bandana under a black baseball cap and as he glares down at me he sucks his teeth loudly. I've seen him before, goading the girls from behind as they pummelled White Shirt, and I realise exactly what he's doing. He opens his mouth but I don't give him a chance to speak. Mother runs for cover as copper wins out. I heel-palm strike him directly in the chest and dart around him as he stumbles backwards in shock.

I set off at a full run after the girls who, luckily for me, are still jogging casually away. I grin as I think of the look on the thug's face, and wonder if it was the ballet shoes, handbag and flowery dress that made him think he could mess with me. As I close the gap between myself and the sisters I feel the familiar rush of adrenalin of a chase. Sirens wail around me. I need to tell them where to go. I can't see them, but knowing they're coming is enough. Knowing that right now, I'm the point at the centre. I'm the point that my colleagues are looking for, the point that's *one of them*. The feeling of camaraderie boosts my nerve and my speed increases. I pick up my commentary.

'Chasing suspects,' I pant into the receiver, 'two girls, around sixteen years, both wearing blue school blazers, grey skirts, black hair tied back, one carrying an orange bag – southwards now on Church Market – they'll be coming out on Angel Street.'

I've closed the gap to about 3 metres when one of the girls looks back over her shoulder. At exactly the same moment, a patrol car appears ahead of them at the end of the street. Their reaction is instantaneous. They sprint to the left and down a side alley. *Shit*.

'Suspects going left – left down an alley towards Sainsbury's car park.'

It's no surprise to me that they're faster. I'm already feeling myself beginning to tire and I pump my legs to maintain speed. As I turn into the alley I see that they're already at the end of it, turning right towards the supermarket. It's as I'm reaching the end of the alley that John runs past me and takes the lead. Running's never been my strong point. I'd rather not let people run in the first place than have to chase them.

'Officers are on scene now. I'm disconnecting.' I hang up and shove my phone back into my bag. I need at least one free hand. Silent and fast, we cross the car park, the girls darting into the side entrance of the store. John follows them in.

'I'll go round the front,' I shout towards him as I run past, planning to catch them as they come out of the main entrance. I race to the front of the store and wait at the bottom of the steps, panting and holding my knees. *God, I need to shift this baby weight.* Five, maybe ten, seconds pass. *They should be out by now.* I stand on the pavement and scan the entrance. No sign of them. I wonder where the uniforms from Church Market have gone. They saw me chasing, why aren't they here?

Frustrated, I wish for the millionth time that I had my radio. That I could communicate directly with the officers around me. I glance up and down the street but can't see any back-up. I hear another siren, but it sounds like it's going the wrong way. *What the fuck?* I can't leave my position. Maybe John has detained them inside the store? I reach once again for my phone and dial his number. No answer. *No surprise there.* I sigh and cross my arms, just as a PCSO wanders around the corner. My temper flares as I look at him. *Is he even listening to his radio?* I gape at the fact that he seems to be bumbling along, lost in his own thoughts, in the middle of a police chase. I grab his shoulder and shove my warrant card in his face. Unlike most of my colleagues, I don't hate PCSOs for the sake of it. I've met some extremely dedicated and professional ones during my time in the Met. But, right now, I hate this one and his lack of any awareness. And I don't have time to be polite.

'I need to borrow your radio,' I say and I twist it off of his Met vest in one smooth motion. He begins to protest but I turn away from him, keeping one eye on the store front as I talk.

'BX, this is 215, I'm using a PCSO's radio. I'm off duty – involved in the Church Market chase.' They really should know all of this, but it doesn't hurt to make sure. 'Suspects are currently inside Sainsbury's, Angel Street. Can I get a unit here please?'

'Received, 215.'

The static cuts out as the operator speaks again.

'215, we have an officer safety update for you.'

My body tenses. 'Go ahead.'

'We have witnesses who claim to have seen a large knife being brandished by a tall IC3 male after you left the scene. You need to be aware that weapons have been seen.'

My blood runs cold. I think of the man that stepped into my path. 'Have you got a description?' I ask, secretly hoping it won't match.

'Yeah – IC3 male, 6 feet plus, skinny, red bandana, baseball cap.'

I close my eyes briefly. 'Has anyone got him detained?'

'That's a negative, 215, he has not been located.'

'Received.' I puff out my cheeks as my mind whirls.

'You have officers in the vicinity – we're going to cancel the urgent assistance, now that you are safe and accounted for.'

And before I have a chance to reply, he is making an all-cars announcement to the borough.

'All cars, all cars, urgent assistance now cancelled to Church Market, officer safe and accounted for.'

Cars start to call out their replies, confirming that they've received the cancellation, blocking the airways, so that I have to repeatedly press the speak button to get back on air. I try and control the anger and panic building inside me as I speak again.

'BX from 215, there is an officer outstanding, I repeat, there is an officer unaccounted for. Do not cancel the urgent assistance.' *My husband's out there somewhere. And there's a guy with a knife looking to spring the girls he's trying to detain.*

'215, confirm which officer please?'

'It's my—' and I nearly say it's my husband. I pull myself back just in time. 'It's DC John Vinten. Last time I saw him he was following the suspects into Sainsbury's.'

I look up at the entrance as a uniformed police officer walks out. I don't recognise him. So many officers go through response team these days it's hard to keep track.

He looks to me and shakes his head, reaching his radio to his lips, and then I can hear his voice on the radio.

'That's a negative in Sainsbury's, BX, they're not in here.' I gape in confusion. *Where the hell are they?* The officers continues. 'The security guards have seen the suspect with the red bandana however. Apparently he ran in and then ran out again, from the side entrance, a few minutes ago.'

I go still as I realise what this means. *He's looking for them.* I fumble my phone from my bag and punch John's number again. *Please pick up.* No answer. The PC joins us and we stand on the street, looking up and down it like John and the girls might just magically appear somewhere. The PCSO coughs to get my attention and asks if he can have his radio back. I look at him like he's insane.

'My driver's out scoping round the block – they'll turn up.' The PC looks concerned. We both know what the result could be if the red bandana reaches John before one of us does.

The radio comes to life again.

'215, receiving Bravo X-ray?'

'Go ahead.'

'999 operators have received a call from the Angel hotel, staff say there's a white male who says he's a police officer detaining two youths.'

'Received, we're on our way.'

I throw the radio back to the PCSO and bolt towards the hotel. I may not think much of his policing skills, but I'm not about to abandon him without a radio, and I'm pretty sure he's not going to follow us. The PC matches me step for step. I hear several units assign themselves, their call signs blaring out from the PC's radio as we run.

Luckily the hotel is just round the corner and we get there a few minutes later. A patrol car has beaten us to it and the sisters stand, handcuffed, against the wall. Another PC that I don't recognise, this one female, is arresting them. She's very formal and I guess that she's new.

'I'm arresting you both on suspicion of affray, assault and assault on police.'

Assault on police. I wander into the reception of the hotel and find John sitting on one of the leather sofas. I note the wet patches on his suit. His tie is twisted and misshapen, the silk wrinkled, and the knot has been pulled so tight it is tiny. I'm just relieved he hasn't been stabbed.

'Didn't I tell you that clip-on ties would be better than real ones?' I say lightly.

He grimaces at me and whispers. 'My balls hurt.'

I stifle a laugh, covering my mouth with my hand. 'Oh God, what did they do to your balls?'

Another PC approaches and offers us a lift back to the station so we can write our statements. 'I'll tell you later,' John mumbles.

As we get into the back of the patrol car I catch him wince as he sits down. I feel a stab of sympathy.

'I'm sorry,' I say, patting him on the hand, quickly, before the other coppers climb in. 'You OK?'

He nods.

As we pull away I lean over to him and whisper, 'At least we've already had kids.'

He rolls his eyes.

*   *   *

As I sit waiting for the case against the sisters to begin, I remember feeling shocked when I learnt just how young they were. It was only after we had arrived back at the station and I was able to access their records on the Police National Computer that I realised they were only thirteen and fourteen. *Thirteen and fourteen.* I felt an odd range of emotions as the information sank in. Shock merged into disbelief, which in turn merged into a vague sense of shame that two girls so young had made me feel so threatened.

I watch the girls walk into court with their solicitor – Fury strutting fiercely ahead of Faith, who shuffles behind, swaggering heavily on her right foot, arms casting wide as she adopts the swagger I see every day on the streets of Brixley. There's no family to support them. They're alone but for a duty solicitor, who looks haggard and over-worked. I stretch and twist in the hard wooden chair, trying to get more comfortable. The waiting room in Brixley magistrate's court is not designed for comfort. Everything is screwed down. The floor is wood, highly varnished; easy to wipe clean. The strip lights cast a pallid orange shade over everyone that has the misfortune to be here. I give up on the chair and stand up, pacing across to the court notices and back again. John's head is still buried in his novel, and I wonder how he can concentrate on it at a time like this.

Despite having giving evidence countless times, I still get nervous. I'm not sure whether it is the fear of public speaking, or the vague feeling that I'm always going to be caught out that makes me perspire before each court appearance. *Why do I always feel like I have something to hide?* I've done nothing wrong. I'm a good copper. Maybe it's the fact that, from day one at Hendon, we're taught that everyone is out to get us. *The press. The public. The barristers.* They'll twist your words. They'll get under your skin. Everyone is looking to bring you down. *Never apologise. Never admit you are at fault.* It's an attitude that's got many an officer in trouble, and it's one that I firmly believe needs to change. *Integrity and transparency.* Yeah, right.

I'm still pacing when the usher pops his head around the door and calls John's name. He walks confidently into the courtroom, throwing me a smile over his shoulder as he goes. I lower myself back into the torture instruments that pass as chairs and cup my face in my hands. I just can't shake the feeling that I'm not supposed to be here. I know what I'm here to do. I'm here to give evidence, state what I've witnessed, so that the suspects inside that court room can be prosecuted. I'm fully aware of my role. Trouble is, I just can't see the point of it. More than that; I don't actually believe that I'm doing the right thing.

I think back to the day of the incident. After we'd written our statements and handed the sisters detention over to the on-duty CID team, we headed home. Four hours after our shift was originally due to end, we stepped once more into Church Market. The stalls were gone and the street was nearly empty. We headed home in weary silence. By the time we got there, Freddy and Arnie were already in bed, tucked in and cared for by my mother-in-law. I headed straight for their bedroom, and stood over them, watching their chests rise and fall. Listening to their snuffled breathing. I gazed at their clean, soft bedding, their brightly painted bunk bed. Their toys, their books, and their freshly combed hair. And, as I kissed each of their foreheads, whispering 'I love you' into their ears, I thought of the girls. I wondered if anyone had ever told them they were loved. I wondered if their sheets were freshly laundered, if they had someone to comb their hair.

The next day I looked the girls up. I trawled the Police National Computer, reading each and every offence they had ever been arrested for. *Shoplifting, drunk and disorderly, public order, assaults, possession cannabis.* I searched Merlin, the system used to record concerns about children's welfare, missing people and child protection issues. Each time an officer attends a call where children are present, or that concerns a child, or where a child has been arrested, they must complete a 'come to notice' record. They should assess the child's living conditions and detail any concern they have regarding the child's care. There were pages and pages of reports. In such short lives, the girls had come to the notice of the authorities countless times. I read every single report.

They were placed on the at risk register before they were

even born, due to their mum's drug addictions. By the time Fury was born, police had attended their house multiple times in response to domestic violence calls. They were present as their dad beat up their mother, time and again, throughout their formative early years. It was noted that the girls slept in travel cots with stained bedding. There was a lack of food and toys in the house. Their bedroom smelt like urine. They were placed on the at risk register, but remained in their parents' care. When they were aged around five and six, their mother accused their father of sexually abusing them. I read the crime report, the intelligence report, and the Merlin, and learnt that the allegations were believed to be malicious. It wasn't taken any further.

Their father left the family home a couple of years later. The girls remained in their mother's care for the next few years, as she took in a series of drunk, abusive boyfriends. They were frequently found, underdressed, wandering the streets. Police presence at their house was frequent, as various stepfathers were arrested, dragged from the house stinking of booze, kicking and screaming. The council saw them as a 'problem family' and they were moved around the borough time and again. They were often absent from school. Eventually, aged eleven and twelve, they were taken into care, after their mother refused to split up with a known sex-offender, instead inviting him to live in with her and the girls. There wasn't a foster family who were prepared to take two sisters who were now labelled as 'problems'. So they were put into a home. Fury immediately ran away and was missing for six weeks before the authorities found her sleeping in a seventeen-year-old's flat. Apparently he was her boyfriend.

I needed to see everything, was hooked on the tragic story of their lives. I had spent most of the day hunched over my computer screen, only leaving to visit the loo, where I would rub my face and stare at my reflection in the mirror. I wasn't getting any work done. But I didn't care. I worked hard 99 per cent of the time. I looked at every custody image of them. Watched the soft rounds of their cheeks change to rouged cheekbones. Watched the curly hair stretch straight and slick against their foreheads, as piercings peppered their ears and noses. I had to constantly remind myself of their tender age. They looked so much older. No one would guess they were only in their early teens. As I approached the most recent reports I noticed a shift in tone. Officers were no longer concerned about vulnerable children; instead they warned others of violent and unpredictable criminals.

It's the last few reports that stick in my mind as I sit outside the courtroom, awaiting my turn to damn them. Each one details the girls being found in the company of older boys, some as old as twenty-five. They've been found with condoms in their pockets and have been sexually suggestive to male officers during stops. A few weeks before I chased them down Church Market, police had been called by a concerned member of the public. It was one o'clock in the morning. She stated that there were a group of lads in an alleyway with two young girls. She could hear what she described as sex noises. Police had attended and taken the details of those present. It was the sisters. They denied any sexual activity and no allegations were made. Officers noted that the alley smelt strongly of cannabis. A Come To Notice report was created and no further action was taken by police. I had recounted the intelligence report to one of my colleagues in the office, shaking my head in horror.

'Is that Fury and Faith?' I turned to see a member of the Youth Offending Team I hadn't met before standing behind me. Before I could answer, she continued, 'What a pair of slags!'

I saw red. I was on my feet before I could consider whether it was wise to make a scene.

'They're children.' I stared down at her; she smirked and rolled her eyes.

'They know exactly what they're doing, fucking scum they are.'

'What the *fuck*?' The office went quiet as I swore loudly. 'You're YOTS? You're supposed to be helping kids like these!' I was doing my best not to be aggressive when what I really wanted to do is smack the idiotic bitch in the face.

'They're a lost cause!' She looked shocked at the idea that I would even think of disagreeing with her. 'Trust me, I've been dealing with them for years, they're way past my help.'

'They're *kids*!' I was almost yelling.

'Yeah, and they're out every night fucking anything that moves.' She looked around her, looking for someone to back her up. The office stayed silent.

'I think what you actually mean is they're out every night *getting raped*?' I paused and watched my words take effect.

'Because that's what sex with a thirteen-year-old child is, isn't it?'

I already knew that I wouldn't get an answer. She flung up her arms. 'I don't need to listen to this shit,' she huffed, and stormed out of the office.

I had sunk back into my chair, covering my face in my hands until my skipper suggested I go get some fresh air. 'You can't let these things get to you,' he'd said, and he'd meant it in kindness. But as I had left the office, grabbing my coat and phone on the way, my mind was still churning. Because if we didn't let these things get to us, then who would?

*   *   *

I give my evidence in court that day. I stand in the witness box and will myself to talk to the magistrate. I will myself to speak up. I want to say *what is the point?* I want to ask him how prosecuting these girls will help to break the cycle. I want to tell him about their history, to tell him to let them off. But I am scared. *Am I allowed to say these things? Will I get in trouble?* And as they sit across from me, huddled in the grand wooded panels of the court room, they look incredibly small. Suddenly they look exactly the ages they are. They don't smirk at me, as I thought they might. They just watch. Watch as I answer the solicitors' questions. Watch as I describe their violent behaviour. Watch as I do my job and am excused, leaving the room without so much as a glance over my shoulder.

21

Lily Again

We're sitting in the café at the start of an early shift. I stifle a yawn with my hand and rub my cheeks to try and wake myself up. Arnie has just turned two and still wakes me up in the night. Freddy will be five in July, only two months away. I was up and out of the house this morning before they were even awake. I'm wondering how early I can get to bed tonight when the conversation turns to the next available advanced driving course. The highest level of driving that you can apply for. It's a step up from basic response driving. It puts you in the driver's seat of the most powerful car on team.

'I'm next in line. I should get it,' says Dave, one of the longest-serving response car drivers. Apart from me.

'Yeah, you're probably right. But I'm still going to apply, mate. No offence!' James claps Dave on the back and guffaws loudly, trying to dissipate the tension that is building across the tables. Driving courses are few and far between right now and it's dog eat dog when it comes to getting them.

'Yeah, good luck with that, James,' Dave shrugs him off,

313

his grin not quite reaching his eyes, 'but you actually have to have done something worth writing about in your application to get the course.'

A laugh jostles around the tables. Everybody knows that Dave is desperate for the course. He's been pipped to the post twice and is determined that, this time, the area car course will have his name on it. And no matter what they say about giving the course to the person with the best application, it always comes down to who the top brass thinks deserves it, generally the person with the most service. After my second lot of maternity leave, I was surprised to return to work and find myself with the longest service on team. I've been in the Met for nine years now. Dave comes in a close second, at eight years, but he's transferred into Brixley within the last year and the governor doesn't know him as well as he knows me.

'What about me?' I look Dave right in the eyes as I ask. Watch as they crease with confusion. The rest of the team grow quiet.

'You serious?'

He's still smiling, but the hand that has been fiddling with the sugar packets in the pot in front of him falls still. I smile back, trying to keep the conversation jovial. Acting like I've only just considered it. When, in reality, I've been seriously considering it since the course was advertised. I've even started drafting an application. I've started to think about my long game. I've always loved being on team, being in the thick of it; answering 999 calls and being out and about amongst the public. But things have changed.

I've changed. Most of the time I just want to get the job done and get home to my kids. I don't do team drinking any more – the banter mostly just pisses me off. And I've already dismissed the idea of going to the armed response teams. I doubt I could even get the childcare for the six weeks live-in training that's required, let alone make the shifts work with my childminder. So, I've been thinking about driving. I did well in my response course and I still love to drive. It's the one thing that hasn't grown old in my nine years on the force. The thrill of driving blues and twos. I think I'd like to be a driving instructor, and the first step to achieving that goal would be the advanced driving course.

'Why not?' I keep my voice light, wondering why the fuck I should have to but doing it anyway. 'I've got more service than you. Technically I'm next in line.'

I watch the annoyance crawl across Dave's face as he realises that I could be serious. But it's not just him.

'You're hardly ever here!' This is Ralph, speaking up from the other end of the table. A series of nods from the rest of them. I feel shocked that even the female team members are nodding. But then, before I became a mother, before I had to go part-time, would I have been nodding too?

'I'm here 60 per cent of the time. Although if you look at the figures you couldn't tell me from a full-time officer.' I smirk at this. No one denies it.

'But the course would be wasted on you.' Dave says it gently. Like he's telling a four-year-old she can't have another ice-lolly. 'You're only part-time.'

I feel a wave of rage, nostrils full of bacon fumes, a trickle of hot sweat tracking down behind my Met vest.

'So, what? I'm not a valued member of this team because I'm *only* part-time?' I look up and down the table and meet the eyes of the young female probationers. A long way from settling down, they have glazed and disinterested eyes. This isn't their problem. And I think, *Just wait. Just you wait.*

Nobody answers, so I carry on. 'So that's it for me, is it? I'm done?' I know I'm raising my voice but I don't care any more. I've spent my whole career not speaking up. And suddenly it's all about not being able to eat a banana in the police canteen without being subjected to blow-job comments. It's about being called a Doris. It's being pulled aside at Hendon and told not to get too drunk, in case you *encourage* unwanted attention from the groups of men that you work with, because they can't possibly be responsible for their own urges. It's being pulled off a suspect that you're doing a perfectly good job restraining, because *the boys* are here now. It's the comments about the team *bike* and how many coppers she's had. It's the covert radio signals that share the location of a scantily clad office worker in summer. It's being *one of the lads* until you realise that you're not, because you can't bend over in uniform without someone commenting on your arse. It's the intimate pictures of ex-girlfriends that get passed around the nick. It's being told to deal with the calls involving kids of female rape victims because *that's what women do.* It's sitting on a carrier and listening to the hard-core porn someone is sharing at the front of the bus and having to be fine with it. And then having it shoved in your face and trying to pretend that it doesn't make you uncomfortable. Sometimes, it's just being the only woman in the room.

The rest of the team are staring at the table-top and shifting in their seats. I stand up, in full flow. 'Well, sod my career aspirations then – I'll just put my career on hold because I'm part-time and *heaven forbid* I *should* want to take a course from you full-timers who do all the sodding work? Is that it?'

I finally stop and glare around the café, hands on my hips, our area at the back thankfully clear of the public. I'm almost willing someone to make a joke about my having my period so that I can really let rip. A beat of silence before I feel a warm hand on my shoulder. It's Andy. 'That's pretty much it, girl, yeah.'

He seems to have relieved the tension and the team deflates into chuckles. But I'm not in the mood to acquiesce. I stalk from the café, pausing only to bark at my operator as I walk out of the door. 'Julia!' I hear a chair scrape back as Julia jumps up to follow me. We climb into the car together and I smile at her to ease the tension. It's not her fault.

It's a Sunday early turn and it's quiet. We spend the first few hours of the shift clearing up left-over calls from the night before. Attending burglaries, taking reports. But even while going about my duties, the conversation in the café runs through my mind. I realise that this could be one of the first times I've really experienced the consequences of sexism. The viscerally disappointing, tangibly debilitating effect it has on women.

Sure, I've been surrounded by it throughout my entire career; I've seen it, watched it, heard about it and probably even contributed to it. But I've never actually felt it. So far, it's slid right by me. *Because now you're a mother, too. How dare you want it all?* My attitude towards it during my twenties, like the probationers who sat silently in the café this morning, was nothing more than that's the way it is. But now, as we drive up and down the borough of Brixley, my fingers gripping the steering wheel so that my knuckles glow white, I'm furious. I'm furious at the Met for letting it happen. I'm furious at a world that puts people in categorised boxes and then stacks them, one on top of each other, in worthiness height-order. And I'm ashamed. Ashamed at myself for not caring until it affected me directly.

It's nearly 10 a.m. when the first 'I' graded call of the day comes out over the radio.

'I grade now to Wellington Park where a member of the public is concerned about a drunk male in charge of two very young children.'

I nod to Julia and she assigns us to the call as I flip on the lights and sirens, pulling a wide U-turn. The location is only a couple of minutes away and Julia reads out the description of the male as we quickly approach – a white male, dressed in blue jeans and a red hoody, pushing a black pram with a baby and a small, blonde-haired girl.

When I first saw Wellington Park I remember being surprised that a sparse patch of grass surrounded by heavily graffitied benches actually had a name. Barely a park at all, it's known for attracting groups of youths who like to smoke cannabis there at night. Despite it being fairly early on a Sunday morning, the traffic is still thick on London Road, the main north/south route of Brixley. I weave my way through the cars and vans as patiently as I can. I desperately don't want the male to have left the scene before we get there. I need to know those kids are OK. As usual, when dealing with any call that involves kids, my two boys pop into my mind, and I push them to the back. *They're not here. They're fine.*

As the entrance of the park comes into view, I can see the man with the pram standing at the edge of the road. I cut my sirens. I don't want to startle him, especially when he's so close to the traffic. It only takes a glance to see that he is inebriated. His feet are glued to the pavement but the top half of his body waves like a sapling in the breeze. He's looking down at a small girl who is standing beside him. She has one hand placed obediently on the side of the buggy. He's got one hand on the handle and the other is clutching a beer can. I park as close as it's safe to do so, not intending to block up the traffic any more than I have to, and we both hop out of the car. It doesn't look like the man has even noticed our presence, and as we walk towards him he begins to push the pram out into the road.

Immediately a horn sounds and the male jolts the buggy to the side, causing the baby within to jerk forward onto the soft bar that thankfully encloses it. I realise that the male isn't going to stop trying to cross the road. I start running towards him. The baby looks around eighteen months old and he's not strapped in. The man continues to swerve the buggy into the traffic as I start shouting at him to stop. He groggily looks at me as I close in on him.

'Get off the road!' I shout at him as I place a hand on the buggy, pushing it backwards onto the pavement. He tries to focus on my face but his eyes don't seem to be cooperating. I look to the girl, hoping that I haven't scared her. She looks around seven years old, with blonde hair that's cut in a short bob. She's extremely cute, and she doesn't appear scared of me at all. In fact, she looks at me like I'm the cavalry. And as I look at her face, which is round and grubby, an odd sensation of déjà vu overcomes me.

I saw Daddy hitting Mummy and now I'm panicking.

The words I'll always remember, and she's standing in front of me. I push my foot down onto the brake of the buggy and turn to look at the male. A vision of him shouting and spitting at the back of the police van. The purple welts on his girlfriend's face. Julia has him engaged and he's fully compliant. I turn back to the girl and bend over so that my face is level with hers.

'Lily?' Her eyes widen and her mouth forms a tiny 'o'.

'How do you know my name?' She stares at me like I'm a magician.

'I was once at your house, a long time ago. You were very little then.'

'I don't think I remember.' She twists her mouth as if she's trying to think. 'Lots of policemen come to our house.'

I can hear Julia talking to the male behind me. He's slurring his words.

'How old are you, Lily?'

'I'm eight.' She smiles proudly. She is small for her age, but her voice is every inch the eight-year-old.

'Is that your dad?'

'Yes.' Lily rolls her eyes.

'And who's this?' I turn to the baby in the buggy. He's wearing a short-sleeved vest with thin bottoms. His feet are bare. It's a chilly morning in May and his fair skin is red and blotchy from the cold.

'Bobby. He's my baby brother.' Lily pats one of his chubby hands and he starts to cry.

I coo at Bobby, leaning forward to scoop him out of the buggy. I turn to see how his father will react to me holding his child, but he is staggering towards a nearby bench with Julia in tow. I notice a dark stain on the back of his trousers and wrinkle my nose. Bobby starts to squirm against me and I can feel his heavy nappy squishing under my hands. Instinctively I start to bob him up and down, shushing him under my breath. His soft skin presses against the Kevlar of my Met vest and I unzip it, pulling the front flaps open to nestle him against the warm cotton of my shirt. As I hold him to me I can smell his nappy, the acrid smell of stale urine. He starts to quiet. I look back to Lily and something tugs at my memory.

Two girls, messy blonde mops framing their round faces, one bigger than the other.

'Where's your little sister, Lily?'

'She lives with my grandma now.' She twists her little hands together and tugs at the light material of her dress. It's pretty; covered in pink and blue flowers, but it's far too small for her. Over the top she wears an oversized, dirty denim jacket. Her feet are covered by battered trainers. No socks. I'm thankful she at least has a coat. Bobby starts to cry again and wriggles furiously against my chest. He is stuffing his fists into his mouth, gumming at them wildly. I peer underneath the buggy in the hope that there will be a bottle for him somewhere. But the net underneath is completely empty. There's no blankets, no changing bag, nothing. When did these children last eat?

Over my shoulder, I can hear Julia conducting a name check on Lily's dad. I switch my radio over to channel two to listen to the result, making sure to keep it low and close to my ear.

"Mark JACOBS, known to police, not currently wanted, flashes "V" and "M"."

The letters refer to warning signals. 'V' tells me that the male is known for violent offences, something I already know, and the 'M' refers to mental health issues. The model father. I switch back to the main channel, keeping my back to Lily, and speak low into my radio.

'BX, receiving 215.'

'Go ahead, 215.'

'I need the van to Wellington Park please. Can you also check that there's space in custody for an adult male, coming in for child neglect?'

'That's all received, 215.'

'Can you also let BX3 know that we'll be taking two children into police protection, a girl aged eight and a boy aged approximately one and a half – can you get in touch with social services, please?'

'Will do, 215, all received and noted.'

There's no way I'm leaving these kids with their father. BX3 are the on-duty sergeants and I'm notifying them as part of procedure. I look over to where Julia is standing over Jacobs. She's looking at me with her hand on her radio. She gives me a slight nod and I know that she's heard. I hold out my palm to her, signalling her to wait for me before she makes a move.

Bobby is still crying and it breaks my heart to have to put him back in his cold buggy. But I can't let Julia deal with Jacobs on her own, and I can't risk taking him over to his father. I plop him down on the seat and pull the straps across his chest and up between his legs, clicking the buckles into place, and giving them a little tug to make sure they're secure. I turn to Lily. 'Can you watch your brother for a moment while I go speak to your daddy?'

Lily nods and places her hand on Bobby's shoulder. She starts rubbing and hushing him and she's good at it. Something tells me she's had to be. I walk across to Julia and Jacobs. I stand in front of him and he looks up at me from his slumped position on the bench.

'Mr Jacobs states that he has only had a couple of cans of beer this morning.' Julia folds her arms and tilts her head at Jacobs, who nods at me hopefully.

'Well that's a load of rubbish, isn't it, Mr Jacobs?' I point to the wet patch on his jeans. 'You're wasted.'

He starts shaking his head, 'No, officer, no, no,' and he repeats the word no over and over again as he covers his face with his hands, shaking and shaking his head. I look back at the kids and think about Bobby's stinking nappy. I think about his hungry cries and his cold little toes. I think about everything that Lily has seen in her short life. And anger boils up in my chest. I'd usually try and keep a suspect calm until the van arrives. Keep them agreeable with small talk and smiles, until the last minute, until the moment the cuffs go on. But something about this call has snapped the reasonable person inside me.

'When did Bobby last eat?' My fists are balled at my sides, arms straight.

Jacobs continues to shake his head.

I bend over and grab him by the shoulders roughly. I shout into his face. 'When did you last feed your children?' *You wife-beating piece of shit.*

He opens his hands and gapes at me, his face streaked with tears. 'I – I don't know, d-dinner time?'

'Dinner time last fucking night?' I'm still shouting. Still holding his shoulders, my face inches from his. For the first time in my career I feel dangerously close to punching a suspect in the face.

Julia clears her throat. I glance to her and she nods towards the other side of the street, where a few people have stopped to watch us. I immediately let go of Jacobs and stand back, panting. *What the fuck just happened?* I turn to look at Lily and she looks away as I meet her gaze. *Shit.* My chest aches. My chest aches and I'm sweating and all I want to do is get in the sodding car and drive back to the nick. Chuck my uniform in my locker and get on a train back to my boys. And never come back.

I hear the roar of a heavy diesel engine as the van pulls up behind me. I look back to Jacobs. He's openly sobbing. 'I'm sorry, I'm sorry,' he shouts towards Lily and Bobby, 'Daddy's sorry!' he stands and staggers towards them.

'Woah, there.' I take hold of his left arm and Julia is there grabbing his right. He pushes against us, starts calling Lily's name. Her face is small and pale, and she moves behind the buggy, her hand still resting on Bobby's shoulder. I bring my mouth close to Jacobs's ear.

'Mark.' He stops calling and looks at me. 'Just get in the van. I don't want to have to cuff you in front of them. You know you're in no state to look after them like this.'

He pushes forward another step and for a moment I think he's going to make a break towards them. But then his shoulders sag and he nods. 'I was doing better.' His voice is wet and snot is dripping from his nose. As we walk him round to the rear of the van, and out of sight of the kids, his body begins to rack with sobs. 'I was on the wagon.'

I reach up and open the cage. Mark climbs in obediently. He sits on the bench and turns to me as I push the grille closed. He looks me right in the eye. 'Please. Don't take my kids.'

'You know it's not up to me, Mark.' I step back and take hold of the van doors, 'It's up to social services. But, right now, they're better off without you.'

* * *

Lily is excited to be in a police car. She's chatted non-stop since we got in and is showing no signs of stopping as I drive slowly through the Sunday traffic. Sitting in the back with Julia and Bobby, she fiddles with her seatbelt as she talks.

'Can you put the lights and nee-naws on?'

I glance at her over my shoulder. 'Honey, can you leave your seatbelt alone, please? It's there to keep you safe.'

Her hands drop into her lap. Her little face falls and I instantly feel guilty for chastising her. 'I tell you what, when we get to the police station I'll let you press the magic button that turns all the lights and sirens on. Would you like that?'

She beams at me and her feet jiggle. I keep my eyes on the road and repeatedly check my mirrors. Julia is in the other rear seat, strapped in, with Bobby on her lap. It's making me extremely uncomfortable that the children aren't in suitable child seats. We are allowed to carry children in emergency vehicles without safety restraints. I keep telling myself that this is necessary. I need to get the kids to the station. I need to feed them. I need to change that awful nappy. Before we got in the car, I radioed ahead and asked the station officer to pop to the local supermarket for nappies. I told her I'd cover the cost but she refused to even discuss it. *Maybe I'll claim the money back.* We both knew she wouldn't. I grip the wheel and concentrate on my driving. *Precious cargo.*

I can hear loud sucking noises in the back and I glance at Julia in the rear-view mirror. She's sitting very still, looking down at the top of Bobby's head. 'That banana going down well, then?'

She nods and looks up at me. 'He's absolutely stuffing it down.'

I smile and think about my boys. They both love bananas. They'd eat three a day if they could. Freddy eats them so quick you could be mistaken for thinking he inhales them. I've never been so grateful for the banana I'd put in with my refs as I am today. I'd tried to offer Lily some, but she'd refused. *Feed Bobby first.* I can't believe how mature she is. We arrive at the rear gates of the police station and, as I drive slowly through, I breathe a sigh of relief.

The prisoner van is parked by the gate, which means that Jacobs should already be in custody. Julia had formally arrested him in the back of the van, on suspicion of being drunk in charge of a minor. Or, in this case, two.

'OK,' I look to Julia. 'You head in to deal with Jacobs and I'll sort out the kids. Suit you?'

'Yes.' Julia passes Bobby to me and practically skips into the custody suite. She doesn't have kids.

I head into the station office, Bobby on my hip and Lily holding my hand. 'First things first, let's get this horrid nappy off you.' I look at Bobby and he giggles. It never ceases to amaze me how fast children can bounce back. He's a totally different child to the hungry thing we found in the street. Sasha, the civilian station officer, is ready and waiting. She makes a big fuss over Lily, handing her some paper and highlighter pens that she's clearly dug up from somewhere.

'Why don't you draw us a nice picture while Alice changes your brother's nappy?' Lily sits down eagerly.

I look at the carpet and Sasha shakes her head. 'Oh no, we are not baring that baby's butt to a Met carpet.' She reaches for an old fluorescent jacket that is hanging on the hat stand by the door. 'It's been in here for ages,' she explains as she lays it out on the floor so that the inside lining is facing up. I lower Bobby onto the now covered carpet and he immediately begins to writhe and whine. As I unpop his vest and unfasten his nappy the festering smell almost makes me gag. Sasha tuts from behind me. She lays out a pack of nappies, a packet of wipes and some nappy cream. She's thought of everything. I suck in my breath at the sight of the red raw rash across Bobby's bottom. It looks painful.

'No wonder you've been so upset, you poor thing.'

He begins to wail loudly as I wipe around the rash. I wince at the sound. I'd rather do this with cooled boiled water and cotton pads, but wipes are all I have. Once I'm done I soothe over the nappy cream and get a fresh nappy on. I wish I had clean clothes to put him in as I button up his filthy vest. He starts to calm as I place him back on my hip and bob around the room. Lily is totally absorbed in her drawing but her head shoots up as I mention food.

'What do you and your brother like to eat?'

'Chips!' She punches the air.

'Well, chips it is then.' I take her hand and lead her to the canteen.

After I'm happy that they've eaten, I take them back to Sasha. Lily doesn't want me to leave. I kneel down in front of her, taking her little hands in mine.

'Honey, I have to go and sort some things out. I promise I'll come back and see you in a bit.'

'OK. I'm going to draw a picture, just for you.' She hops over to Sasha's desk and picks up the blue highlighter pen. I head out of the station office and into the PC's writing room, where I find Julia. She's entering the crime report.

'Any word from social services?' I ask hopefully.

'Not a thing.' She doesn't look up from the screen, her fingers jabbing hard at the keys. 'Control contacted them over an hour ago.'

'Brilliant.' I rub my face and smell nappy cream. 'I'll chase them up.'

Just as I'm about to start hunting for a quiet room with an available phone, my mobile rings. A flustered voice on the other end. It's the social worker; she's outside the station. I rush through the station office and intercept her before she reaches Sasha. I want to speak to her before she gets to Lily and Bobby. I usher her into one of the available interview rooms and offer her a seat. She's around forty years old and plump, with a stern face. Her handshake is strong and she gets straight down to business.

'Where are the children?' She glances around the room as if they might pop out from some cleverly concealed hiding place.

'I wanted to speak to you first.'

She takes a deep breath and I get the distinct impression that she's trying to stop herself rolling her eyes. 'OK.'

'They're not going back to their father, are they?'

Her mouth opens, then shuts. She tilts her head to the side and considers me. 'Look, I know this family,' she says. 'I know Dad's a waste of space. But he was on the wagon up until not very long ago and I genuinely think he's doing his best.'

'Doing his best?' It comes out louder than I'd intended and her eyes widen. I take a breath to calm myself down. 'He's been drinking all morning. Probably all night too. He hasn't fed them since last night, he's got piss all down his pants and he very nearly pushed Bobby's buggy into oncoming traffic.'

'Shit.' She scribbles some notes on the jotter she's holding.

'What about Joanne? That's Mum's name, isn't it?'

The social worker snorts. 'Mum's not been on the scene

for about two years now. She's a total junkie, last we heard she was in Birmingham. And good riddance.'

'The grandparents?'

'They've already got Lily's sister. They're old. Grandad's in a wheelchair and Grandma's not exactly mobile herself. They could only cope with one and Bobby needs too much care. I doubt they'd even be able to lift him.'

I stare at the floor.

'Look, officer, I appreciate that you want the best for these kids, but, please be assured, so do I.'

I nod, opening the door to the interview room and pointing her in the direction of the station office. I'm about to follow her when I hear the governor's voice behind me.

'215. Debrief, please. In my office.'

I gaze into the station office and see the social worker bend over to greet Lily. She doesn't see me.

'Yes, sir.'

* * *

I fill in the governor as quick as I can but he just keeps on asking questions. Taking children into custody isn't something we do every day and he wants to make sure everything's shipshape. Usually, his fastidious nature is one of the reasons I like him, but today I just want him to shut up so I can go and say goodbye to Lily. Finally, he's satisfied and I storm towards the stairs that will take me back down to the ground floor, taking them two at a time. Once down, I race into the station office. It's empty. Sasha's at the front desk dealing with a member of the public. I stand in the middle of the room until something colourful catches my eyes.

The picture sits in the centre of Sasha's desk. A wobbly police officer with a wide smile. My uniform is the fluorescent blue of office highlighters and my pink smile matches its luminosity perfectly. The rest of me is scribbled in black biro. Next to me is a little girl with bright orange flowers on her dress, and bright yellow hair. Floating above our heads is a pink heart.

I snatch the paper off the table, fold it quickly and stuff it into my Met vest pocket. My eyes prickle and I pinch the bridge of my nose.

I broke my promise.

*   *   *

I'm hiding in the locker room. There's still an hour to go before the end of my shift but I can't seem to pull myself together enough to go back out there. I've wedged myself on the end of a wooden bench, my head resting between two heavy-weather police coats. I'm partially hidden from view and I'm not planning on moving any time soon. All I can think about is Lily. About how her life hasn't changed since I first met her, years before. About how nothing we did made a difference. *Nothing we do ever does.* I know for certain that tomorrow, she'll be sent back to her father, once he's sobered up. And there's nothing I can do about it. I try to keep them out but they're always with me. Leanne and the knife her four-year-old son brought for her. Francine and her silk scarf. A newborn baby that was never born. Hilda's eyeless gaze. Rosa's screams. Selina and her empty eyes. Trevor's lifeless body. Faith and Fury and all the other girls who are forced to become women too soon. The bodies ravaged by drugs. Broken people, broken lives, broken fucking society.

I feel dizzy and sick. My tongue is stuck to the roof of my mouth and there's a pressure in my chest that's hard to describe. It's not an inward pressure, a pressure you might feel if someone was squeezing you – it's more like a pressure from the inside trying to get out. Like I've taken a giant gulp of air and I don't know how to release it. Like something waiting to explode. I rub my wet eyes fiercely. *Get a fucking grip.* My heart is beating so fast I feel sure I'm about to have a heart attack. Sweat breaks out on my top lip and I lean forward, positive that I'm about to throw up. Saliva builds in my mouth and I sit there, head in my hands, willing myself not to vomit, because I'm too dizzy right now to make it to the toilets. *What the fuck is happening to me?* I'm terrified.

And just as I'm about to call out. Shout out for someone to help me because I'm 100 per cent certain I'm about to die, a thought pops into my head. *You're having a panic attack.* Suddenly it all makes sense. I'm not dying, I'm panicking. It's so ridiculous I almost laugh. But the power of knowing what's going on enables me to bring my breathing under control. The dizziness subsides and I sit, taking slow steady breaths, my fingertips tingling like they're on fire.

The locker room door swings open and I sink further back in to the coats, hoping whoever it is won't notice I'm here.

'Alice, you in here?' It's Julia.

I think about staying silent but responsibility makes me call out. 'Back here.'

She wanders over and looks down at me. 'You OK?'

'Yeah,' I stop. 'Actually, no.'

She waits. A useful tactic I've used many times myself. People need to fill the silence.

'You know what? I think I'm done for the day.'

She nods. 'Tough job.'

'Yeah.' I stand up and smooth my hair back from my forehead. 'It's just – kids – you know?'

'Yeah, I know.'

But, she doesn't know. She doesn't know. How can she? *Everything changes once you become a mother.*

Julia glances at the door and I can tell she wants to leave.

I slap on a smile. 'I'm going to get changed – I'll let the skippers know I'm leaving.'

'OK,' she grins. 'See you tomorrow.'

I watch her leave and wonder how I used to be just like her. I can't remember what it felt like to be so carefree. *So invincible.*

But she's wrong about one thing.

She won't be seeing me tomorrow.

Acknowledgements

Although this story is mine, the book you are holding would not have been possible without the help of many kind and dedicated people.

I'd like to start by thanking the wonderful team at Two Roads Books. To Kate and Lisa for taking a chance on an unknown, un-agented writer, for having a direct submissions portal in the first place, for letting me prattle on about my book (and joining in!) and providing lovely chats in bookish surroundings with tea and cakes. To Kat, Alice and Emma, and of course to all of those behind the scenes at Two Roads, thank you for all your hard work!

To Kate Latham for early editorial advice and encouragement, and for having faith in my writing from your first read; thank you for giving your precious time to a new and unsure writer.

To 'Marc the Legend' for the T-cut, random question-and-answer sessions, and, always, for the laughs. To Drew and Caz for the memories. Hey you guys!

Thank you to the original D team massive (you know who you are) for being there during the highs and the lows, and refs at the beach. To the sometimes weird and always wonderful guys and girls of the BIU, thanks for making office work the best it could be (the doughnuts helped).

Thank you to all of the inspirational female officers who rose through the ranks and inspired me throughout my career. Thank you to the Met for being my home for ten years.

And last, but by no means least, thank you to my family, without whom I couldn't have found the strength and confidence to write in the first place. Mum and Dad, thanks for the babysitting (and the love). John, thanks for being a friend, an excellent father and the best ex-husband one could have. To my boys: you are, and always will be, my inspiration.

About the Author

Alice Vinten spent ten years as an officer in the Metropolitan Police. Now in her thirties, she lives in Leigh-on-Sea with her two sons.